# dancing *with* fear

IIIIIIIIIIIIIIIIIIIIIIIIIIIIIIIIIIIIIIIIIIIIIIIIII

### Praise for the First Edition of *Dancing with Fear*

"There have been endless books written by countless authors on the subject of anxiety and how best to identify and cope with its paralyzing manifestations. What makes *Dancing with Fear* so special and so welcome is that Paul Foxman speaks eloquently and intelligently to the two key people involved in accomplishing full recovery from this insidious problem: the sufferer and his therapist. Because Dr. Foxman knows, firsthand, what gut-wrenching anxiety feels like, he never minimizes its impact nor does he hide his own humanness behind his degree. It become obvious from the first chapter that Dr. Foxman is a consummate professional who, thank heavens, can honestly teach from his heart."

— ANN SEAGRAVE
coauthor of *Free from Fears*

"Dr. Foxman's book, *Dancing with Fear,* is a comprehensive and compassionate overview of the most crippling of our 'social diseases'—fear—with a wealth of practical approaches to loosening its hold on us. The work will find a wide and appreciative audience."

— JOSEPH CHILTON PEARCE
author of *Magical Child, The Crack in the Cosmic Egg,*
*The Biology of Transcendence,* and *Evolution's End*

"For anybody who recognizes that stress can't be avoided, only managed, psychologist Paul Foxman's *Dancing with Fear* is a splendid resource. Dr. Foxman delivers the coping tools and techniques all the more effectively for his wisdom, compassion, insight, and graceful prose."

— JOHN STICKNEY
Senior Features Editor, *Fitness* magazine

"This book by Dr. Paul Foxman has all but paved the path to peace, the way to freedom from anxiety. He offers a clear exposition of what severe anxiety is, where it comes from, and what to do about it. He shares his personal experience with trauma and anxiety, as well as his understandings gained from decades of helping others. Is his easy style, Dr. Foxman provides unlimited hope and specific information on how anxiety can be overcome."

— JOHN R. PULLEN, PH.D., National Director of CHAANGE
(Center for Help for Anxiety/Agoraphobia
through New Growth Experiences)
www.chaange.com

### Praise for the New Edition of *Dancing with Fear*

"Undoubtedly the finest book ever on this topic....You will feel greatly rewarded by reading this best of all possible books on anxiety and its cure. You will be excited by this powerful book."

— JOHN R. PULLEN, PH.D., National Director of CHAANGE
www.chaange.com

"Paul Foxman offers not only inspiration and hope, but also a practical road map that explores the various aspects of recovery from anxiety. Readers will be in good hands as Foxman compassionately shares his hard-won wisdom, starting with the sometimes-brutal origins of his own anxiety and continuing with his personal and professional journeys. This timely book is a godsend to those struggling to find inner peace in an ever-shrinking world of accelerating changes."

— ERIKA B. HILLIARD, MSW, RSW
author of *Living Fully with Shyness and Social Anxiety*

## Dedication

*For Sheryl, my wife and soul mate, whose companionship and love have been the best rewards for facing my fears. And for my two children, Kali Dawn and Leah Sunset, who are my greatest pride and joy.*

## IMPORTANT NOTE
||||||||||||||||||||||||||||||||

The material in this book is intended to provide a review of information regarding anxiety. Every effort has been made to provide accurate and dependable information. The contents of this book have been compiled through professional research and in consultation with medical professionals. However, mental-health professionals have differing opinions, and advances in medical and scientific research are made very quickly, so some of the information may become outdated.

Therefore, the publisher, author, and editors, as well as the professionals quoted in the book, cannot be held responsible for any error, omission, or dated material. The author and publisher assume no responsibility for any outcome of applying the information in this book in a program of self-care or under the care of a licensed practitioner. If you have questions concerning anxiety or about the application of the information described in this book, consult a qualified mental-health professional.

## ORDERING

Trade bookstores in the U.S. and Canada please contact:

Publishers Group West
1700 Fourth Street, Berkeley CA 94710
Phone: (800) 788-3123       Fax: (800) 351-5073

Hunter House books are available at bulk discounts for textbook course adoptions; to qualifying community, health-care, and government organizations; and for special promotions and fund-raising.
For details please contact:

Special Sales Department
Hunter House Inc., PO Box 2914, Alameda CA 94501-0914
Phone: (510) 865-5282       Fax: (510) 865-4295
E-mail: ordering@hunterhouse.com

Individuals can order our books from most bookstores, by calling **(800) 266-5592,** or from our website at **www.hunterhouse.com**

# dancing *with* fear

||||||||||||||||||||||||||||||||||||||||||||||||||||||||||||||||||||||||||||||||||||||||||||

## Controlling Stress and Creating a Life
## Beyond Panic and Anxiety

*Second Edition*

**PAUL FOXMAN, PH.D.**

Hunter House Inc., Publishers
PO Box 2914
Alameda CA 94501-0914

**LIBRARY OF CONGRESS CATALOGING-IN-PUBLICATION DATA**

Foxman, Paul.
Dancing with fear : controlling stress and creating a life beyond panic and anxiety / Paul Foxman. — 2nd ed.
p. cm.
Includes bibliographical references and index.
ISBN-13: 978-0-89793-476-3 (pbk.)
ISBN-10: 0-89793-476-8 (pbk.)
1. Anxiety. 2. Fear. 3. Stress (Psychology) 4. Stress management. I. Title.
BF575.A6F68 2006
152.4'6—dc22                                        2006030063

**PROJECT CREDITS**

Cover Design: Brian Dittmar Graphic Design
Book Production: Hunter House, Jinni Fontana
Developmental and Copy Editor: Jude Berman
Proofreader: Herman Leung
Indexer: Nancy D. Peterson
Interns: Blair Cavagrotti, Faith Merino
Acquisitions Editor: Jeanne Brondino
Editor: Alexandra Mummery
Senior Marketing Associate: Reina Santana
Customer Service Manager: Christina Sverdrup
Order Fulfillment: Washul Lakdhon
Administrator: Theresa Nelson
Computer Support: Peter Eichelberger
Publisher: Kiran S. Rana

Printed and Bound by Bang Printing, Brainerd, Minnesota

Manufactured in the United States of America

9  8  7  6  5  4  3  2      Second Edition      09  10  11  12  13

# Contents

## Part I: Insight: How to Understand Anxiety

What Is Anxiety and Why Is It So Prevalent Today?
The Anatomy of Fear
Differences Between Animal and Human Survival Reactions
The Role of Stress in Anxiety
Strong Emotions and the Fight/Flight Response
Thought Patterns and Anxiety
Conclusion

Panic Disorder
Generalized Anxiety Disorder
Social Anxiety
Specific Phobia
Separation Anxiety
Obsessive-Compulsive Disorder
Post-Traumatic Stress Disorder
Acute Stress Disorder
Anxiety Associated with Medical Conditions
Substance-Induced Anxiety Disorder
Depression and Anxiety
Conclusion

### Part II: Strategies and Skills for Creating a Life Beyond Anxiety

# Foreword

Anxiety disorders are among the most common emotional conditions, but they are also the most underrecognized and undertreated. According to the U.S. Surgeon General, 16 percent of adults and 13 percent of children and adolescents experience signs and symptoms of an anxiety disorder each year. Unfortunately, fewer than one person in four receives help. As a result, it is estimated that anxiety disorders cost the United States more than $42 billion a year, with approximately half this amount attributable to increased expenses for general medical care.

Nobody's life is completely devoid of anxiety, nor should it be. Anxiety is an instinctual emotion that evolved to help us recognize danger and ensure survival. In the normal course of life, anxiety can also motivate people to achieve and succeed. However, in the extreme, anxiety can be disruptive, debilitating, and even paralyzing. A child may refuse to go to school. An adolescent may avoid sports, music, or social activities. Self-esteem and school performance may suffer. And during adulthood, anxiety can interfere with career choices, job performance, and family relationships.

As with many other mental-health conditions, we tend to wait much too long before seeking help for problems with anxiety. On average, the signs and symptoms of an anxiety disorder have been present for more than ten years before people finally get treatment. This book, by a widely respected expert on anxiety, is particularly valuable because it helps readers avoid unnecessary suffering and minimize the loss of precious time.

In his previous book, *The Worried Child,* Dr. Foxman skillfully described how anxiety typically begins in childhood and how parents, teachers, therapists, and others can help young people heal. In *Dancing with Fear,* Dr. Foxman offers a helpful and reassuring guide for the millions of adults whose lives are touched by anxiety disorders. Drawing on both his personal experience and his extensive clinical practice, he empowers readers to learn about and master their own anxieties. His key message is that treatment works and that you can successfully over-come anxiety and achieve your full potential.

By conceptualizing the "dance" of fear, Dr. Foxman acknowledges the complexities of this emotion and the reality that professional help may be necessary. Many of the skills and insights you will find in this book are based on Dr. Foxman's work as a practicing psychologist and director of the Center for Anxiety Disorders. You are taking a time-saving step forward by reading this book, but if necessary, you are advised to follow up by seeking professional help. If you have family members with anxiety disorders, encourage them to read this book and to get help, if needed. Finally, if you are a clinician, use this book and other resources to learn as much as you can about the presentation, evaluation, and treatment of anxiety-related problems.

— David Fassler, M.D.
Clinical Professor of Psychiatry
University of Vermont College of Medicine
Burlington, Vermont

# Preface to the New Edition

When *Dancing with Fear* was first published in 1996, it was my hope that the book would reach its intended audience and provide hope and help. I had no idea that the book would become a publisher's best-seller or a stock item at major bookstores, such as Barnes and Noble Booksellers, Borders, and Amazon.com. I have received hundreds of thankful letters and phone calls from readers who have said the book provides inspiration, insight, and effective strategies for anxiety recovery. One reader went so far as to describe the book as his personal "bible." Naturally, such positive feedback has been gratifying, especially since it has included appreciation for my personal anxiety recovery story.

It has been almost a decade since publication of the first edition of *Dancing with Fear*. A second edition is now warranted for updating the material with new knowledge from mental-health research and clinical practice. For example, exciting results from brain research during the last decade indicate that cognitive therapy can change brain chemistry as much as drugs. This gives more credence to the techniques included throughout the book. There have also been advances in medications for treatment of anxiety symptoms and these newer drugs are discussed in Chapter 17, "Should You Take Medication for Anxiety — or Not?" A growing interest in alternative medicine, such as herbal treatment and homeopathy, is also addressed in this updated edition.

New technology now permits scientists to view the astonishing biochemistry involved in emotions and how our minds communicate with our bodies. It has become apparent that anxiety is created primarily by our thinking patterns and habits, and that we can reduce symptoms by literally changing our minds. Meditation and a state of "flow," for example, are associated with relaxation and "antianxiety" brain chemicals. Relaxation and meditation practices can alter the messenger molecules that translate our thoughts into symptoms and behavior. Such new findings are discussed in this edition.

My understanding of how and why anxiety develops has stood the test of time but it has been refined in this new edition. Each of the "three ingredients" in anxiety—genetic temperament, anxiety personality traits, and stress overload—is addressed in depth in Chapter 4, which brings these components together in an integrated explanation of how and why anxiety disorders emerge. A self-test of the anxiety personality traits was developed since the first edition and is found in Chapter 4. I have also added a chapter (Chapter 3) on anxiety disorders, which includes the criteria used to diagnose each anxiety disorder.

Some core information has not changed. For example, stress overload remains the key "why now?" factor in anxiety, and emphasis continues to be placed on methods for controlling stress. However, based on what I have learned from further clinical work with my patients and my workshops with mental-health professionals, I have included some new and interesting approaches, such as the "Triple-S Method for Stress Control." In addition, some new high-tech approaches are discussed.

A long chapter in the first edition focused on anxiety in children. I have opted to eliminate this chapter in the new edition because anxiety in children is addressed in depth in my recent book, *The Worried Child* (Hunter House, 2003). However, children and adults suffer from the same anxiety conditions, and most of the techniques for reducing anxiety in adults are applicable to children. This book, therefore, provides insight and help for children and adolescents as well as the primary audience of adults. Readers are referred to *The Worried Child* for information on how parents, therapists, health-care providers, educators, and even children themselves can reduce anxiety in young people.

The exercises and suggestions for anxiety recovery in this new edition of *Dancing with Fear* have been reformatted for aesthetics and ease of use. Shaded text boxes set the how-to techniques apart from other information, and bulleted lists are incorporated to help readers learn and recall helpful information. The goal was to create a helpful, user-friendly book that supports self-help and anxiety-recovery work. Approximately 35 exercises are included, some of which are new to the second edition. These are self-help skills that can be practiced without professional help. On the other hand, this edition includes information on a how to decide when professional help is advisable.

My original goal for the book remains unchanged. It is to help you understand and reduce your anxiety in less time that it took me to succeed in my own recovery. As you will note in my own anxiety story (Chapter 1), this type of information was not available when I most needed it. It took many years of experimentation and practice to discover life beyond anxiety.

Finally, the ultimate purpose of this book is to enable you to create a life beyond stress and anxiety. The last chapter describes what this might look like. To begin the journey now, ask yourself, "With what will I replace stress and anxiety and what would such a life be like?"

With best wishes for discovering the answers and creating a life beyond anxiety,

— PAUL FOXMAN, PH.D.
Williston, Vermont
May 2006

# Acknowledgments

Many kind people deserve recognition for their time and support during the creation of this book. Let me begin by thanking those who reviewed chapters of the book-in-progress: Lynn Murray, Jeanne Albertson, R.D., Katie Lessor, Leslie Purple, Ron McConnell, Gail Shaw, Debra Lopez, M.D., Lynn Almon, Anne Clegg, M.D., and Rabbi James Glazier.

Special thanks to Barry Weiss, for his support throughout the years and for the inspiring dialogues we had while skiing at Stowe, Vermont. There are not enough lifetimes to write the many books we outlined on those rides up the mountain.

Many thanks go to John Pullen, Ph.D., who is the National Director of CHAANGE and who reviewed most of the original chapters and encouraged me to share the good news about anxiety recovery.

Thanks also to Ann Seagrave, cofounder of the first and best cognitive-behavioral self-help program for anxiety, who felt at the outset that my work was important to share with others. Ann also encouraged me to include my personal recovery story.

I will be forever grateful to Saul Neidorf, M.D., whose trusted ears were the first to hear about my painful childhood and anxiety condition. As therapist, teacher, and mentor *par excellence,* Saul demonstrated that therapy heals by shared heart, and he had a significant influence on my therapeutic style.

I am grateful to my colleagues at the Center for Anxiety Disorders in Vermont. I may be the Director, but I have learned as much as I have taught. My heart is warmed by their competence, dedication to the work, and eagerness to grow professionally.

I also wish to thank the many patients I have had the privilege to serve. They offer living proof that creating a life beyond panic and anxiety is possible. Some of my patients, whose names and identities have been changed to protect their confidentiality, appear in the following pages to help illustrate the information and material. I respect my patients and I rejoice in their growth and recovery from stress and anxiety.

Thanks to Hunter House Publishers for the opportunity to breathe new life into *Dancing with Fear*. May this second edition transform a cult classic into a mainstream hit.

I can only begin to express my appreciation to Sheryl Anne Foxman, my soul mate and wife, whose support and faith in me had helped immeasurably in making this book possible.

Finally, thanks to the One whose patient presence reminds me that every experience has a higher purpose and that whatever happens, everything will be okay. Thanks for the opportunity to serve through writing, clinical practice, and teaching.

# Introduction

This book was written for everyone who has experienced anxiety and would like to live without its limitations and constraints. The intended audience also includes mental-health professionals, health-care providers, and others who are called on to treat patients with anxiety disorders. In addition, family and friends will find valuable information with which to understand and support loved ones with anxiety.

Approximately thirty-seven million American adults now suffer from severe anxiety and at some point in their lifetime nearly one-quarter of the adult population—some sixty-five million people—will suffer from an anxiety disorder. Panic attacks, phobias, avoidant behavior, worrying, compulsive behavior, unwanted obsessions, and frightening body symptoms such as racing heart, breathing difficulties, sweating, shaking, nausea, numbness, and weakness are some of the many forms of anxiety. In addition, millions of children experience anxiety severe enough to affect school attendance, concentration, sleep, and learning ability.

Anxiety is increasing at a startling rate as a result of many kinds of stress in society. Divorce, economic instability, health hazards from environmental toxicity, violent crime, and terrorism are just some of the conditions fostering insecurity and anxiety. Terrorism, for example, is no longer a remote threat, as the bombings of the World Trade Center in New York City in 1993 and 2001 made devastatingly clear. Unfortunately, when the media—television, newspapers, magazines, movies, and the Internet—broadcasts the world news, it tends to contribute to our anxiety, insecurity, and sense of vulnerability. The violence it portrays has been shown to increase our fear of the world around us. Even video games can be violent, and some branches of the military train soldiers in methods of killing using commercially available video games that can be purchased at a local mall.

Fear and feelings of vulnerability are a normal reaction under threatening or stressful circumstances. For those who are already anxious, such external conditions can intensify this reaction. Furthermore, certain personality styles increase the chances for anxiety reactions. This book includes an examination of how anxiety develops from the interaction of personal characteristics and external pressures.

This book proposes that anxiety is primarily a pattern of learned cognitive, emotional, and behavioral habits, and that these habits can be changed. The change process involves replacing old, nonproductive habits with more effective patterns.

Anxiety recovery usually requires insight combined with regular practice of new skills. Anxiety sufferers typically exhibit nonproductive habits that create and reinforce their anxiety, such as worrying, trying to predict the future, negative thinking, and attempts to always be in control. This book contains the concepts and skills that can be practiced to replace such unproductive thinking and behavior.

Although medications can be helpful in the short run in certain cases, they are not usually necessary for long-term success. New research demonstrates that changes in thinking can reduce or eliminate anxiety symptoms as well as alter brain chemistry to the same extent as antianxiety medication. There is good reason to be optimistic about the chances for a lasting recovery from anxiety.

This book suggests that several ingredients combine to create an anxiety disorder: genetics (I call this "biological sensitivity"), a specific personality type, and stress overload. An anxiety disorder usually signals an overload of stress in sensitive people. We discuss this view of anxiety and focus on those factors that can be changed, such as how we think and behave, and how we deal with stress.

This book was written from a personal as well as professional perspective. My own story of recovery from an anxiety-ridden childhood and early adulthood, and my discovery of how to live without anxiety, is included. This book was undertaken to reduce significantly the recovery time for readers whose lives, like mine, have been impaired by anxiety.

I had already begun my career as a clinical psychologist when I addressed my personal anxiety issues. In fact, it was a resonance with my patients' anxiety that brought my anxiety issues into focus. The insights I uncovered and the skills I developed became the foundation for my specialty in anxiety treatment.

I work directly with patients and train other therapists in anxiety treatment. This is gratifying work, because people can and do recover, often in a relatively short period of time. As I share in the joy of each patient's new freedom, I am continually reminded that anxiety can be "unlearned." You will meet some of the patients I have worked with throughout the book and hopefully appreciate their triumph over fear and anxiety. If you see yourself reflected in any of these patients' stories, there is a high likelihood that you, too, can recover from anxiety. The skills described in this book have been personally tested and used to enhance and maintain my own recovery.

This book is not a substitute for professional help. No book on anxiety can replace the healing relationship with a therapist, someone who knows the territory of anxiety and how to guide you through it. On the other hand, understanding your anxiety condition, knowing you are not alone, and having concrete skills to practice can make a difference. In fact, just having a proper diagnosis of an anxiety disorder is usually a relief for people who are afraid of what is happening when they are anxious. Many people with anxiety disorders have spent years seeking professional help before a correct diagnosis was made. Fear of having a heart attack, going "crazy," having a fatal illness or dying, or fear of losing control, all begin to subside when people understand what is happening, and why. My main purpose in writing this book, therefore, is to offer information and concrete suggestions to help you understand anxiety and why it developed in your particular case.

You will most likely be able to identify your anxiety symptoms and diagnose yourself with the information contained in Part I. The criteria for diagnosing anxiety disorders (Chapter 3) and the Anxiety Personality Self-Test (Chapter 4), along with other resources throughout the book, should go a long way toward helping you identify your particular form of anxiety. Throughout Part II, you will find specific self-help practices for creating a life with more ease, joy, and trust. A concluding chapter describes what it is like to live without anxiety.

How did I choose the title of this book? "Dancing" refers to the rituals and tactics we may use to cope with anxiety. For example, we may habitually avoid certain situations or places in which we anticipate feeling anxious. We may develop a passive communication style because we fear rejection or conflict. We may develop compulsive behavior patterns and "busywork" in order to distract ourselves from anxiety. Or, we may repeatedly engage in "what-if" thinking in an effort to anticipate what may happen in the future. We want to feel in control and safe, so we develop a kind of dance—and waste a lot of energy—in our effort to manage anxiety.

Dancing, however, also has more positive connotations. Dancing is usually associated with freedom of movement, having fun, enjoying music, letting go, and celebrating. This book is about overcoming anxiety and increasing your ability to "dance" with life. Living without anxiety is about learning how to "go with the flow," relax, derive satisfaction from work, enjoy peace of mind, and appreciate the gift of life.

Strange as it may seem, many of my patients have remarked that they are fortunate to have had an anxiety condition because in coming for help they re-examined their lives and made positive personal changes. It is not unusual for people to learn that their anxiety was a signal, a message that their lives were out of balance, and that change was needed. Anxiety serves a productive purpose in many cases, leading to greater understanding about oneself, new skills for living, less stress, a more positive attitude, and a higher quality of life. Chapter 16, "Spirituality and Anxiety," explores the idea that anxiety recovery and spiritual development can overlap to a great extent.

There are other books about anxiety. Some are self-help manuals, while others offer insight and understanding about the condition. So why add another book on anxiety? Anxiety disorders are the most prevalent emotional conditions, outranking all others including depression and alcohol/drug abuse. Yet only 25 percent of the millions of people who suffer from anxiety seek professional help, and most receive inappropriate or ineffective care. Considering the epidemic prevalence of anxiety, and the 75 percent of anxiety sufferers who receive no help at all, there are not enough books and resources on the topic.

While some books offer information and help, many are based on a biological and drug-treatment approach to anxiety. Medication can be helpful, but my emphasis is on combining insight with skills for anxiety recovery.

The vast majority of people who seek help for anxiety are treated with medications, such as tranquilizers and antidepressants, often with no significant or enduring improvement. The medication approach is promoted by drug manufacturers who advertise heavily on television and in other media, as well as influence physicians by funding their continuing medical education. Other alternatives need to be promoted, particularly the idea that anxiety is a learned pattern that in many cases can be replaced with new ways of thinking and acting.

There is a growing need and desire for more information about anxiety and effective treatment options. One early example was the incredible response to a Panic Disorder Education Program established in 1994 by the National Institute of Mental Health (NIMH). The main goal of the program was to increase the number of people with panic disorder who are properly diagnosed and treated. The NIMH reports that when properly treated, there is approximately an 80 percent partial or complete recovery rate for panic disorder sufferers. When the U.S. government agency installed a toll-free telephone number, (800) 64-PANIC (647-2642), they received *thirty thousand* calls in the first three months of operation! And when the telephone number was mentioned on August 20, 1994, on the ABC television show *Good Morning America*, twelve thousand calls were received, three thousand of which were placed within five minutes after the broadcast, causing a temporary circuit jam. Another three thousand calls were generated by a CNN broadcast, *Sonja Live,* that featured the personal stories of panic disorder patients in New York and Los Angeles.

I recall a professional experience that validated the need for more information and effective programs for anxiety recovery, and therefore a place for this book. I was interviewed on a Vermont Public Radio program, *Switchboard,* accompanied by two former patients who had recovered from anxiety. After the interview, the public was invited to call in with questions or comments. Calls flooded in from Vermont, New Hampshire, Canada, and New York. Beginning the next day, my office received over 150 phone calls from people seeking more information. Listeners also requested that information be sent to friends and relatives as far away from Vermont as Alaska, South Carolina, and North Dakota.

In addition, the radio station received a record number of calls for taped copies of the program. I sent an information packet to all callers and spoke with many individuals. In some cases, the individual had never received help or a diagnosis of their anxiety condition. In other cases, people had received help but were still feeling anxious. What amazed me most was how many people were willing to travel considerable distances, in spite of their fears of driving, travel, and new situations, to get specialized help.

Another example is the response to the annual National Anxiety Disorders Screening Day, sponsored by several grassroots organizations. Even in its 1995 startup year, thirty-five thousand people visited more than twelve hundred anxiety-screening sites in all fifty states for information and guidance about coping with anxiety disorders. Each year thousands of people show up for no-cost anxiety screenings and referral information.

In addition, there are a growing number of organizations devoted to public information about anxiety disorders. They include the Anxiety Disorders Association of America (ADAA), Freedom From Fear (FFF), The Obsessive-Compulsive Foundation (OCF), The Center for Help for Anxiety/Agoraphobia through New Growth Experiences (CHAANGE), the National Anxiety Foundation, and the Council on Anxiety Disorders. Information about these organizations is included in the Resources section at the end of this book.

About twice as many women as men seek help for anxiety. There are two possible explanations for this discrepancy. One is that more women than men develop anxiety disorders. However, it is also possible that both men and women are equally susceptible to anxiety, but men are less inclined to reveal their anxiety or ask for help. There may be a greater barrier to seeking help for men, who are conditioned to hide their feelings and not show weakness or fear. Hopefully, a book written by a man who is willing to reveal his own anxiety story will open the door for other men. I would like to increase the number of both men and women who find effective help and learn how to live without anxiety.

The need is apparent, so let us begin...

# PART I
||||||||||||||

# *insight: how to understand anxiety*

During my early training as a psychologist, the prevailing professional assumption was that insight was powerful enough to change behavior and heal human suffering. This belief was at the core of psychoanalysis, which evolved into "insight-oriented psychotherapy." This therapy method analyzes the root of a person's symptoms in the hopes that such an understanding will have a healing effect.

What I have learned since that time is that insight is necessary but usually not sufficient to resolve an anxiety disorder. Many of my patients are experts in anxiety. They know as much, if not more, about anxiety than the doctors who refer them to me. In many cases, they have read the literature and conducted Internet research on the topic of anxiety. They may have extensive insight into their anxiety. Yet despite this knowledge, they are unable to control their irrational anxiety and they continue to suffer from its limiting effects.

I now view insight as the first step in overcoming anxiety. Insight is a form of deep knowing and understanding, and it is usually experienced as reassuring. Insight also opens the door to the second step in anxiety recovery, which is to learn new ways to relate to anxiety (this in itself can reduce anxiety), manage its causes, and create a more fulfilling life. The second step could be called the new skills stage of recovery.

Part I, then, provides the first step in anxiety recovery by offering insight into the nature of anxiety. You will learn to distinguish between fear and anxiety (toward the goal of eliminating fear of anxiety) and to recognize the three ingredients in the development of abnormal anxiety. The three ingredients consist of genetics (I use the term "biological sensitivity"), personality style (traits and habits that contribute to anxiety), and stress overload (which influences the timing of anxiety symptoms). The various anxiety disorders are discussed and illustrated with brief case examples. You should be reassured by data that show a high success rate (greater than 80 percent) for anxiety recovery with appropriate information and skills. The insights found in Part I set the stage for Part II, which addresses the skills for controlling the causes of anxiety and creating a life beyond anxiety.

||||||||||||||||

# CHAPTER 1

||||||||||||||||||||||

# *My Anxiety Story*

> I realize that it requires a tremendous leap of faith to imagine that your childhood—punctuated with pain, loss, and hurt—may, in fact, be a gift.
>
> — WAYNE MULLER, *Legacy of the Heart*

Fear haunted me since childhood, and as I grew up, I sensed I was more sensitive and anxious than other people. My life story is an example of how an anxiety disorder can develop and how to overcome it.

A number of conditions and traumatic experiences were responsible for my anxiety. One strong influence was exposure to violence in the volatile community in which I was raised. It was the 1950s in New York City, in a neighborhood known as "Hell's Kitchen." The Broadway play, *West Side Story*, portrays the kind of tension and violence I experienced in this primarily Puerto Rican and black community.

Some sharp images and memories stand out about this aspect of my childhood. Racial tension was high and, as a white boy, I was an easy target for racial hostility. When I dated a Puerto Rican girl, for example, I was threatened and physically harassed up by a group of Puerto Rican boys who said, "We don't want you messing around with our women." In high school, a black member of the track team punched me in the face in the locker room, and claimed, "I don't want no white boy hanging out with my friends."

Many other forms of violence surrounded me in Hell's Kitchen. I recall a hunting knife being thrown into the lobby of my apartment building, entering blade first into a wall near me. While bicycling in Central Park, my brother, Marc, was mugged and had his bicycle stolen.

One boy pushed another from a pier to his death in the Hudson River. A friend of mine, whom I can still vividly picture, was beaten regularly by a brutal father. He finally ran away from home, and I never saw him again. Although I never witnessed it, there were stories of violent gangs from "uptown," with names such as Viceroys and Marlboros, who fought with pipes and chains. These violent images certainly contributed to my unease and anxiety.

I was myself a victim of violent abuse. On the way to school at the age of twelve, I was raped in an abandoned building by a man who threatened to "smash my head" with the brick he held over me, if I did not do what he said or if I ever told anyone. I was so frightened that I not only complied but was unable to tell anyone about the humiliating and painful trauma for more than ten years. I was always on the lookout for that man, and unbelievably, I did see him on one occasion roaming the neighborhood. There must have been other victims.

There were more subtle incidents that also contributed to my anxiety. I recall, for example, my father telling me he had joined the Army to fight against Hitler. I learned at a young age that because of their beliefs, millions of Jews were systematically exterminated in gas chambers and ovens. Because my father was Jewish, the Holocaust struck even closer to home. As I matured, I learned that racism, war, economic exploitation, and political oppression have occurred throughout history, and that the world is indeed unstable and often dangerous.

A near-death experience I had when I was ten years old added to my anxiety. I had a cold, which developed into croup. During the night, I was awakened by a phlegm obstruction in my windpipe that was blocking my breathing. I tried to scream for help, but could make no sound. Due to oxygen deprivation, I fell unconscious. Waking up the next day, after an emergency tracheotomy operation, I found myself strapped to a hospital bed, breathing through an opening in my throat. I was unable to speak, and my parents were told I might never speak again due to surgical damage to my vocal chords. The only pleasant part of the following two weeks in the hospital was a caring nurse named Peggy, toward whom I felt my first feelings of falling in love. The life-threatening episode was a frightening brush with death, leaving me with a sense of vulnerability and life's fragility.

Another source of anxiety was the separation and divorce of my parents when I was ten years old. From this destabilizing process, I learned relationships can be tense, unstable, and hostile. Avoiding commitment and intimacy became a pattern by which I protected myself in relationships for many years to follow.

How did the traumas of my childhood show up in my personality and in my problem with anxiety? Many of my early experiences naturally evoked fear and anxiety. But I was also ashamed of my fear and anxiety. In Hell's Kitchen (as in the larger society), a sensitive or fearful boy would be considered a chicken, a sissy, or a weakling. To avoid the stigma of anxiety and to cope with shame, I compensated by working hard to be successful in academics and sports. I became a high-achieving student and athlete who could hide anxiety behind visible accomplishments. For example, I was the captain of my high school track team, medaled frequently, and earned a reputation as the "fastest white boy" in New York City. I also became editor of the high school yearbook, and I was accepted as a scholarship student to Yale University, where I became a ranking scholar (top 10 percent of the class) and repeatedly made dean's list. At Yale, I had a research project published in a prestigious psychology journal and went on to earn a Ph.D. in clinical psychology. Although not all high achievers are driven by anxiety, it is a common strategy for counteracting shame, low self-esteem, and self-doubt.

In my relationships, I was hesitant to make commitments, but I was also afraid to be alone. Hiding my fear led to difficulty expressing other feelings. My external accomplishments seemed possible only if there was someone to cheer, admire, and approve. I was too dependent on others for my self-esteem, and I worked overly hard to please them. I was unusually sensitive to criticism and rejection, and I avoided conflict whenever possible. I had intense separation anxiety and fears of abandonment. These traits are common in people who tend to develop anxiety disorders.

I also had difficulty relaxing. I was restless, impatient, and tense, and frequently distracted myself from anxiety by engaging in activity. I was certainly not enjoying life, except for a sense of gratification in my accomplishments. My stress level was high due to my perfectionism and need to "prove myself" through my achievements.

This approach to life was exhausting. However, I did not realize there was a problem until this stressful style took a toll on my energy and I began to feel depressed as a young adult.

Depression, as we will see later in the book, often arises as a response to anxiety, and in some cases, an anxiety disorder is misdiagnosed as depression. The symptoms of depression include low energy, low motivation, and loss of interest in activities that have been associated with joy, pleasure, or satisfaction. Particularly when frequent worry is involved, chronic anxiety can also lead to these symptoms.

In my case, fear of being alone was at the heart of the depression that occurred when I was without a companion. At one point, I found myself without a romantic relationship, and both my anxiety and depression intensified. I began to have panic attacks, with accompanying fears of losing control. The worst period consisted of daily panic attacks for several weeks, during which I thought I was going to die, go crazy, or disintegrate.

After college, I experimented with drugs and experienced some relief. The drugs consisted of marijuana and psychedelics, such as mescaline, peyote, and LSD. Use of mind-altering drugs was both a line of defense against anxiety and depression as well as a source of pleasure. Marijuana, for example, helped me relax and slow down. I was able to "let go" and begin to experience an inner peace previously unknown to me. Relaxation through drugs marked the beginning of my anxiety recovery. However, I paid the price: My social life suffered, my efficiency dropped, and I had some "bad trips" that reinforced my anxiety. For these reasons, I would not recommend hallucinogenic or psychedelic drugs for anxiety. In many cases, the altered state of mind induced by these drugs can directly precipitate an anxiety disorder. In fact, there is a formal diagnosis for this response—Substance-Induced Anxiety Disorder—which I discuss in Chapter 3. Fortunately, I discovered healthier methods for relaxing and experiencing inner peace, which I emphasize in Part II.

My anxiety recovery was an eclectic, trial-and-error process. I experimented with many techniques and methods, concentrating on those I found useful. I share them in greater detail with you in later chapters.

I discovered, for example, that I could relax and find inner peace not only through drugs but also through meditation. I studied meditation with a Sufi group in San Francisco, where I began to understand the role of the mind in anxiety. I received teachings and training in meditation from a variety of sources. Through regular "sitting" practice, which I describe in Chapter 8, I was able to face and let go of my anxiety-producing thoughts. I developed the ability to empty my mind and experience my true nature. I frequently enjoyed a state of inner peace, with a quiet mind and open heart. At first, my mind resisted vigorously because it had served for so long as a vigilant guard against threats and danger. It was necessary to diligently practice the yoga and meditation skills I acquired.

Spiritual studies became part of my recovery from fear and anxiety. I explored many wisdom traditions, including Buddhism, Hinduism, Christianity, Judaism, and Native American teachings. In addition to my yoga and meditation practices, I studied many aspects of health and the healing arts, such as massage, herbology, reflexology, and various forms of body work. As I released my body's tension, I was able to experience deeper trust, peace, and feelings of security. I also resumed regular exercise, and I gradually adopted a vegetarian diet, which enhanced my peacefulness. In addition, I sought psychotherapy, where I could talk openly and safely about my anxiety and other feelings.

Equipped with these tools for relaxing my body, controlling my mind, understanding myself, and tapping into spiritual power, I was able to desensitize myself and recover from anxiety. At one point, I faced my biggest fear by taking a year off and traveling by myself, with no itinerary or plans. During this psychological pilgrimage, I spent considerable time by myself, facing my anxiety about being alone, and letting go of the past. At another point, I relocated by myself from San Francisco, California, to Nashville, Tennessee—where I knew no one—to further my professional training. By taking such risks and testing my skills and faith, I experienced a quantum leap forward in my recovery.

One specific incident stands out as an example of the benefits of my anxiety recovery practices. While asleep one night at home, someone broke into my house. When I awoke to the unusual noise, the intruder threatened to shoot me with what appeared to be a shiny weapon. I was able to keep my presence of mind, negotiate with the intruder, who turned out to be a teenage boy, and overpower him through focused attention to his body language and weapon (which was actually a knife). As he pleaded to be released, a profound feeling of compassion overcame me and I let him go. I am certain my life was saved by the mind-body practices that allowed me to stay focused and calm in this life-threatening situation.

What is the reward for working at recovery from anxiety, apart from sheer relief? Anxiety recovery boosted my self-confidence, energy level, and general enjoyment of life. In the recovery process, I learned how to express my feelings more openly, as well as how to deal with conflict. I learned how to love, forgive, and let go of negativity. Anxiety recovery prepared me for a healthy intimate relationship and the joys of marriage and raising children. Through recovery methods such as meditation and relaxation, I now control my mind, rather than having my mind control me. I do not fear aging, or even dying, although I am in no rush to pass on. While I may plan for the future, I live much more in the present. My hope is that more anxiety sufferers will, through their successful recovery, experience these rewards and blessings. I also hope *Dancing with Fear* will help.

# CHAPTER 2

||||||||||||||||||||||

# *What Is Anxiety?*

Anxiety is a normal part of life for everyone. Taking an exam, meeting with a boss or authority figure, having a near accident, starting a new job, or traveling by airplane can all evoke anxiety. Anxiety can even be helpful in preparing for a challenge or change. However, persistent or intense anxiety is abnormal, especially when it interferes with daily life. In such cases, it can become an anxiety disorder requiring professional help.

Anxiety disorders are surprisingly common, and their incidence appears to be rising due to increasing stress and uncertainty in the world. Approximately thirty-seven million American adults suffer from anxiety severe enough to warrant professional help. It is estimated that one out of every four adults will have some form of severe anxiety at some point in their lifetime. Anxiety is the most common emotional disorder, outranking all others, including depression and substance abuse. Indeed, it is estimated that up to 40 percent of those who are dependent on drugs or alcohol have a severe anxiety disorder they are attempting to "self-medicate" and control.

## What Is Anxiety and Why Is It So Prevalent Today?

Anxiety is related to our survival instinct. Normally, when we are confronted with danger or a life-threatening situation, our bodies react quickly with an automatic survival mechanism, known as the fight/flight response. Briefly, this is an energized state that enables us to effectively confront or flee from a life threat. In response to danger, a survival command center in the brain calls for release of activating hormones that organize all body systems for survival. A more detailed

15

description of the fight/flight response is found in the next section, entitled "The Anatomy of Fear."

Many situations can trigger the fight/flight reaction, particularly in sensitive people, even if those situations are not life-threatening. This is precisely what happens in most cases of anxiety: A person reacts as though there is a life-threatening situation when no actual danger exists.

It is normal to fear danger or a threat to our lives. As part of our survival instinct, fear is a natural and adaptive reaction. Anxiety, on the other hand, can be understood as a fear response when there is no actual danger or threat. Anxiety is a maladaptive response because it is a reaction to imagined or perceived threat, or an anticipated threat that is not occurring in the present.

In many cases, anxiety develops as a learned reaction to past fears and extreme stress. For example, if you have a traumatic experience in a particular situation—say, a panic attack while driving a car or a nervous feeling while giving a presentation in front of other people—you may begin to perceive that activity as "dangerous." Thereafter, just thinking about entering the situation—driving a car or giving a presentation—will set the fight/flight survival reaction in motion. In other words, certain situations or places become linked to a negative emotional experience and its associated body reactions, and these situations are then perceived as threatening. Some typical "phobic situations" are traveling away from home, flying, being alone, shopping in crowded stores or malls, meetings, and social gatherings. In these situations, the body reaction itself is normal, but it is triggered by a false alarm.

A common denominator in most anxiety conditions is a fight/flight reaction to a place, thought, feeling, or situation, accompanied by an irrational fear of losing control, "going crazy," embarrassing oneself, having a serious illness, or dying. Worry enters the scene as a form of anticipation of future events in an effort to feel in control. We try to predict what will happen in order to feel prepared. But frequent worry keeps us in a state of anxiety. In the next chapter, we explore the anxiety disorders that develop when this pattern persists.

Sensitivity is a key ingredient in the development of anxiety, and it is important to understand the process of "sensitization." We can turn to Claire Weekes, a pioneer in writing about panic disorder and agoraphobia, for help. Weekes suggests that in sensitive people the reaction to a fight/flight response can become a greater source of fear than the stress originally triggering it. It is this sensitivity that accounts for the "unusual intensity and disconcerting swiftness" of certain people's reaction to stress. She explains, "Most of us have felt the first fear in response to danger. It comes quickly, is normal in intensity and passes with the danger. However, the sensitized person's first fear is so electric, so out of proportion to the danger causing it, he usually recoils from it and at the same time adds a second flash—*fear of the first fear.* He is usually more concerned with the feeling of panic than with the original danger. And because sensitization prolongs the first flash, the second may seem to join it and the two fears are experienced as one." Weekes adds that this is why we may feel "bewildered" by anxiety and have difficulty coping with it.

Many everyday experiences involve the same body activation as in the fight/flight response. Consider, for example, the autonomic arousal involved in sexual excitement: heart rate increases, breathing intensifies, body temperature rises, perspiration is profuse, muscles tense, and arousal escalates until orgasm is reached. Another example is exercise, during which heart rate and respiration increase, perspiration is profuse, body temperature rises, and so on. These are virtually the same reactions as the fight/flight response, although they are not triggered by stress or danger. Most people do not perceive these body reactions as a sign of stress or danger, but for the sensitized person, this type of reaction can trigger anxiety. In such cases, people may avoid exercise or sexual activity because the arousal effects are too similar to anxiety.

Some anxiety symptoms are actually attempts to avoid anxiety. Worrying, for example, is an attempt to anticipate events in order to prepare for what might happen and to feel in control. Similarly, compulsive behaviors, such as double-checking and hoarding things, are ritualized attempts to prevent anxiety. Avoiding anxiety-arousing situations, such as social gatherings, travel, public speaking, standing in lines, and being alone, is another mechanism of defense against anxiety. Some of these behavior patterns do, in fact, succeed in warding off anxiety.

I believe anxiety has become so common today because there is so much stress and so many *potential* threats in the world. Based on increases in actual global threats, such as terrorism and natural disasters, the amount of perceived danger is also increasing. This is reinforced by the media, particularly television, which brings vivid images of threat and disaster into our daily lives.

## The Anatomy of Fear

Fear and anxiety exist on a continuum. They are rooted in the same physiology and can have similar consequences. To get at the essence of anxiety, we must start with the anatomy of fear.

The survival command center is the amygdala, a small, almond-shaped structure that rests at the center of our brain and is elaborately tied to other regions through nerve fibers. When activated, the amygdala triggers a body-wide emergency response within milliseconds. Jolted by impulses from the amygdala, the nearby hypothalamus produces a hormone called *corticotrophin releasing factor,* or CRF, which signals the pituitary and adrenal glands to flood the bloodstream with activating hormones, such as epinephrine (adrenaline), norepinephrine, and cortisol. These "stress hormones" then shut down nonemergency services, such as digestion and immunity, and direct the body's resources to fighting or fleeing. The heart pounds to supply extra oxygen, the lungs pump to assist in oxygen supply, muscles get an energizing blast of glucose and tense up to prepare for fight or flight, vision and hearing become acute and focused, and posture assumes a defensive mode. In an instant, the body becomes charged and energized for self-protection, and all this takes place instinctively and without conscious thought.

Stress hormones also act on the brain, creating a state of heightened alertness and supercharging the circuitry involved in memory formation. The amygdala, in effect, tells the brain to remember the relationship between the fight/flight reaction and the event that triggered it.

It is important to note that, once the chemical messengers are released into the bloodstream, the fight/flight response is launched and cannot readily be stopped. Unlike insulin, the chemical that counteracts high blood sugar, our body produces no chemicals to neutralize the activating hormones. This means we need some time to calm down after a fight/flight reaction to allow for the dissipation of the hormones, even though danger may no longer exist. It is important to allow for some de-escalation time as part of recovery.

### Differences Between Animal and Human Survival Reactions

Imagine for a moment you are an animal, such as a rabbit, living in a natural environment where there is a clearly established pecking order of predators and prey. As a rabbit, you are prey to other animals, such as hawks and foxes. On a typical day, you spend time foraging for food—eating and storing berries, leaves, and roots. However, when you are approached even remotely by a predator, you "sense" danger. Your survival instinct is so attuned that your body reacts without your knowing the specific threat. You immediately respond to the subtle warning signals of danger by taking refuge. You run for cover until danger subsides. When the danger passes, your body relaxes and you resume foraging for food.

The survival instinct described above is a conservative mechanism that takes no chances. Making no distinction between a *possible* and an *actual* threat, it assumes subtle signs of potential danger are real. An activated amygdala does not wait for instructions from the conscious mind. It bypasses conscious thought, because time spent evaluating a threat before responding could result in death.

The fight/flight response in animals is deactivated when danger or threat subsides. As far as we know, animals in natural habitats do not carry tension and anxiety, as we humans often do. They do not worry about future danger or "obsess" about past threats. They recover from the arousal response quickly and they live fully in the present.

The situation is more complex and less reliable for human beings because, for us, danger is often ambiguous. Of course, when the survival reaction occurs in response to a life-threatening situation, such as an assault, fire, riot, or tornado, the fight/flight reaction is normal and appropriate. But, based on prior traumatic or threatening experiences, we tend to perceive danger in response to cues that remind us of threat or danger. In addition, we often interpret ambiguous situations as threatening because we have been sensitized to situations like those in which we had a strongly negative experience.

## The Role of Stress in Anxiety

*Stress* can activate the arousal reaction to the same extent as can danger or life threat. The topic of stress, and its role in anxiety, can be confusing because stress has been defined in terms of both external situations and internal responses. Does stress consist of outside "stressors" that cause certain physical reactions or does stress consist of those internal reactions? Should we understand stress by looking outside or by looking inside?

I think it is necessary to take both external circumstances and internal responses into consideration. Certainly, external events exist that are "stressful" for most people. One measure of stress, in fact, consists of rating a list of life events for their stress value. The Life Change Scale (shown in Chapter 4), as it is called, assumes such events involve demands, adjustments, or change for most people. The test even includes some positive events, such as marriage and job promotions, that are considered stressful because of the adjustments they require.

On the other hand, it is also useful to view stress in terms of the effects of outside pressures that can activate the fight/flight reaction. Let's explore this further.

Generally speaking, an arousal reaction helps us rise to the occasion and cope effectively when we are faced with stressful demands or pressures. If the arousal reaction is focused and short-term, the effect can be beneficial. However, health is jeopardized when the arousal reaction is prolonged. It is known, for example, that stress hormones are toxic to tissue, particularly the heart. Constant, low-grade adrenaline "baths" can damage the heart and raise the long-term risk of cardiovascular disease. Continuous exposure to activating hormones can also dampen the immune system, leaving stressed people more vulnerable to infections. Stress hormones can harm the brain, too, severing connections between neurons. In both human and animal studies, researchers have found that prolonged stress shrinks the hippocampus, a brain structure that plays a critical role in processing and storing information.

The most important thing to understand about the role of stress in anxiety is that stress produces many of the same body reactions as fear does. In Chapter 4, stress is discussed in more depth because it is one of the key ingredients in the development of an anxiety disorder. In that chapter, stress is considered the ingredient that determines when anxiety symptoms will show up.

## Strong Emotions and the Fight/Flight Response

Strong emotions can also trigger the fight/flight mechanism. Actually, it would be more accurate to say that emotional arousal and the fight/flight response involve the same body reactions. Anger, for example, involves arousal in the form of muscle tension, increased heart rate, increased blood pressure, and intensification of breathing. Excitement is another recognizable example.

The sensitive or anxious person tends to fear such strong emotions because of the body reactions associated with them. In addition, many anxiety sufferers have been reared in families where feelings were not discussed or expressed or, even more damaging, actively discouraged or punished. In some families, feelings are associated with out-of-control behavior or violence. For all these reasons, most people who develop anxiety disorders tend to be fearful of strong feelings. Chapter 4, "The Three Key Ingredients in Anxiety Disorders," addresses in more depth the issues associated with feelings. Chapters 13 and 14 deal with feelings and anxiety, and include helpful techniques for safe and appropriate expression of feelings.

## Thought Patterns and Anxiety

Finally, there are a number of *thought patterns* that can trigger the fight/flight reaction. These patterns include worrying, "shoulds," perfectionistic thinking, negative thinking, and all-or-nothing thinking. Let's discuss each of these cognitive styles briefly and see how they contribute to stress, arousal, and anxiety. Chapter 11 includes suggestions for replacing each of these thought patterns with more positive alternatives as a way to reduce anxiety.

Worrying involves "what-if" thoughts, which are negative anticipations about what might happen in the near or distant future. "What-if" thoughts are the primary feature of generalized anxiety disorder, and are found in most other anxiety disorders. Some examples are:

"What if the school bus goes off the road with my child on it?"

"What if I forgot to turn off the oven?"

"What if I have a panic attack in the mall?"

"What if I have a serious but undetected illness?"

Since the survival instinct takes no chances in the face of danger, it treats "what-if" thoughts as signals of *definite* rather than *possible* threat. Therefore, worrying can lead to high arousal, fight/flight reactions.

"Shoulds" are a related thought pattern common to many anxious persons. These are internalized rules that drive behavior. Like perfectionistic thinking, shoulds are unreasonable expectations of ourselves that create stress. Some sample shoulds are:

"I should be more productive."

"I should eat a healthier diet or lose weight."

"I should be a better parent."

"I shouldn't procrastinate so much."

"I should be in control of myself at all times."

"I should keep a cleaner home."

Perfectionistic thinking is another pattern that can trigger body reactions and anxiety. Perfectionism is based on a need to have everything "just right." Perfectionistic people tend to push and drive themselves, often to the point of exhaustion, as they strive to attain the elusive goal of perfection. Unfortunately, when they "fail," perfectionistic people tend to feel frustrated and disappointed. They can also become self-critical or blame problems on forces beyond their control. Perfection may be possible once in awhile, but not all the time. Expecting it creates stress and anxiety.

Negative thinking reflects low self-esteem and contributes to anxiety because it leads to feelings of helplessness and powerlessness. Negative thinking is associated with pessimism about the future. This thought pattern also contributes to gloomy feelings and depression. Some examples of negative thoughts are: "I never finish things," "I'm not motivated enough to succeed," "This is going to be a bad day, I can just feel it," and "I have bad luck." If our thoughts create our reality, then negative thinking makes us unhappy and ineffective.

Yet another thought pattern that contributes to body reactions and anxiety is "all-or-nothing" thinking. This is a habit whereby everything is judged as good or bad—right or wrong—with nothing in between. Some examples of "all-or-nothing" thinking are:

"If I do not know what will happen, then it will probably be bad."

"If I make a mistake, then I am 'stupid.'"

"If you are not friendly to me one day, then you must be an unfriendly person."

"If I cannot learn something on the first try, then it is too difficult for me to learn no matter how hard I try."

"If you did not do a great job, then you must have done a bad job."

These examples of all-or-nothing thinking are common among anxious people, who frequently monitor the environment for safety and danger. When danger cues are unclear, these individuals prepare for the worst.

### Conclusion

It should now be apparent that the fight/flight reaction is a natural response to danger, but can be aroused by perceived danger, stress, strong emotions, and certain thought patterns. Obviously, when danger is clear and present, the fight/flight reaction serves a life-saving purpose. And when stress is the trigger, the fight/flight reaction can serve the useful function of providing energy to cope. However, the anxious person creates stress through worry, perfectionism, unreasonable expectations, and a tendency to perceive threat when it does not actually exist. In addition, the anxious person tends to be highly sensitive to arousal reactions. For these reasons, the fight/flight reaction can set off a cycle of anxiety involving body reactions, followed by fear of those reactions, leading to more reactions. Secondary fears—of having a heart attack, going crazy, or losing control—further feed into the pattern, causing a vicious cycle of anxiety.

In the next chapter, we look at the consequences of prolonged anxiety. We identify various patterns of anxiety, or anxiety disorders, that can develop when a person lives in a state of heightened arousal.

# CHAPTER 3

|||||||||||||||||||||||||

# The Anxiety Disorders

Anumber of patterns can develop when anxiety becomes intense or chronic. These recurrent symptom patterns are referred to as *anxiety disorders,* to distinguish them from normal or transient anxiety. Each anxiety disorder consists of a distinct set of symptoms and can be diagnosed on the basis of those symptoms. Anxiety crosses the line and becomes a disorder when it interferes consistently with day-to-day functioning.

I have included this information to help you recognize typical signs and symptoms of anxiety disorders. However, a diagnosis of anxiety should be confirmed by an experienced mental-health professional, who can distinguish between normal and abnormal anxiety as well as determine if professional help is advisable.

In describing each anxiety disorder, I summarize the primary symptoms, followed by a brief case example. In addition to the specific anxiety disorders, I discuss the relationship between depression and anxiety.

Until recently, child and adult anxiety disorders were listed separately, based on the belief that children do not experience the same types of anxiety as adults do. We now know that children and adults experience the same anxiety conditions. For example, contrary to old myths, children can experience panic attacks, and adults can suffer from separation anxiety. Therefore, in the most recently revised *Diagnostic and Statistical Manual of Mental Disorders* (1994), published by the American Psychiatric Association, there is no distinction between child and adult anxiety disorders, with the exception of separation anxiety disorder. However, many mental-health professionals, including myself, have encountered separation anxiety disorder in adults and this exception is likely to be eliminated in the next edition of the diagnostic system. I am, therefore, including separation anxiety disorder in this discussion.

Children, adolescents, and adults can develop any of the following anxiety disorders:

- Panic disorder (with or without agoraphobia)

- Generalized anxiety disorder (GAD)

- Social anxiety

- Specific phobias

- Separation anxiety disorder

- Obsessive-compulsive disorder (OCD)

- Post-traumatic stress disorder (PTSD)

- Acute anxiety disorder

- Anxiety associated with a medical condition

- Substance-induced anxiety disorder

A List of Common Anxiety Disorders

When there is more than one distinct anxiety disorder present, it is appropriate to diagnose each separately. Mental-health professionals have a "multi-axis" coding system for recording more than one disorder.

### Panic Disorder

Panic disorder is known for episodes of intense anxiety—or panic attacks—that seem to come "out of the blue." Panic disorder can occur with or without agoraphobia—a pattern of avoiding situations in which one might expect to have an anxiety attack. We will discuss the agoraphobia component later in this section. But first, what is a panic attack?

Panic attacks consist of sudden and intense arousal symptoms, such as heart palpitations or pounding, chest pain, shortness of breath or difficulty breathing, choking sensations, shaking, weakness, sweating, nausea, dizziness, and faintness. These symptoms can be so physically intense that people often fear they are having a heart attack or other life-threatening medical condition.

There are also some corresponding psychological reactions, such as racing thoughts and feelings of unreality or detachment. These psychological symptoms make some people with panic disorder fear they will "go crazy," lose their minds, or embarrass themselves by losing control in public. Essentially, a panic attack is a sudden, unwanted fight/flight reaction with a corresponding fear of losing control.

People who experience panic attacks usually seek help from a medical doctor or go to a hospital emergency room. Typically, they are medically evaluated and told there is nothing physically wrong. They may receive a prescription for a tranquilizer to help with "stress." Unfortunately, a referral to a mental-health professional is not usually made. Without appropriate help, this anxiety disorder usually progresses, and the agoraphobia component can emerge.

It is natural for people experiencing panic disorder to begin avoiding situations in which they anticipate further attacks. This component is known as *agoraphobia,* the Greek term for fear *(phobia)* of the marketplace *(agora),* or in more modern terms, "fear of being in public." A diagnosis of panic disorder with agoraphobia is used when people show a pattern of avoiding situations, such as shopping, travel, or public places, or avoiding separation from a security figure, in an effort to manage their anticipatory anxiety. The person fears that being in one of these situations will lead to another anxiety attack, loss of control, or embarrassment. In extreme cases, people can become severely restricted or even "house-bound," but in most cases avoidance is limited to specific situations.

The symptoms of panic disorder are as follows:

**The Symptoms of Panic Disorder**

- Heart palpitations, pounding heart, or accelerated heart rate

- Sweating

- Trembling or shaking

- Shortness of breath or smothering/choking sensations

- Chest pain or discomfort

- Nausea or abdominal distress

- Feeling dizzy, unsteady, lightheaded, or faint
- Feelings of unreality
- Fear of losing control, going crazy, or dying
- Numbness or tingling
- Chills or hot flashes

### Harriet

*Harriet, who was referred to me for help by her physician, had the classic symptoms of panic disorder. Her panic attacks frequently occurred while she was driving, so she was afraid to get into the car by herself. This fear was so intense that she was unable to come by herself to the first few appointments. In fact, her life had become increasingly limited, to the point that she needed her husband to accompany her to any new situation. She was a school teacher, and to get to work, she often offered to pick up a colleague who lived on the way, in order to avoid being alone in her car. "All day long I would panic just thinking about the drive home," she told me. Harriet spent considerable time anticipating and worrying about every trip out of the house.*

*When I first saw Harriet, she was tearful and depressed about her inability to control her fear. Fortunately, Harriet's therapy was successful. In just sixteen weeks, she went from fifteen to twenty panic attacks a day to only occasional attacks; instead of being "troubled by anxiety" several hours a day, that feeling lasted five minutes at most. She was also able to discontinue the tranquilizing medication she was taking when she first came for help.*

### Daniel

*Daniel, a sensitive, thoughtful young man and father of two children, came to me with an agoraphobia pattern. At the beginning of his treatment for panic disorder with agoraphobia, he avoided shopping malls, large stores, and church (about which he felt extremely guilty). Daniel said, "Currently, everywhere I go and every-*

*thing I do I need to think about how the anxiety might affect me during the activity. Fear has almost total control over my life, and I feel that it has enveloped me and is smothering me. I do not want to spend the rest of my life with this fear."*

## Generalized Anxiety Disorder

This anxiety disorder is characterized by unrealistic worry about future and past events, excessive concern about performing competently, and significant self-consciousness. People with this form of anxiety often seek reassurance from others, and they may limit their involvement to activities in which they feel confident of success and positive feedback. Due to their excessive need for reassurance, people with this disorder easily feel slighted and are highly sensitive to criticism. They also tend to have physical complaints during periods of increased anxiety, such as stomachaches and headaches. In addition, generalized anxiety disorder often involves sleep disturbance, which in turn, leads to fatigue and low energy.

A diagnosis of generalized anxiety disorder can be made if a person experiences four or more of the following symptoms for six months or longer:

- Excessive or unrealistic worry about future events

- Excessive or unrealistic worry about the appropriateness of past events

**The Symptoms of GAD**

- Excessive or unrealistic concern about competence in one or more areas, including academic, athletic, and social

- Bodily complaints with no established physical basis

- Excessive self-consciousness

- Excessive need for reassurance about many things

- Difficulty relaxing and a high level of tension

### Lisa

*Lisa's generalized anxiety disorder consisted of spending twelve to sixteen hours a day worrying excessively and anticipating negative events. A homemaker and mother of three children, Lisa focused on all the "bad things" that could happen and felt she had little control over her life. Lisa often woke up feeling tired, as though she could not get enough sleep, no matter how many hours she slept, and she felt tense during the day. Lisa could relax only temporarily when reassured her worrying was unreasonable and unnecessary. Therapy, however, was effective in helping her replace worrying with more positive and realistic thinking.*

## Social Anxiety

Social phobia, or social anxiety disorder, is characterized by a marked fear of social or performance situations, especially when exposed to unfamiliar people or to possible scrutiny by others. Socially anxious people fear they will act in a way that is humiliating or embarrassing, such as showing anxiety symptoms or blushing. Social anxiety is triggered by situations, such as meetings, public speaking, parties, classes, and other activities involving interaction with or proximity to people.

Avoidance of such situations, if possible, is usually the first line of defense against anxiety. When phobic situations cannot be avoided, they are experienced as extremely stressful, and the anxious anticipation escalates. Some of my patients have used the term "white knuckling it" to refer to the tension involved in suffering through a phobic situation. The criteria for a diagnosis of social phobia are as follows:

**Diagnostic Criteria for Social Phobia**

- Persistent and significant fear of one or more social or performance situations involving unfamiliar people or possible scrutiny by others

- Fear of humiliation or embarrassment as a result of own behavior

- Exposure to feared social situation provokes anxiety (e.g., panic, freezing, crying or tantrums in children, attempts to avoid)

- Avoidance of social or performance situations, or intense anxiety if unable to avoid

- Anxious anticipation, avoidance, or anxiety reaction interferes with normal routines (e.g., work, school, social)

- Physical manifestations that include muscle tension, dry mouth, cracking voice, the urge to urinate, trembling hands or legs, blushing, racing heart, and difficulty breathing

A history of shyness can be associated with social phobia. One way to distinguish between the two is to think of shyness as a personality trait. Shy people are usually cautious and inhibited, and tend to avoid social interaction in order to prevent anxiety. Social phobia, on the other hand, involves more intense anxiety that can be aroused by just the thought of interacting socially. In spite of these subtle distinctions, shyness and social anxiety often go hand in hand.

### Fred

*Fred, who was painfully afraid of meetings, social events, and dating, suffered from social phobia. He was convinced he would say something foolish and people would laugh or think he was "stupid." Fred told me he sometimes went for several days without interacting with another human being, even at work. Although he felt more comfortable avoiding social contact, he revealed how lonely and isolated he was. Fred yearned for a special relationship, but his anxiety inhibited him from making any efforts to socialize. To help Fred, I first focused on his negative view of himself, which seemed to be the basis of his concern that others would judge him negatively. I then encouraged him to participate in one of my weekly therapy groups, where he was able to practice social interactions and reduce the intensity of his anxiety.*

## Specific Phobia

This anxiety disorder involves excessive and persistent fear, triggered by exposure or anticipated exposure to a specific object or situation, such as flying, heights, being alone, darkness, particular animals, medical offices or hospitals, and speaking in front of other people. Proximity to the feared object or situation usually leads to an immediate anxiety reaction, which can appear as a panic attack or other intense arousal response. Phobias are often embedded in other anxiety disorders, such as panic disorder and obsessive-compulsive disorder (discussed below). Phobias are considered the most common anxiety disorder. The criteria for a diagnosis of specific phobia are listed below.

With children, it is important to distinguish between specific phobias and developmentally normal fears. Readers are referred to the chapter on childhood anxiety disorders in my book, *The Worried Child*, for a chart that shows the common fears in children for each age group.

The symptoms of specific phobia are as follows:

- Persistent, excessive, or unreasonable fear triggered by presence or anticipation of a specific object or situation (e.g., visiting the doctor, storms, heights, water, animals)

**The Symptoms of Specific Phobia**

- Exposure to the phobic situation provokes an immediate anxiety reaction (e.g., panic, freezing)

- Attempts to avoid the situation, or intense anxiety if unable to avoid

- Anxious anticipation, avoidance, or anxiety reactions that interfere with normal routines (e.g., work, school, social, family)

### Maria

*Specific phobia is exemplified by Maria, who came to see me about her fear of flying. Approximately five years earlier, she had experienced panic anxiety, triggered by an extremely rough airplane ride, on a trip to Florida. "It was the worst experience of my life, and when I got off that plane I vowed I would never fly again," she told me. After the incident, Maria could not even think about flying without intense anxiety, and avoided flying in spite of a love of travel. As a supervisor at work, Maria functioned effectively with people and job pressure. She had no other problems with anxiety, but felt strongly that she was restricted by her fear of flying. Her goal was to be able to go again on vacations to des-*

*tinations requiring air travel. Maria did achieve this goal through a combination of mentally rehearsing air travel while relaxed, as well as having appropriate medication available as back-up when she did begin to fly again. See Chapter 17 for a discussion about the medication used in Maria's case.*

## Separation Anxiety

Although the American Psychiatric Association reserves the diagnosis of separation anxiety for children, I am convinced adults can and do suffer from this disorder. In fact, in the cases of some children experiencing separation anxiety disorder, I have found that the parents were also experiencing anxiety about letting go of their children.

Separation anxiety consists of excessive, persistent, and intense worry associated with separation from a security figure. Anxiety symptoms usually emerge in anticipation of separation, followed by worry about losing control and not being able to function without the presence of the security figure. The adult symptoms of separation anxiety, which is usually noted in children, are as follows:

**The Adult Symptoms of Separation Anxiety**

- Fear or worry that a destructive event will befall the security figure, thereby preventing their return

- Fear that the attachment figure will leave permanently

- Avoidance of being alone or without the security figure

- Somatic symptoms (nausea or gastrointestinal distress, loss of appetite, difficulty sleeping), especially in anticipation of being without the attachment figure

### Hugh

*Hugh, a competent special education teacher, functioned without anxiety on the job. However, he came to me for help because he experienced severe anxiety, including panic attacks, whenever his wife was late coming home from her job. Hugh's anxiety peaked*

*when she was scheduled to travel on business, and he found it nec-*
*essary to stay with a friend or have one of their adult children come*
*home for the night. No one would have guessed that Hugh suf-*
*fered from this anxiety disorder because he seemed to be in control*
*whenever other people were around. I helped Hugh by teaching*
*him how to tolerate the anxious feelings that arose under condi-*
*tions of separation from his wife, as well as by drawing his atten-*
*tion to the issue of control. He learned to accept that he was not in*
*control of many aspects of life and to focus on those areas where he*
*could have control, such as his thoughts and body reactions.*

## Obsessive-Compulsive Disorder

Obsessive-compulsive disorder (OCD) has received considerable public attention in the media. The movies *As Good as It Gets* and *The Aviator,* as well as the television series *Monk,* have dramatized OCD, even in an endearing way in some cases. Nevertheless, OCD is a serious condition that is usually troubling and disabling. What is OCD all about?

OCD is a pattern of anxiety involving either unwanted thoughts (obsessions) or compulsions to engage in repetitive behaviors aimed at preventing or controlling anxious feelings. The focus of obsessive think-ing can be on many different things, but is often sexual or aggressive in nature. Common compulsions include excessive cleaning, double-check-ing, and hoarding things. Often both obsessive and compulsive com-ponents are involved. In fact, compulsive behavior is usually driven by obsessive fears that something bad will happen or that the anxiety will escalate out of control if the compulsive behavior is inhibited or resisted. For example, a person might excessively engage in hand washing due to fear of contamination and illness.

The person with this condition usually knows that the thoughts and behaviors are exaggerated and unreasonable, but is unable to stop them. Shame and secrecy about this pattern cause people to hide it and delay seeking help.

I find it useful to think of OCD patterns as attempts to control or prevent anxiety. This is particularly apparent with respect to compulsive behavior, such as checking, ordering, hoarding, and cleaning. The per-son usually feels relieved and more relaxed after engaging in the OCD behavior pattern, but feels more anxious if he or she tries to resist it. In terms of overcoming this form of anxiety, it is important to replace the symptomatic behavior with other methods of achieving relaxation.

OCD can consist of either obsessions or compulsions, or both, as defined below:

### Obsessions

- Recurrent or persistent thoughts or images that are experienced as intrusive and inappropriate

  Obsessions are defined as …

- The thoughts or images cause anxiety or distress

- Person attempts to ignore or suppress the thoughts or images, or to neutralize them with other thoughts or action

- Recognition that such thoughts and images are from the person's own mind

- Obsessions are often time-consuming (take up more than one hour per day) or interfere with normal routines

### Compulsions

- Driven to perform repetitive behaviors (e.g., hand washing, checking, arranging things) or acts (e.g., counting, repeating words silently), usually according to rigid rules

  Compulsions are defined as …

- The behaviors or acts are aimed at preventing or reducing distress

- The behaviors or acts are not a realistic way of preventing or reducing distress

- Compulsions are often time-consuming (take up more than one hour per day) or interfere with normal routines

Some experts believe OCD is caused by a disorder of brain chemistry. Indeed, a specific area of the brain involved in OCD, called the caudate nucleus, has been identified. However, I prefer to interpret the findings of recent brain research as revealing the biochemical mechanisms involved in anxiety disorders, rather than their cause. One reason this makes sense to me is that OCD research has found that brain chemistry can be changed by cognitive-behavioral techniques to the same extent as it can be by medications used to treat OCD. This suggests a reciprocal relationship between brain chemistry and thought processes, and implies that negative patterns of thought can cause aberrations in brain chemistry. In other words, a two-way relationship may exist between thought process and brain chemistry. Thought patterns can both wound and heal the brain.

Cognitive-behavioral techniques for counteracting OCD are discussed in Chapter 11. The pros and cons of medication for treating anxiety disorders, such as OCD, are reviewed in Chapter 17.

### Olivia

*Olivia was unable to leave her home without checking to make sure she had not left any fire hazards. She checked every electrical outlet in the house to make sure no curtain or other flammable material was near enough to catch fire and unplugged numerous appliances (toaster, hair dryer, lamps). She spent an inordinate amount of time performing these safety rituals, and her anxiety persisted even when she was reassured that curtains could not catch fire by touching the outside of a wall outlet, and that modern electrical systems have circuit breakers to cut off power in the event of a short circuit. On one occasion, Olivia put her toaster in the trunk of her car before coming to a therapy appointment as the only way to ensure that a kitchen fire would not occur while she was out of the house. Olivia was habitually late for appointments and work due to the unreasonable time she spent protecting her home from fire. This was a severe case of OCD that took time to overcome. I was able to help her by explaining that the issue was her low tolerance for anxiety-producing thoughts ("My house might burn down") and that she needed to be able to experience such thoughts without engaging in excessive checking.*

Another aspect of OCD seen in many cases is an attempt to manage anxiety through keeping things as predictable and controlled as possible. For example, some of my patients have reported they eat the same foods at the same time every day. For example, Bruce feared that if he changed his eating habits and deviated from his routine diet, he might get food poisoning. Although Bruce complained his diet was "boring," he needed help to overcome his irrational fear and add more interest to his diet and life in general. I have seen variations on this issue, some of which involved a full-fledged eating disorder, such as anorexia (intentional undereating to control body weight).

## Post-Traumatic Stress Disorder

The term *post-traumatic stress disorder* was originally coined in reference to Vietnam veterans who were deeply psychologically scarred by the horrors of war. In my clinical practice, this anxiety disorder is most commonly seen as a reaction to physical and sexual abuse, and is often accompanied by depression and other symptoms. However, any event that involves threat or injury or is outside the normal range of human experience can be traumatic and produce this pattern of anxiety. Traumatic events include rape, school shootings, automobile accidents, violence within a family, terrorist attacks, and natural disasters. Preoccupation with the traumatic experiences, recurring nightmares and/or flashbacks, unprovoked anger, difficulty relaxing, irritability, inability to concentrate, and sleep difficulties are common symptoms of this anxiety disorder. The symptoms of PTSD are as follows:

- Response to the trauma involving intense fear, helplessness, or horror, which may be expressed as disorganized or agitated behavior

> The Symptoms of Post-Traumatic Stress Disorder

- Persistent re-experiencing of the event, in the form of distressing memories, disturbing dreams, acting or feeling as if the event were recurring, reenactment of specific aspects of the trauma, or strong physical or emotional reactions to reminders of the trauma

- Avoidance of reminders of the trauma

- Numbing of general responsiveness, such as detachment from others, limited emotions, and difficulty feeling love

- Symptoms of increased arousal, such as sleep disturbance, impaired concentration, irritability, and angry outbursts

Approximately half of the clients I see who complain of anxiety have experienced a trauma in childhood.

### Roberto

*During his childhood, Roberto was a victim of brutal physical abuse by his father. Not surprisingly, Roberto was also emotionally abused: His father called him names such as "stupid," "good for nothing," "queer," and "son of a bitch." Roberto had two sisters who were also abused, except their cases included incest. The abuse was profound, and the effects were devastating.*

*Roberto developed several anxiety conditions that persisted well into adulthood, when he came in for help. In addition to PTSD, he had a stuttering disorder, social phobia, fear of male authority figures, and OCD. His self-esteem suffered, and he had lingering feelings of shame.*

*As a youth, Roberto's primary escape from the traumatic family situation was going to the movies. He would spend an entire day watching movies at a theater, which temporarily took his mind off his abusive home life. He ran away from home at age sixteen and did not return to visit until he was an adult. When he first became my client, he was unable to visit his hometown or parents without having intense anxiety symptoms. I worked with Roberto for approximately ten years to counteract the effects of his traumatic family history, eventually tapering off to monthly appointments to maintain positive results. Roberto has learned how to relax, and while in therapy, he met a sensitive and accepting woman with whom he now has a fulfilling relationship. He is able to visit his family and parents without anxiety.*

### Carrie

*Another client with PTSD is Carrie, who was sexually abused by her stepfather. The abuse was repeated many times. One episode occurred on her thirteenth birthday, when her stepfather invited some male "friends" to participate. Carrie suffered a long history of PTSD as well as panic attacks with agoraphobia. Her relationships were affected, and anxiety was a problem in many areas, including difficulty trusting other people (especially men), travel avoidance, and low self-esteem. Yet in spite of the overwhelming childhood trauma, Carrie functioned effectively in her job, and was an exceptionally sensitive parent. She was referred to me by a female counselor when it was determined that working with a male therapist might be beneficial.*

*One successful aspect of Carrie's therapy was her ability to trust me and feel comfortable discussing her traumatic history. Talking about past trauma is a form of exposure therapy, which can help reduce anxiety associated with the memory or reminders of the trauma. One of the goals in Carrie's therapy was to be able to travel so she could help her children select colleges and visit them after they left home. We used the power of Carrie's bond with her children to help her face the anxiety associated with travel, and to learn she could handle the stress if it meant she would gain the joy of visiting her children.*

## Acute Stress Disorder

A diagnosis of acute stress disorder is used if symptoms of PTSD are apparent within a month of a traumatic event. All other criteria for diagnosing this anxiety disorder are the same as for PTSD.

### Doris

*Doris was referred to me by an attorney who was representing her in a lawsuit against a hair salon. Apparently, a hair stylist mismanaged the type and exposure time of chemicals used to color Doris's hair. Her hair was so badly burned that it was necessary to remove virtually all of it. Because she herself was a hair stylist, Doris felt ashamed and unable to face her clients. She reluctantly wore a wig and stopped working. Doris presented with many of the symptoms of PTSD, such as anger, agitation, and irritability, sleep disturbance, distressing memories, flashbacks of the trauma, and avoidance of everything associated with her work as a hairstylist.*

## Anxiety Associated with Medical Conditions

Anxiety can develop in conjunction with a serious medical condition or disease. Symptoms can include panic attacks, obsessions or compulsions, phobias, or excessive worry. A diagnosis of anxiety due to a medical condition can be used if there is evidence the anxiety is the direct consequence of a specific medical problem. Virtually any serious medical condition can trigger anxiety, especially if associated with pain or suffering, periodic relapses, or life threat. In my practice, I find anxiety associated with many medical issues, such as chronic fatigue immune deficiency syndrome (CFIDS), Crohn's disease, fibromyalgia, and anticipation of surgery.

### Harold

*Harold was a youthful and energetic sixty-year-old professor who suffered from pain when urinating. He was advised by his urologist to have prostate surgery to relieve the painful condition, but he postponed the procedure for several years due to intense fear of anesthesia and surgery. In fact, he chose to live with a highly restricted diet, dehydration from limited water intake, and daily urination pain, rather than face the treatment that promised to relieve the problem. I helped Harold focus on the positive benefits and outcome, instead of the details and risks of surgery. I also suggested he provide the anesthesiologist with a set of affirmations to be spoken during this phase of the procedure (to help develop trust). Furthermore, I taught Harold how to relax and combine relaxation with positive imagery of the medical procedure. The outcome was positive and Harold said he gained a "new lease on life" by facing his fear and having the surgery. After recovering from the surgery, he was able to once again eat the foods he loved and function normally when going to the bathroom.*

The relationship between medical conditions and anxiety can be reciprocal. Not only can a medical condition trigger anxiety, but anxiety can intensify or cause a flare-up of a medical condition. For example, when one of my clients felt stressed, she experienced an intensification of her fibromyalgia pain. She would then panic and rush to the hospital emergency room, thinking, "What if this is the beginning of a panic attack or a heart attack?" Her anxiety reaction then reactivated her pain symptoms.

Another patient of mine, Kelly, presented with an unusual phobia about being touched by other people. At the time I saw her in therapy, she was a high school senior with little insight into the nature or cause of her anxiety disorder. In just one interview, however, the basis for her anxiety became clear to me. Kelly had a brain tumor at age ten, and a medical intervention to drain fluid from her brain resulted in an infection. She had undergone four brain surgeries by age eleven, in addition to eye surgery at age nine. Kelly became "sensitized" to being touched as a result of traumatic surgeries on two vital organs.

There are also a number of medical conditions whose features overlap with anxiety symptoms. In some of these cases, the medical condition can be misdiagnosed as an anxiety disorder. A few examples are hyperthyroidism, hypoglycemia, asthma, and mitral valve prolapse.

## Substance-Induced Anxiety Disorder

Anxiety can be induced by prescription or illegal drugs, such as inhalants, amphetamines, marijuana, cocaine, and sedatives. Caffeine and alcohol can also have similar effects. The anxiety symptoms can occur during or within a month of drug use or withdrawal. Under these circumstances, a diagnosis of substance-induced anxiety disorder may be applicable.

### Quinn

*Quinn was a bright, college-bound high-school senior who was referred to me with intense anxiety about "losing his mind." He worried frequently about memory loss, especially around other people, and was distressed about not being able to control these thoughts. I learned that Quinn had experimented just once with marijuana and had had a "bad experience" involving mild visual hallucinations in which he "saw himself from outside himself." Although some people might experience this state as entertaining, Quinn was terrified it would recur or become permanent. He was not readily reassured that this was unlikely to happen because he had no such history. With some time and therapy, Quinn stopped worrying about losing his mind, although he relapsed briefly during his first semester at college when the stress of leaving home and starting a new stage of life became high. We met a few times when he was home from college for holidays and school breaks. The anxiety disorder subsided again and I have not heard from Quinn in several years.*

### Depression and Anxiety

Depression is a separate set of emotional disorders that generally exist without anxiety. Typical signs and symptoms of depression include low energy, loss of motivation and interest, sleep disturbance, and social withdrawal. This emotional problem is often severe enough to interfere with friendships and family relationships, job productivity, and overall health.

In some cases, depression develops as the result of a prolonged anxiety disorder. For example, people with social anxiety who have few close friends or a limited social support system may feel isolated and become depressed. Similarly, those who have panic disorder with agoraphobia may become depressed because they limit their exposure to social or other situations they associate with anxiety. And victims of abuse who develop PTSD may develop depression as a result of anger that is turned inward or as a result of difficulty with trust and intimate relationships. Finally, the frequent worry involved in generalized anxiety disorder usually results in difficulty sleeping, low energy, and fatigue—all symptoms of depression. In all these cases, depression is considered secondary to the primary anxiety disorder.

Depression becomes part of the anxiety picture when some of the signs and symptoms shown in the following list are involved:

- Social withdrawal
- Sleep disturbance
- Fatigue or low energy
- Poor appetite or overeating
- Loss of interest in activities usually associated with pleasure
- Having medically unexplained aches and pains

The
Signs and
Symptoms of
Depression

- Low motivation

- Difficulty concentrating or memory problems

- Feeling worthless or guilty

- Restlessness or fidgety movement

- Feeling anxious

If the primary condition is an anxiety disorder, any secondary symptoms of depression usually subside when the anxiety is properly addressed. In other cases, both an anxiety disorder and a depressive disorder may coexist, and may need to be addressed separately.

### Harriet

*You may recall Harriet, one of my patients who had panic disorder with agoraphobia. Harriet experienced depression as a secondary consequence of her dependency on her husband and coworkers. She could not go shopping or run errands by herself, and was exhausted from frequent worry about when her next panic attack would occur. This was demoralizing and depressing for a forty-year-old woman with three children. On a self-evaluation at the outset of therapy, she rated herself as 9 on a 10-point scale for depression. By the 16-week point in therapy, she had not only reduced the frequency of her anxiety, but also the degree to which she felt depressed and out of control. At that point, Harriet rated herself as 2 on the same 10-point depression scale. In short, her depression subsided when she addressed her anxiety.*

## Conclusion

Anxiety recovery begins with an understanding of what is happening in the body and mind, and what is triggering the anxiety reactions. It is important to realize that anxiety is not a life-threatening disorder. Except for "anxiety disorder due to a medical condition," your physician has probably ruled out a medical problem and you do not have a fatal illness. You are not losing your mind and you are not "mental" or psychotic. You can change this learned pattern and recover from anxiety. May the rest of this book deepen your understanding of anxiety and show you the way out.

# CHAPTER 4

# The Three Key Ingredients in Anxiety Disorders

Anxiety disorders, as we know, develop in some people and not in others. If you have experienced any of the anxiety disorders or symptoms discussed in the previous chapter, it is likely the model presented in this chapter will apply to you. I created this model based on many years as a clinical psychologist working with anxiety patients, and it invariably fits my clients. It is useful in understanding why anxiety develops in some of us, and also suggests what we can do to manage, and even prevent, an anxiety disorder. I have named this understanding of anxiety development the Three Ingredients Model. Let's see if it fits you.

There are three basic ingredients in the development of anxiety:

1. Biological sensitivity

2. Personality type

3. Stress overload

In this chapter, we explore each of these three ingredients and begin to identify what we can do to manage anxiety.

## Biological Sensitivity

The disposition to develop anxiety begins with a genetic factor, which could be called *biological sensitivity*. This refers to the fact that some of us are born with a high level of sensitivity to both external stimulation (such as lights and sounds) as well as to internal stimulation (such as our own bodily reactions and feelings). Due to such sensitivity, we tend to react intensely to many forms of stimulation, including vivid movies, news reports, other people's feelings and behavior, and even our own thoughts. Biological sensitivity is present at birth, but it does not mean we are born fearful or anxious. We are simply born with a sensitive temperament—a disposition toward reacting to stimuli with higher than average intensity. We are especially sensitive to stress, which, as will we see, is the key to determining *when* we may become symptomatic with anxiety.

I can personally identify with the qualities of the highly sensitive person. I am affected strongly by many different kinds of internal and external stimuli, such as noisy environments, strong odors, fatigue and hunger, low blood sugar, other people's moods, violence seen on television and in the movies, and even the weather.

This aspect of genetic temperament has led psychotherapist and author Elaine Aron to use the term "highly sensitive person." In her books, Aron details the advantages and pitfalls of high sensitivity and refers to this temperament as a mixed blessing. On the positive side, those who are highly sensitive tend to be keen observers of human behavior and are effective as teachers, social workers, nurses, parents, health-care professionals, and other roles that involve interpersonal sensitivity. They tend to be creative and respond positively to art and music. On the other hand, they are easily thrown off balance and need to take precautions in order to maintain their health and function effectively in a not-so-sensitive world. In Part II, we address some of the precautions and recommendations for managing the high sensitivity factor.

Biological sensitivity has been identified in children as young as four months of age. In research settings, such children are observed to react more strongly to unfamiliar sounds and objects. By age seven, they show symptoms of anxiety. However, if their parents help them to refocus their attention away from the unfamiliar stimuli, these children are less likely to develop an anxiety disorder.

Brain research during the past ten years suggests that the genetic component in anxiety may also include an overactive emotional center, or limbic system. The limbic system is associated with how we react to what we see, hear, smell, think, and feel. The research does not indicate with certainty that an oversensitive limbic system causes anxiety, but there does seem to be a correlation between the two.

Brain research also suggests a biochemical basis for some anxiety disorders, such as OCD. This idea is discussed in Chapter 17, when we address the role of medication in treatment of anxiety.

## The Anxiety Personality Style

The second ingredient in the development of an anxiety disorder is a pattern of personality traits I call the *anxiety personality style*. Let's start with a brief definition of personality and then look at the specific personality traits that seem to be common in anxious people, noting how this type of personality creates stress and anxiety symptoms. After that, we consider the kinds of family background and childhood experiences that combine with genetics to form the anxiety personality style.

Personality is the combination of traits and qualities that makes each of us unique. Yet, there seem to be recognizable types of personalities—patterns shared by people who have certain traits in common. Some psychological tests attempt to determine an individual's personality type based on patterns of behavior, thought, and emotional style. For example, based on a theory of personality developed by Carl Jung, the Myers-Briggs Type Indicator is widely used to distinguish between sixteen different personality types. Likewise, students of astrology believe there are twelve personality types based on sun signs and other cosmic conditions at birth.

I have found a common pattern of personality traits in my anxiety patients. Here is a brief profile. Generally speaking, my anxious patients are sensitive, hard working, and dependable. They are perfectionistic and try to live up to high standards. They aim to please others and are fearful of rejection. In wanting to be liked and appreciated, they tend to focus on the needs and feelings of other people and avoid conflict whenever possible. In going the extra mile, they tend to take on too many commitments and they have difficulty setting reasonable limits. Consequently, they often feel stressed (and sometimes resentful because not everyone has the same work ethic). Due to their innate sensitivity, they are also suggestible; that is, they are readily affected by their environment and other people. Finally, they strive to be in control and they prefer structure and predictability.

One of the great ironies of the anxiety personality style is that, despite their sensitivity to stress, people with this style actually create more stress. For example, a fear of rejection and a strong need to please others can cause them to say "yes" when they feel "no." They may work too hard to earn acceptance and praise. At their own expense, they may focus too much on the needs and feelings of other people. They may take on too much and have difficulty setting reasonable limits for themselves. In short, this personality style creates unnecessary stress.

The personality traits of the anxiety-prone person are summarized below:

- Is responsible, dependable, hard working

- Is perfectionistic and has high expectations

- Aims to please and seeks approval

- Is sensitive to criticism and fearful of rejection

- Is suggestible (easily influenced by the opinions/actions of others)

- Needs to feel in control

- Has difficulty relaxing

- Has difficulty with strong emotions

- Has problems with assertiveness

The
Anxiety
Personality
Traits

Difficulty with assertiveness is related to some of the personality traits listed above, such as difficulty with strong emotions, sensitivity to criticism, and a strong need to please others. Although important for effective communication and satisfying relationships, being assertive can create conflict and, therefore, anxiety. This trait can be addressed by changing how we think about conflict and by learning new communication skills, as discussed in Chapters 13 and 14.

If you identify with the personality type described above, you may be predisposed to developing an anxiety disorder. Let's examine some of the traits found in the anxiety-prone personality in more detail. Because these traits apply to me as well as to most people with anxiety potential, I use the terms "us" and "we." It is not necessary to have all of these traits to qualify as having the anxiety personality style. Those who develop an anxiety disorder, however, usually have a majority of these traits.

### Is Responsible, Dependable, Hard Working

Generally speaking, the anxiety-prone person is responsible, dependable, and hard working. We can be counted on to do what we say and to do a good job. We are also loyal and reliable, and this makes us excellent and valued employees, as well as good entrepreneurs when we are willing to take risks. Our values and ethics include keeping our word and fulfilling our promises. In part, we are dependable and hard working because we do not want to disappoint others or let them down. As we will see, this is related to another trait: our need to please others. Unfortunately, we are not good at setting reasonable goals and limits or taking care of ourselves. We often take on too many commitments and responsibilities. Therefore, our potential for burnout, resentment, and symptoms of stress is exceptionally high.

### Is Perfectionistic and Has High Expectations

The anxious personality type is often perfectionistic. We have high standards and expectations for ourselves. We want to do well in everything and are willing to push ourselves to the limit in an effort to meet our own expectations and attain perfection. When this trait is combined with our dependability and strong work ethic, we often do achieve excellence in fulfilling our responsibilities, whatever they happen to be. For some, this trait manifests in the way we keep house, while for others it is apparent in the competence with which we do our jobs or perform in our professions. However, because it is impossible to attain perfection at all times, we may find ourselves pushing even harder to reach this goal or feeling frustrated or disappointed in ourselves when we fail to meet our unreasonably high expectations. It should be obvious that our perfectionism creates stress, but we find it difficult to control this deeply ingrained trait.

### Aims to Please and Seeks Approval

The anxiety-prone person seeks approval and reassurance from others. We have an excessive need to receive positive feedback in order to feel appreciated, secure, and at ease. Thus, we are "people-pleasers," willing to go the extra mile for recognition.

### Is Sensitive to Criticism and Fearful of Rejection

This trait is related to our desire to please and approval-seeking style. We try to avoid negative feedback by working hard to please and impress others. If possible, we avoid conflict with others because we do not want anyone to be angry with or disapprove of us. As a result, we tend to be somewhat passive in relationships, particularly with people who are in positions of authority, such as supervisors and managers. Our need for approval also interferes with our ability to be assertive, even when it is important and appropriate to speak up for ourselves.

### Is Suggestible

The anxiety-prone person is highly suggestible. This is due in part to our natural sensitivity, which causes us to react intensely to many stimuli, including the feelings and behaviors of other people. Thus, we may find ourselves absorbing the concerns of others or being easily influenced by their desires or needs. Combined with our excessive need for approval and fear of rejection, we are likely to be strongly influenced by those around us.

### Needs to Feel in Control

A strong need to feel in control is a marked personality trait of anxious people. As one of my anxious patients announced, "I'll be the first to admit that I'm a control freak." What is the control issue all about?

Control gives us a feeling of power and safety, but in most cases, our need to feel in control is based on lack of confidence in our ability to handle ourselves in ambiguous or unstructured situations. We like to know what is going to happen in the future—but we also want options. Control means having choices, such as the ability to leave an uncomfortable situation. On the other hand, we like structure and predictability, conditions we may have had as children. In an effort to feel prepared for whatever may happen, we try to predict the future. This leads to worry when we try to anticipate what may happen. We habitually "what-if" or try to second-guess the future.

Naturally, to feel in control, we may tend to foresee all the negative possibilities. It is as though we are continually preparing for threat or danger. Threat includes not only the sudden panic attack or anxiety we fear, but also the possibility of criticism, rejection, mistakes, and failure. This keeps us in a continual state of fight/flight arousal. Inevitably, our need for control leads to anxiety.

Because we value control, we tend to conceal our vulnerabilities from other people. We do not want others to be aware of our flaws or inadequacies because we fear they will think less of us or reject us. Our need to impress others to attain approval leads us to pretend we have it all together, whereas we may be anxious or insecure inside. Many clients I see for anxiety treatment report that when they tell others about their anxiety problem, the response is one of surprise: "You're kidding. You always seem to be in control. You do your job so well and you always seem to have it together. I never would have guessed you feel inadequate or insecure or have a problem with anxiety."

### Has Difficulty Relaxing

Despite our desire to relax, we find it difficult to calm down, take time out, and let go. We tend to be physically active on a continual basis, and our minds are busy almost all the time. High gear is a habit, and it is hard to shift into neutral. There is no time to relax when we are busy proving our self-worth, taking care of others, avoiding criticism, and always striving to do a good job.

What compounds the problem is the increase in anxiety we may feel when we begin to relax. Relaxing threatens our sense of control and self-protection. Some people simply do not know how to relax or believe relaxation is a waste of time. There is, after all, always another item on the "to do" list. To truly let go and relax requires *being*, which is a different attitude from *doing*, as we discuss in Chapter 7.

When we cannot relax, we deprive ourselves of the stress recovery required to live without symptoms. Our difficulty relaxing, therefore, compromises our physical needs and overall health. Our preoccupation with doing well, looking good and pleasing others, and avoiding rejection and criticism creates a great deal of stress, but we tend to deny these symptoms while we keep up the pace. When our bodies alert us with stress signals, such as fatigue, we may consider them annoying distractions. Only when our stress warnings intensify into severe physical symptoms do we begin to take notice. But we may not realize the connection between our personality style and physical symptoms, and instead focus on the symptoms themselves, often fearing loss of control or a life-threatening illness. This adds to our stress and makes matters worse.

### Has Difficulty with Strong Emotions

Difficulty with—and even fear of—strong emotions is another feature of the anxiety personality style. As we discuss later in this chapter, feelings present a problem for those of us who were raised in families with inappropriate expression of feelings or with little emotional communication. In some cases, feelings within the family were associated with out-of-control behavior. Frustration expressed as yelling or physical violence is a common example. In other cases, feelings were discouraged or even punished. These family background experiences have left many of us without the skills for appropriate identification and expression of our feelings.

Some feelings, such as anger, involve physical arousal similar to the fight/flight response, and can be confused with anxiety or fear. Anger can be frightening if it was associated with violence or out-of-control behavior as we were growing up. Anger also threatens us because we fear disapproval and rejection, and assume that relationships will be jeopardized by conflict or anger.

Other feelings, such as guilt and sadness, can also be difficult if our emotional management skills are limited. We may fear such strong feelings will take over or last indefinitely.

When we deny or repress our feelings, we experience a buildup of emotional tension. If that tension is not released, an internal pressure accumulates that can lead to anxiety about losing control emotionally.

Thus, our personality creates a paradox in which we may deny feelings to prevent anxiety, but experience anxiety when we deny our feelings.

Our difficulty with strong feelings can lead us to avoid situations that could trigger emotional arousal. We may have a strong emotional reaction to poignant movies, televised news (especially about violence, injury, or suffering), social events, and other situations. In our personal and professional relationships, we may avoid conflict or behavior that could lead to disapproval or rejection. We are careful to not offend, hurt, or anger others because of our extreme sensitivity to how they view us. Thus, we may end up hiding our feelings or going against them, as we seek to keep peace and not make waves. In this way we are not always true to ourselves and make choices that are not necessarily in our own best interests.

Strategies and exercises for managing our feelings without anxiety are discussed in Chapter 13. For example, I include an exercise for developing a "feelings vocabulary," as well as skills for communicating emotionally with others when conflict is anticipated.

## The Anxiety Personality Self-Test

I created this test as an informal screening tool to help identify people with the anxiety personality style (see the facing page). The questions in the self-test will help you determine the degree to which you match the anxiety personality profile discussed so far in this chapter. Answer each question by putting a check mark in one of the three boxes ("often," "sometimes," or "seldom"). At the end of the test, add up all the points to get your anxiety personality score. There is a scoring key at the bottom of the self-test.

## The Positive Side of the Anxiety Personality Style

Obviously, there are many pitfalls to possessing the personality traits discussed above. However, the anxiety personality style also has a positive side. People with this type of personality tend to be sensitive, caring, nurturing, gentle, and kind. Compassionate and sensitive to the needs of others, they are good listeners and they make good friends. They care about the earth and other living beings, including animals

# THE ANXIETY PERSONALITY SELF-TEST

| | OFTEN | SOMETIMES | SELDOM |
|---|---|---|---|
| 1. Do you worry about things you can't control? | ☑ | ☐ | ☐ |
| 2. Do you have difficulty relaxing or taking time off? | ☑ | ☐ | ☐ |
| 3. Do you avoid telling other people how you feel when you think it will upset them? | ☑ | ☐ | ☐ |
| 4. Do you try to be perfect in your work or at home? | ☐ | ☑ | ☐ |
| 5. Do you tend to push yourself to exhaustion to get things done? | ☐ | ☑ | ☐ |
| 6. Do you tend to judge other people, or categorize things as good or bad? | ☐ | ☑ | ☐ |
| 7. Do you try to anticipate what will happen in the future? | ☑ | ☐ | ☐ |
| 8. Do you prefer structured or predictable situations more than unstructured or ambiguous situations? | ☑ | ☐ | ☐ |
| 9. Do you have "what-if" thoughts, such as "What if something bad happens?" | ☑ | ☐ | ☐ |
| 10. Do you make "to do" lists or lists of things you feel you should do? | ☐ | ☑ | ☐ |
| 11. Do you try to please or impress other people? | ☑ | ☐ | ☐ |

*(cont'd.)*

## THE ANXIETY PERSONALITY SELF-TEST (cont'd.)

|  | OFTEN | SOMETIMES | SELDOM |
|---|---|---|---|
| 12. Do you feel there is not enough time to do all the things you want to do? | ☑ | ☐ | ☐ |
| 13. Do you find yourself agreeing to do things even when you don't want to? | ☐ | ☑ | ☐ |
| 14. Do you feel stressed or anxious? | ☑ | ☐ | ☐ |
| 15. Are you easily influenced by other people's actions or statements? | ☐ | ☑ | ☐ |
| 16. Do you need to be in control of situations in order to feel comfortable? | ☐ | ☑ | ☐ |
| 17. Do you tend to take on too much responsibility? | ☐ | ☑ | ☐ |
| 18. Do you need to finish things before you can relax or feel good? | ☐ | ☑ | ☐ |
| 19. Do you have difficulty expressing your true feelings to other people? | ☑ | ☐ | ☐ |
| 20. Do you have difficulty finding time, energy, or interest in physical exercise? | ☑ | ☐ | ☐ |
| 21. Do you eat in a rush—or avoid eating—because you are too busy? | ☐ | ☑ | ☐ |
| 22. Are you concerned about how other people feel about you? | ☑ | ☐ | ☐ |

## ANXIETY PERSONALITY SELF-TEST (cont'd.)
||||||||||||||||||||||||||||||||||||||||||||||||||||||||||||||||||||||||||||||

|  | OFTEN | SOMETIMES | SELDOM |
|---|---|---|---|
| 23. Do you have difficulty expressing anger? | ☐ | ☐ | ☑ |
| 24. Do you wish you had more time to engage in recreational activities or enjoyable hobbies? | ☑ | ☐ | ☐ |
| 25. Do you feel your life is out of balance? | ☑ | ☐ | ☐ |
| **SUBTOTALS** | 18 | 10 | 1 |

**TOTAL SCORE** Multiply the number of checkmarks you placed in the "often" column by 4 and multiply the number of checkmarks placed in the "Sometimes" column by 2. The sum of these two numbers is your total score.

$$4(\;14\;) + 2(\;10\;) = \;78\;$$

*(handwritten: 56 + 20)*

**SCORE INTERPRETATION** A total score of 50 to 100 puts you in the anxiety personality range. The higher the score, the more closely you match the anxiety personality profile.

Name _____ Age _____ Gender _____

Have you had any form of psychological counseling in the past? _____

If yes, please briefly describe: _____

_____

_____

Do you think your score would be higher without the benefit of previous counseling? _____

and plants. These qualities can be found in the way they parent, provide community service, and maintain friendships. These traits stem from an innate sensitivity and attunement to their surroundings. Frankly, I would like to see more of these qualities in the world.

I observe these positive traits in many of my patients. For example, a friendly and talkative woman named Phyllis suffered from panic disorder with agoraphobia before she came for help. Her phobic situations included driving and crowded stores. One interesting thing about Phyllis was her ability to take any kind of plant, no matter how neglected and withered, and bring it back to health. She also loved animals. And she did many thoughtful things in group therapy, such as offering a kind word and remembering the birthdays of other members with a card or little gift.

Some other positive dimensions to this personality type are dependability, dedication, strong work ethic, competence, and high standards of achievement. The person with this personality profile is typically a valued worker and responsible person. Achievement at work and competence in home life are characteristics of this type, who is always striving for excellence.

Finally, the anxiety-prone personality tends to be spiritually oriented. While I cannot fully explain it, I notice that the majority of anxiety sufferers are people with spiritual inclinations. Surprisingly, many anxiety sufferers have faith in a higher power, but this is not always enough to help reduce their anxiety. This quality may be related to our sensitivity and empathy. Perhaps we are spiritually inclined because we are sensitive and empathetic toward other living beings. Fortunately, spirituality is a great resource to be drawn upon in anxiety management, and I discuss this further in Chapter 17.

To summarize this analysis of the anxiety personality profile, I created the table on the facing page, which shows the assets and liabilities of the anxiety personality style.

Overcoming anxiety usually requires a thorough look at the personality traits that contribute to the anxiety condition. While it is not possible or even desirable to change our personality altogether, we can become aware of specific habits and traits that limit us or interfere with healthy behavior. I take the view that my personality has many positive

## THE ASSETS AND LIABILITIES OF THE ANXIETY PERSONALITY STYLE

IIIIIIIIIIIIIIIIIIIIIIIIIIIIIIIIIIIIIIIIIIIIIIIIIIIIIIIIII

| ASSETS | LIABILITIES |
| --- | --- |
| Caring/kind/supportive | Produces high stress |
| Loyal to friends | Overreacts to stimuli |
| Outstanding employee/worker | Difficulty setting reasonable limits |
| Good listener | Not assertive/can be exploited |
| Competent and high-achieving | Fearful of strong emotions |
| Spiritually oriented | Becomes resentful |

aspects and that I want to modify the negative aspects. I want to be in control of my personality, rather than have my personality be in control of me.

For example, I have a tendency toward perfectionism. However, I know this creates stress, especially when I do not have the time to do things according to my high standards. I have learned to simply get the job done in some cases and to be selective about which tasks or projects I approach with greater attention to detail. I strive for excellence, rather than perfection, and accept that doing my best sometimes means working within less than ideal conditions. In Part II, I offer some techniques and skills for modifying the anxiety- and stress-producing aspects of the anxiety personality style.

### Stress Overload

If you have the biological sensitivity and anxiety personality style discussed so far, you are an anxiety disorder waiting to happen. The third ingredient, stress overload, determines *when* the anxiety will surface. If you understand the role of stress in triggering anxiety, you are likely to appreciate the importance of the stress management practices recommended in Part II.

As discussed in Chapter 2, stress can consist of both (a) the situation causing the stress response and (b) the resulting feeling of stress. One useful and widely used measure of stress, the Life Change Scale, emphasizes the situations causing the stress response. This screening tool defines stress as any situation that involves demands, adjustments, or change. Such situations can be both positive and negative.

The Life Change Scale lists approximately forty life events considered stressful, ranked according to the degree of stress and likelihood of producing body reactions. At the top of the list are the death of a loved one, divorce, separation, and serious illness in the family. Lower on the list are increased responsibilities at work, financial problems, and family relocation. At the bottom of the list are a minor traffic violation, holiday stress, and even planning and taking a vacation. The Life Change Scale is reproduced below. You can use it to estimate your stress level and to determine if you are experiencing stress overload.

Notice in the instructions that you should consider a period of at least one year when measuring your stress level. A one-year period is used because it has been found that stress is cumulative. In addition, there is often a delay between a period of high stress and the onset of stress symptoms. People do not always realize they are under stress overload until their stress level reaches a critical threshold and they "crash" with symptoms.

## The Life Change Scale

This widely reprinted self-test lists forty-three stressful life events and the value of each in "stress points." To use the Life Change Scale, you check off events that have happened in your life within the last twelve to twenty-four months, then add up the total number of stress points. Add your own events, assigning the appropriate number of points by comparing them to the events ranked on the chart. A score of 150 gives you a 50 percent chance of developing an illness. A score of 300 or more gives you a 90 percent chance. This scale provides an estimate only, and other factors may affect your chances of developing an illness. A stress recovery program can significantly reduce your vulnerability.

## THE LIFE CHANGE SCALE
||||||||||||||||||||||||||||||||||||||||||||||||

| LIFE EVENT | CHECK | POINTS | YOUR SCORE |
|---|---|---|---|
| Death of spouse | ☐ | 100 | _____ |
| Divorce | ☐ | 73 | _____ |
| Marital separation | ☐ | 65 | _____ |
| Jail term | ☐ | 63 | _____ |
| Death of close family member | ☐ | 63 | _____ |
| Personal injury or illness | ☐ | 53 | _____ |
| Marriage | ☐ | 50 | _____ |
| Terminated at work | ☐ | 47 | _____ |
| Marital reconciliation | ☐ | 45 | _____ |
| Change in health of family member | ☐ | 45 | _____ |
| Pregnancy | ☐ | 44 | _____ |
| Sexual problem | ☐ | 40 | _____ |
| Gain of new family member | ☐ | 39 | _____ |
| Business readjustment | ☐ | 39 | _____ |
| Change in financial state | ☐ | 38 | _____ |
| Death of close friend | ☐ | 37 | _____ |
| Change to different line of work | ☐ | 36 | _____ |
| Change in number of arguments with spouse | ☐ | 35 | _____ |
| New mortgage or existing mortgage over $100,000 | ☐ | 35 | _____ |
| Foreclosure of mortgage or loan | ☐ | 30 | _____ |
| Son or daughter leaving home/ starting college | ☐ | 29 | _____ |

*(cont'd.)*

## THE LIFE CHANGE SCALE  (cont'd.)

| LIFE EVENT | CHECK | POINTS | YOUR SCORE |
|---|---|---|---|
| Trouble with in-laws | ☐ | 29 | _____ |
| Outstanding personal achievement | ☐ | 28 | _____ |
| Spouse begins or stops work | ☐ | 26 | _____ |
| Begin or end school | ☐ | 26 | _____ |
| Change in living conditions | ☐ | 25 | _____ |
| Revision in personal habits | ☐ | 24 | _____ |
| Conflict with supervisor or boss | ☐ | 23 | _____ |
| Change in work hours or conditions | ☐ | 20 | _____ |
| Change in residence | ☐ | 20 | _____ |
| Change in school | ☐ | 20 | _____ |
| Change in recreation | ☐ | 19 | _____ |
| Change in church activities | ☐ | 19 | _____ |
| Change in social activities | ☐ | 18 | _____ |
| New loan or mortgage under $50,000 | ☐ | 17 | _____ |
| Change in sleeping habits | ☐ | 16 | _____ |
| Change in frequency of family get-togethers | ☐ | 15 | _____ |
| Change in eating habits | ☐ | 15 | _____ |
| Vacation | ☐ | 13 | _____ |
| Major holiday | ☐ | 12 | _____ |
| Minor violation of the law (e.g., driving citation) | ☐ | 11 | _____ |

I do not routinely administer the Life Change Scale, but I always ask new clients to tell me about any stress that might be affecting them. I am amazed at the number of people who are unaware of the amount of stress in their lives. One example was a youthful-looking, fifty-nine-year-old woman who sought help for an uncontrollable fear of panic attacks. When I interviewed Cynthia and took her history, I learned she had experienced seven deaths of relatives in the last four years, as well as numerous relocations due to her husband's military job. In addition, a son was going through a divorce and she was experiencing some medical problems that required a special restrictive diet. In spite of all this, Cynthia never thought she was under stress and felt she should be able to handle her life without a problem. In fact, she was upset and disappointed in herself for experiencing anxiety symptoms.

In my opinion, one of the most common sources of stress is the recurring demands of daily life that we assume are normal and that fill our schedules with increasing speed and intensity. Working for a living, raising children, maintaining a home, doing the laundry, food shopping, cooking and kitchen cleanup, recreation, and even socializing can all combine to yield an overload of stress. As a society, we are so overloaded with stress that many people have little time for basic activities such as, cooking, home maintenance, rest, or spending time with friends and family. I recently received a mailing from a business that offers to send birthday, holiday, and occasional cards to your friends and family for an annual fee. Even our efforts to recover from stress—whether through recreational activities, exercise, or vacations—are often approached with the same rush and time pressure as the rest of our daily life.

Hans Selye, a biologist who wrote the now classic book, *The Stress of Life,* asserts that stress is an inherent and inevitable part of life. He suggests that stress is vital to growth, but only if it is kept within certain limits. Otherwise, it can cause a breakdown of the body and lead to other symptoms, including anxiety.

Stress, therefore, does not have to be a problem, as long as we manage stress and maintain our health. We are designed biologically to handle enormous amounts of stress, as evidenced by childbirth and the athletic feats involved in running marathons and triathlons. Every summer, I am impressed by the athletic endurance of cyclists in the Tour de France who ride more than a hundred miles per day for three weeks, sometimes up the steepest mountains in the Alps, with just one or two rest days. But these triumphs over stress require training and preparation, as well as stress recovery.

As mentioned at the beginning of this section, we must view stress not just in terms of external events, but also in terms of the unique impact of stress on each person. A specific event may be stressful to some people but not others. The difference may be due to stress recovery practices, as well as the degree to which people create additional stress by virtue of their personality style. We have already seen how the anxiety personality style creates stress, and noted that it would be helpful to control the personality traits that create stress. In addition, if we restore ourselves at regular intervals, preferably daily, our stress-recovery pattern becomes balanced, our energy reserves remain stocked, and we can deal effectively with more stress.

When our recovery practices do not keep pace with stress demands, we gradually deplete our energy reserves and wear down our resilience. We then lose our balance and develop early warning signals of stress overload in the form of mild symptoms. Headaches, backaches, difficulty relaxing, muscle twitches, and low energy can all be early warning signals of stress overload. When these signals are ignored, they intensify until we are forced to notice them. This often occurs as an anxiety disorder, such as panic attacks, generalized anxiety, acute stress disorder, or phobias.

## Conclusion

There are three ingredients in the development of an anxiety disorder: biological sensitivity, personality style, and stress overload. But there are also three things you can do to reduce or even prevent an anxiety disorder:

- Accommodate your biological sensitivity (for example, get enough sleep, limit exposure to disturbing stimulation)

- Control your personality traits (for example, replace perfectionism with excellence, replace worry with optimism and positive self-talk)

- Manage your stress (for example, exercise, learn to relax, eat a healthy diet)

In Part II, you will find many suggestions and recommendations for accomplishing these vital steps toward anxiety control.

# CHAPTER 5

||||||||||||||||||||||||

# *How Anxiety Develops*

One of the three ingredients in the development of an anxiety disorder is the anxiety personality style. What causes this type of personality to develop?

Research tells us that genetics account for approximately 40 percent of our personality style. This means that about 60 percent of who we are and how we behave is the result of learning. Let's consider this environmental side of the equation, the learned aspect of personality style. This involves specific family and childhood background factors that could help us understand why anxiety develops in some of us and not others.

As a psychologist, one of my first steps with each patient involves taking a family history to identify any background experiences that may have contributed to the anxiety condition. The purpose of this step is also to help my patients understand that anxiety does not suddenly show up in adulthood—there is usually a history leading up to it. Most of my anxiety patients recognize the role played by their family and childhood history and conclude that their anxiety disorder was virtually "waiting to happen." Of course, anxiety can also be triggered at any time by traumatic experiences, but the basic template for anxiety usually exists already as a result of genetics, background experiences, and personality type.

It is also important to understand that, in many cases, adult anxiety begins in childhood but is not recognized or addressed at the time. In fact, mental-health professionals now realize there is a continuum of anxiety from childhood through adolescence to adulthood. The background factors we explore in this chapter typically have led to anxiety relatively early in the life of adults with an anxiety disorder.

As my own anxiety story illustrates, early life experiences, particularly traumatic experiences during the formative years of childhood, can have a profound impact on our personality and subsequent behavior patterns. Our emotional and behavior patterns as adults are largely determined by experiences earlier in life.

In this sense, anxiety disorders are *developmental*. They do not appear suddenly, although that is how it feels in some cases. Although some symptoms of anxiety, such as feelings of panic, nightmares, and unreasonable fears may seem to appear "out of the blue," there is usually a developmental history leading up to them, beginning with an inborn sensitivity that combines with early family experiences.

Let's think developmentally before we look at the specific childhood and family experiences that contribute to anxiety potential. Development implies a process that takes place over a period of time and involves a relatively predictable sequence of events, leading to a specific outcome. The figure below illustrates the sequence of anxiety development:

### SEQUENCE OF ANXIETY DEVELOPMENT

**Biological Sensitivity**

+

**Family/Childhood Experience**

↓

**Anxiety Personality Style**

+

**Stress Overload**

↓

**Stress Symptoms**

↓

**Fear of Symptoms**

↓

**ANXIETY DISORDER**

With this developmental picture in mind, we can begin to fill in details of the family and childhood background risks for anxiety. As we review them, you might want to make mental notes about which ones seem to apply in your case. In my work with patients, this step adds some structure to the process of learning how the condition developed. The insights from this discussion often result in reassurance and relief. Taking the mystery out of anxiety and having a logical explanation is the first step in recovery.

The family and childhood experiences known to contribute to the development of anxiety are as follows:

**Family / Childhood Experiences That Can Lead to Anxiety in Adulthood**

- Inadequate bonding
- Separation anxiety in childhood
- Emotional repression/inhibition
- Critical or overcontrolling parents
- Parent alcoholism or drug abuse
- Child abuse
- Sexual abuse
- Divorce
- Limited mind-body knowledge including of sexuality
- Anxiety in parents
- Stress in parents and families
- Parents with mental illness or psychological instability
- Death or serious illness of a parent or other family member

## Inadequate Bonding

Our first concern is the quality of bonding between a child and parents (or primary caretakers). Bonding is the physical and emotional connection between people that serves as a basis for security. A strong and positive child-parent bond is the single most effective defense against anxiety. Conversely, inadequate or disrupted bonding is a risk factor for anxiety.

This bonding process actually begins before birth. During embryonic development, mother and child are intimately connected in a biological relationship in which the fetus depends on the mother's body for oxygen, growth nutrients, disease prevention, and so on. "Communication" between mother and fetus also takes place during pregnancy, long before verbal interaction occurs. Such communication occurs at a cellular level, through the sympathetic pulsing of the heart cells of mother and embryo. This has been demonstrated in the laboratory: If two living heart cells are placed a distance apart on a microscopic slide, they pulsate randomly, each at its own rate. However, if moved closer together (they do not have to touch), they arc the gap between them and "communicate" with each other by pulsing in unison, as one heart. At another level of communication, the infant *in utero* responds immediately with body movements to sounds from the mother and the surrounding environment. Those movements, it turns out, match precisely the mother's sound inputs in a predictable, one-to-one pattern. Thus, the bonding process between mother and child begins long before birth.

Although we may not remember such an early stage of development, our sense of security was established to a great extent at a very young age. Strong and positive bonding helps us to feel the world and human relationships are safe, predictable within limits, and worthy of trust. To a great extent, successful bonding immunizes us against future anxiety. Furthermore, successful bonding is the foundation for our identity as lovable, worthy of attention, and powerful. This is the basis for self-esteem, without which all future praise and positive reinforcement will leak through an apparent "hole in the bucket."

On the other hand, an unhealthy degree of attachment between parent and child occurs in some cases that interferes with normal development and fosters anxiety. Due to a *parent*'s separation anxiety, or concerns about the child's ability to function independently, normal exploratory behavior and interaction with the world may be discouraged. When a parent projects his or her own insecurity, vulnerability, or need for protection onto a child, the child can absorb that anxiety, with resulting fear and guilt about growth and independence. Such unhealthy attachment is seen in some single-parent families, particularly when custodial parents turn to one of the children for friendship and companionship following a divorce. This puts a burden of responsibility on the child, who is likely to develop stress symptoms and anxiety.

There are a number of other threats to successful bonding. Bonding can be disrupted or broken by divorce, child abuse and neglect, harsh or corporal punishment, loss of a parent through death or abandonment, premature separation of a child from parents, and medically complicated or mismanaged birth experiences. Generally speaking, the earlier the disruption to bonding, the more likely will be the risk for anxiety as the child grows up, or later in life. As we discuss the risk factors, the theme of disruption to normal bonding will resurface.

## Separation Anxiety in Childhood

Looking back on their childhood, some adult anxiety sufferers can pinpoint episodes of separation anxiety. This is one of the first experiences in life in which we may feel out of control. For children, security is based on the emotional relationship and close proximity to parents, particularly with the mother during the early bonding period. Unprepared for separation from their security base, children in certain situations experience symptoms of severe anxiety, such as accelerated heart rate, breathing difficulties, warm flush, and nervous stomach, along with secondary fears about losing control, being ridiculed, or feeling embarrassed. The situations in which such anxiety is most likely to occur are day care, preschool, sleepovers at a friend's house, overnight camp, and hospitalizations.

Anxiety triggered by separation can be traumatic and become imprinted in memory. This lays the foundation for future anxiety, insecurity, and dependency. If you have experienced separation anxiety at some point in childhood, you are more likely to develop an anxiety disorder later in life.

As I indicated in Chapter 3, I have seen separation anxiety disorders in adults. Some of these individuals had a history of separation anxiety in childhood. However, separation anxiety in childhood does not necessarily lead to adult separation anxiety, although it tends to be correlated with other anxiety disorders.

## Emotional Repression/Inhibition

In families in which feelings are not readily expressed or welcomed, children may adapt by emotionally shutting down. In some cases, children are aware of their feelings, but learn to hold them in. Or they lose touch altogether with their feelings. Children raised in emotionally repressed or inhibited family environments do not acquire the language of feelings—the vocabulary for emotional communication.

This family style serves to increase the likelihood of relationship problems later in life. Many of my anxiety patients do not have satisfying relationships because they lack knowledge and skills in emotional communication. It is apparent such deficiencies add to the potential for anxiety.

Success in work and personal relationships requires "emotional intelligence," or EQ. Emotional intelligence refers to awareness of feelings and how to use them effectively for problem solving and communication. In his popular book, *Emotional Intelligence,* Goleman asserts that successful people tend to possess these emotional competencies. They are higher performers at work, school, and home because they have emotional knowledge and skills, not because they are more intelligent or better educated than their peers. Those with lower emotional intelligence tend to be more depressed, more anxious, less productive, and less satisfied with their relationships.

Problems dealing with feelings contribute to anxiety in a number of ways. For example, one of the personality traits of anxiety sufferers is difficulty relaxing. Because getting in touch with feelings is easiest when we slow down and relax, anxiety sufferers may not give themselves enough space to really acknowledge what they are feeling. Conversely, they may have difficulty relaxing due to their anxiety about feelings. Difficulty relaxing thus interferes with one of the most important steps in stress management and anxiety control. What's more, being emotionally aware and in touch with feelings is necessary for reading early warning signals of stress.

## Critical Parenting

Frequent or severe criticism by parents hurts children's self-esteem. Children who are frequently criticized develop not only a poor self-image, but also anxiety about taking risks as learners. Furthermore, children raised by critical parents may mistakenly believe that if they try harder or do better, they will receive love, praise, and positive attention. This can contribute directly to anxiety personality traits, such as perfectionism, difficulty relaxing or setting reasonable limits, and approval-seeking behavior. In addition to high anxiety potential, depression is likely to develop in adults who were raised by difficult-to-please or highly critical parents.

Approval and love in some families are provided primarily on the basis of achievement, rather than because of the essence or inner qualities of a child. This pattern encourages children to "perform" for acceptance and affection, and gives a subtle message they are not intrinsically lovable. This parenting pattern reinforces high achievement, perfectionism, and a tendency to focus on external accomplishments as the basis of self-worth. The pattern can create high stress later in life and make it difficult for adults to set realistic goals and limits. Of course, it is important to praise children for their accomplishments because this helps establish self-esteem. However, when approval, love, and praise are given conditionally, the stage is set for problems with self-esteem as well as future stress and anxiety.

Low self-esteem is the basis for social anxiety disorder. When asked what arouses anxiety in social situations, adults with this form of anxiety typically say they are concerned about "what others will think of me" or "negative judgments by others." These concerns are usually a projection of the person's negative self-judgments onto others—who, it is presumed, would reciprocate the same negative judgments. To help adults with social anxiety, my therapy focuses on building positive self-esteem as well as developing communication skills and skills to handle emotions.

### Alcoholism or Drug Abuse

Alcoholism or drug abuse in a family creates anxiety in a number of ways. First, alcoholism and drug abuse are associated with unpredictable and inconsistent parenting. Where such an atmosphere exists, children can become confused and anxious. In many cases, alcoholic or drug-dependent parents do not recognize their impairment, and they may actively deny the problem. This makes the environment even more confusing and anxiety arousing for children.

Violence is often associated with alcoholism. In fact, it is estimated that approximately 90 percent of all domestic violence is alcohol related, and it is known that alcoholism and drug abuse are responsible for the majority of violence against children, including child abuse. Naturally, many adults turn to alcohol or drugs to cope with their own anxiety or other psychological problems. Nevertheless, violence and out-of-control behavior raise children's anxiety levels because they threaten the children's basic safety and security. Children who witness violence, or who are direct victims of violence, usually adapt by remaining in a constant state of psychological arousal and fear. They become tense and vigilant and are likely to develop many of the anxiety personality traits. Children of alcoholic or drug-abusing parents are at risk for developing anxiety disorders, such as post-traumatic stress disorder, as well as other emotional problems.

In alcoholic or other types of dysfunctional families, children may also adapt by taking on one of several identifiable survival roles. A survival role is a personality pattern whose purpose is to divert attention away from the alcoholism or to compensate for it in some way. The "family hero," for example, is a high-achieving child who acts out the myth that his or her family is stable. This role is often assumed by the oldest child. The role of "mascot" serves to defuse family tension and anxiety. The "lost child" retreats into the background, adopting a passive style often seen by others as simply well behaved. The "scapegoat," or troublemaker, acts out the family's feelings of abandonment, hurt, and anger. As I see it, these roles are ways in which children cope with the anxiety they experience in alcoholic family environments.

The literature on alcoholism recognizes the personality profiles and behavior patterns of "adult children of alcoholism." Anxiety is among the key consequences of growing up in an alcoholic or drug-abusing family. Other personality traits of these adult children include "all-or-nothing" thinking, emotional dependency, difficulty relaxing or experiencing pleasure, approval-seeking, and other patterns that overlap with the anxiety personality style.

## Physical Abuse

Being abused as a child (physically, sexually, or emotionally) is one of the most significant risk factors for the development of anxiety. Sadly, the majority of child abuse is perpetrated within the family. Sixty percent of domestic child-abuse cases involve parental neglect, 10 percent involve sexual abuse by a family member, and 19 percent involve physical abuse. In the United States, in the year 2000, an estimated nine hundred thousand children were abused in their own families—in the very environment where protection, security, and safety should be greatest. Every one of these children is at risk for the full range of anxiety disorders, including PTSD, OCD, panic disorder, phobias, and GAD.

Each year in this country, thousands of children are hospitalized due to physical abuse by their own parents. Another two to three thousand young children are actually killed by their parents. Where abuse of a child occurs, anxiety is virtually guaranteed. All biological and psychological systems are affected in cases of physical abuse. When abuse occurs within the family, the most obvious damages include betrayal of trust and broken bonding—with vast implications for anxiety, especially if the abuse is kept secret or not stopped by an informed adult.

PTSD is the most likely anxiety disorder to develop as a result of child abuse. Readers may recall that the symptoms of this anxiety disorder include acute anxiety upon exposure to reminders of the abuse, feelings of helplessness, nightmares, irritability, angry outbursts, emotional numbing, and high autonomic arousal that interferes with sleep, concentration, and the inability to relax. Abused children are also likely to experience symptoms of depression. The effects of abuse can stay with a child victim for many years, or a lifetime, if proper help is not received.

In order to address their anxiety, many of my adult clients must sort out their history of abuse. They need to understand that abuse is not a reflection of their self-worth, but rather a complex issue involving their parents or the adults who abused them. They also need to tone down their chronic arousal and learn how to relax and trust other people, particularly same-gender authority figures who symbolize their abusers. This was necessary for the two clients with PTSD we met in Chapter 3—

Roberto, a victim of physical abuse, and Carrie, a victim of physical and sexual abuse. Coming to terms with abuse was a vital stage of therapy that took a significant amount of time for both of them.

Two key contexts for physical abuse of children are drug and alcohol abuse by parents, and frustration caused by lack of parenting skills, particularly with respect to discipline. We have already discussed the risks associated with parent alcohol and drug abuse. See the section on discipline for additional comments about this family source of anxiety.

## Sexual Abuse

Like physical abuse, sexual abuse of children can occur in families despite the fact that throughout recorded history and in most cultures there has been a strong social taboo prohibiting it. Such abuse may involve incest by a parent or stepparent, or inappropriate sexual activity by uncles, aunts, or cousins. Sexual abuse in families also includes sibling incest, defined as sexual activity between siblings, where the age difference is greater than five years or where force or threat of violence is used to coerce a younger child sibling. Some researchers believe sibling incest is currently the most common form of childhood sexual abuse and the least reported. One out of every three to four girls, and one out of ten boys, is a victim of sexual abuse by age eighteen, often within the family. Naturally, a family environment in which sexual abuse occurs is unsafe for children, and this adds to the anxiety associated with sexual abuse.

### *Arlene*

*One anxious woman with whom I worked was raised in a family with critical parents, who had a tense marriage with poor communication and virtually no affection. Arlene was the youngest of three children in the family. Unfortunately, Arlene was sexually abused at a young age on several occasions by her older brother, who threatened to hurt her if she told. Several incidents took place in a bedroom closet. The lack of warmth and communication within the family, combined with the brother's threats, inhibited Arlene from reporting the abuse. She told no one about it and repressed her feelings and memories of the trauma. Arlene developed a fear of authority figures, a pattern of pleasing others, difficulty relaxing, and many other traits common to anxiety sufferers. She initially came for help as an adult, following a period of stress, when she began to have panic attacks. Her trauma memories surfaced in therapy, but only after some gains in anxiety recovery.*

Sexual abuse of children is also common outside of the family, and it is one of the most underestimated and underreported sources of severe anxiety. Child victims are typically threatened or manipulated into cooperating, and only a fraction of victims report sexual abuse to responsible adults.

The U.S. Department of Health and Human Services defines sexual abuse as "contacts or interactions between a child and an adult when the child is being used as an object of gratification for adult sexual needs or desires." State laws typically define sexual conduct as any contact between the penis and vulva, penis and anus, mouth and penis, mouth and vulva, masturbation, bestiality, and sadomasochistic abuse for sexual purposes. In some states, sexual abuse is recognized more broadly as any act by any person involving sexual molestation or exploitation of a child, including but not limited to incest, prostitution, rape, sodomy, or any lewd or lascivious conduct with a child. Sexual abuse also involves the aiding, abetting, counseling, hiring, or procuring of a child to perform or participate in any photograph, motion picture, exhibition, show, or other presentation which, in whole or in part, depicts sexual conduct, sexual excitement, or sadomasochistic abuse of a child.

Boys and girls are equally vulnerable to sexual abuse, although girls are more likely to report it. The most vulnerable ages are ten to twelve, and children who are loners, are hungry for affection, or lack adequate supervision are most at risk. In addition, children who are not taught about sex, or whose fathers are psychologically or physically absent, are more vulnerable.

Professionally, I never cease to be amazed by the number of adult clients who were sexually abused as children. The survivors include both men and women, many of whom have never told anyone before. Others have had prior therapy and have been dealing with the effects of sexual abuse for years.

### Divorce

About half of all marriages eventually break up, leaving one million children per year with stress, anxiety, and the unwelcome task of adjusting to change and loss. The divorce rate steadily increased, starting in 1960 when it was 26 percent, and peaked in the late 1980s at 50 percent. Some sources believe the divorce rate has stabilized in recent years for economic reasons: It now takes two incomes to support a middle-class family lifestyle. Considering the millions of children who are affected by divorce, this is a significant source of anxiety for children. Divorce is usually traumatic for the children and is considered the second-highest stressor for children, outranked only by the death of a parent.

I am personally familiar with the effects of divorce because I was ten at the time my parents separated. It was a confusing and frightening time for me, the oldest of three children. We lived with our mother and had "visitations" with our father. Based on my personal experience as well as my work as a psychologist, I can say with confidence that the effects of divorce are long term for parents as well as children. This view is supported by research on divorce: The impact lasts well into adulthood, often peaking when children of divorce deal with commitment and marriage issues of their own. Another wave of impact occurs when children of divorce become parents themselves, if they go that far in their relationships.

Before a divorce occurs, a period of tension and conflict exists between the parents that, even if it doesn't result in outright violence, can create anxiety in children. However, the stress of divorce usually continues well beyond the acute crisis and separation of the parents. Custody and visitation arrangements are frequently unstable, and conflict between divorced parents can linger or even intensify over a period of many years. Stepfamily adjustments also come into play as a source of stress, and according to statistics, half of all children who have been through the trauma of divorce are likely to face the second divorce of at least one of their parents.

The most unique and comprehensive study ever conducted on the effects of divorce was initiated in 1971 by one of my supervisors, Judith Wallerstein, when I was training in San Francisco. She conducted case studies of sixty families from the upper-middle-class community of Marin County, California, and interviewed most of the original family members periodically for up to thirty years. Most of the families were Caucasian, with a total of 131 children. All of the children were doing well in school, and none of the parents were in psychological counseling for any emotional disorders. Most of the parents were college educated, and half of the families attended church or synagogue. In other words, this could be considered a study of divorce under the best of circumstances. The study has been criticized because it did not compare children of divorced families with children of intact families. On the other hand, its value lies in its unprecedented follow-up of the divorced families. In 1989, Judith Wallerstein and Sandra Blakelee published the study's findings in *Second Chances: Men, Women and Children a Decade after Divorce*. What did they find?

At ten years after divorce, 41 percent of the children were doing poorly. They were entering adulthood as worried, underachieving, and angry young men and women with low self-esteem. As young adults, a majority were found to have significant anxiety about commitment, sex, love, marriage, family, and having children. The children who were doing well at that point came from families in which the parents were able to cooperate after divorce, put their differences aside, and allow the children ongoing relationships with both parents.

### Limited Mind-Body Knowledge, Including of Sexuality

It is surprising how frequently children arrive at adulthood with limited knowledge about body functions, including sexuality. Although knowledge of body functions and good health habits are included in most school curriculums, children tend to practice that which is modeled within the family. In families in which body functions are not discussed openly, children may remain naive about the most basic health and stress-management information. Regular exercise, good nutrition, familiarity with the body's systems, and knowledge about the effect of stress on the body can all go a long way toward anxiety prevention. Young adults who are not exposed to these practices are at a disadvantage when it comes to managing anxiety and stress.

Parental anxiety about teen pregnancy is often handled in an authoritarian way or by avoiding the subject altogether. This is unfortunate, because sexual concerns are high on the agenda for most teens. Concerns about masturbation, sexual feelings, dating, intimacy, and falling in love are all developmentally normal, but often confusing and anxiety arousing. These concerns do not necessarily end in adulthood, and the child who is unprepared for sexuality in adolescence is likely to be unprepared and anxious regarding intimacy later in life.

There is also the special circumstance of children who are coming to terms with their own homosexuality or bisexuality. Anxiety is likely to arise about loss of family support, as well as about living with a minority sexual orientation in a society that can be intolerant and even hostile toward gay, lesbian, bisexual, or transgender people. Similarly, children adjusting to a parent coming out as gay or lesbian can experience significant anxiety and confusion.

### Anxiety in Parents

We have considered many family sources of anxiety in children, but we have not yet addressed one of the most obvious: anxiety in parents. Because children learn primarily by imitation, the behavior patterns and habits of anxious parents often serve as a template for anxiety in children. In some cases, parental anxiety has little to do with raising children, but in other cases the anxiety is focused on trying to be a good parent.

I have worked with many anxious patients who were raised by parents with anxiety in the form of excessive worry, compulsiveness, perfectionism, as well as full-blown anxiety disorders. Children tend to internalize anxiety messages, such as "The world is not safe," "Bad things might happen," "Don't relax," "People cannot be trusted," and "There will never be enough."

In one case, a client's mother was so compulsive about keeping the house clean that her children could not bring friends home. Her mother could not tolerate any "dirt" in the house and did not want any children to use the guest bathroom, where they might soil the towels after washing their hands. My client developed her own anxiety as a result of being raised by this compulsive, rigid, and controlling mother. As an adult, she suffered from social phobia, obsessive-compulsive disorder, and generalized anxiety disorder. In addition, she was extremely indecisive, perfectionistic, and anxious about making mistakes.

Some anxious parents overprotect their children. In an effort to ensure their children's safety, they set unreasonable limits or prohibit such activities as overnight camps, social contacts, exploratory behavior, and other normal interests. In some cases, the parents themselves suffer from anxiety about separating from their children.

It is natural for parents to relive their own childhood experiences during the stages of their children's development. A child's first day of school, first summer camp experience, or first driving lesson can reactivate a parent's past emotions that are associated with those experiences. One of my adult clients, for example, was sexually abused at the age of fourteen, and experienced a resurgence of traumatic memories when her own daughter approached the same age.

In some cases, it may be necessary for parents to obtain professional help. I have worked with numerous parents who intuitively recognized that their own anxiety was interfering with their children's development. For example, one mother with social anxiety and low self-esteem knew well before her children started school that unless she addressed her anxiety, she would be unable to attend parent-teacher conferences, participate as a parent volunteer in school, or interact comfortably with parents of other children. Fortunately, through therapy, this mother of two children learned how to be more relaxed and assertive in social situations, and within a year she was able to engage fully in her children's school and extracurricular activities. She participated actively as a teacher's helper in the classroom, hosted play dates for her children at home, and interacted with other parents at sports and recreational activities.

In another case, a mother realized that her perfectionism and worry habits were clouding her judgment about her children's learning and social progress in school. She tended to compare her children to their peers and overreact to any social issues or possible delays in their academic progress. Like many parents, she measured her parenting skills and competence in terms of her children's achievements. This resulted in additional anxiety, as well as depression, whenever one of her children experienced a problem of any kind. Her task in therapy was to notice how her perfectionism was projected onto her children, and to identify her all-or-nothing thinking as it applied to parenting. She also needed to trust the resiliency of her children, and to work with their unique patterns of strengths and weaknesses.

It is important, of course, for parents to know when their children require special help and to advocate effectively for their needs when appropriate. Yet even this can be a problem for parents who have anxiety personality traits of their own, such as fear of conflict, unreasonable concern about being judged negatively, or difficulty communicating assertively.

## Stress in Parents and Families

My comments about anxiety in parents also pertain to stress in parents. Even without anxiety symptoms, highly stressed parents inevitably create a high-stress environment for their children. As discussed in Chapter 4, one source of stress is the recurring demands of daily life that most families consider to be normal. For parents, this can include working for a living, maintaining a home, transporting children, monitoring homework, attending school conferences, shopping, cooking, cleaning house, and other tasks.

Ironically, much of the stress in family life stems from efforts by parents to provide the best opportunities for their children. They value positive experiences, such as sports, music, art, and various other social, religious, educational, and recreational activities. The net result is often stress in children who have too little personal time, relaxation, and stress recovery. When so much stress occurs in children with anxiety personality traits, anxiety symptoms are likely to develop.

Parents rightfully believe that more opportunities and tools will translate into their children reaching their highest potential. But parents may have difficulty setting reasonable limits on extracurricular activities because they do not want their children to miss any opportunities. This has been called "hyperparenting," and it has become a cultural norm, especially in upper-income families.

In order to function on a day-to-day basis, children in high-stress family situations may shut down some or all of their systems, using defense mechanisms such as repression of feelings, social withdrawal, and even denial of reality. As a result, overstressed children become handicapped in coping with other demands, and are at risk for additional anxiety.

Family influences on a child's personality often have their full effect later in life. Many adults who come to therapy with anxiety disorders are unaware of how much stress they are under because it has been a normal part of life since childhood. They lack an objective perspective on stress because they have never lived without it or because they have somehow managed to remain in control in spite of it. The following are some of the indicators of high stress in families:

- Feeling constantly pressed for time or like always falling behind

**Indicators of High Stress in Families**

- Too many commitments

- Impatience, frustration, or conflict

- Fatigue

- Lack of time for play and relaxation

- High expectations

- Difficulty leaving the house on time

- Poor planning

- Lack of communication

## Other Background Issues

Some children are exposed to the idea that people can "go crazy" or "lose their minds." This can take place if they hear about people who were taken to a "mental hospital" or "insane asylum." This idea can be frightening to children and may become imprinted as a fear that, under certain circumstances, it could happen to them. This, of course, can add to the anxiety the person may experience at a later point in time.

Many families have histories they wish to keep secret, usually because of shame or embarrassment. Such information is typically withheld from the children out of a desire to protect them. Some examples of family secrets are suicide or the severe mental illness (such as schizophrenia) of a relative, an extramarital affair, sexual abuse of a child by a parent, an out-of-wedlock child, adoption, alcoholism, or a crime committed by a family member. Such hidden information can contribute to anxiety in children, especially when they intuitively sense something does not fit together or is being avoided. Indeed, confusion and uncertainty are among the most powerful anxiety producers.

A family with many rules and rigid patterns creates an inflexible atmosphere that does not match up with the real world. Children who were raised with the idea that there is only one way to do things have difficulty coping with situations involving choices or requiring flexibility. Such children can develop a problem with "shoulds" or a tendency to be compulsive about what must be done and how to do it. This can lead to stress and interfere with spontaneity and the ability to accept change.

## Conclusion

A variety of family background and childhood issues can contribute to the development of an anxiety disorder. The sequence generally follows a pattern. Initially, biological sensitivity combines with family and early life experiences to form the anxiety personality style discussed in Chapter 4. In response to stress, this type of person tends to react strongly, and anxiety emerges as he or she attempts to manage the feelings and body sensations associated with stress.

Looking back over Part I, we explored the relationship between fear and anxiety and discussed the biology of the survival reaction (Chapter 1). We then looked at the anxiety disorders and the criteria for diagnosing them (Chapter 2). The Three Ingredients Model was introduced to help understand how anxiety disorders develop (Chapter 3), followed by a discussion of the personality traits and family background experiences usually associated with anxiety disorders (Chapters 4 and 5). These concepts and insights are the foundation for Part II, in which you will find many recommendations, strategies, and self-help skills for creating a life beyond panic and anxiety.

# strategies and skills
## for creating a life
## beyond anxiety

Imagine that a miracle occurs in your life, and as a result, you no longer have an anxiety disorder. However, the miracle occurs while you are sleeping, so you don't know it has happened until you wake up in the morning. What would be different, and how would you know you have changed? What new thoughts, feelings, or behaviors would you notice?

To be anxiety free means to feel more relaxed and think more optimistically. It means to enjoy life more, with less concern about making mistakes, being embarrassed, or being judged negatively by others. It means having more energy and better health. It also means having more confidence and willingness to take reasonable risks to achieve personal goals. To create a life beyond anxiety means to find meaning and purpose, pursue your dreams, and realize your potential.

Part II is about the changes needed to create this outcome. Here, you will find a wide range of strategies, skills, and solutions for coping with anxiety and moving beyond it. You will be encouraged to create a personal program of practices that address your particular needs.

The recommendations I make are based on the information from Part I. For example, stress was identified as one of the key ingredients in the development of anxiety disorders, and many of the suggestions in Part II are directed toward managing stress. You will also find recommended steps for modifying the personality traits and cognitive style discussed in Part I as sources of anxiety. Many of these steps are preventive. They help not only with recovery from an anxiety disorder but also with preventing relapses and future anxiety.

I also include several chapters that deal with the biological aspect of anxiety. For example, Chapter 10 addresses dietary recommendations for reducing and preventing anxiety. The very next chapter (on stress control) includes recommendations for improving sleep. Chapter 17 addresses the pros and cons of medication, and the use of herbal remedies for anxiety.

||||||||||||||||||

# CHAPTER 6

||||||||||||||||||||||||

# Controlling Stress

In the story of creation, according to the Christian tradition, God took a day off after six days of work to rest and behold the fruits of His labor. Virtually all wisdom traditions and religions have such a weekly day of rest and reflection—a Sabbath day. Why?

Daily life requires energy that must be restored regularly in order to stay in the game. Without regular recovery from even the normal stress of everyday life, we become vulnerable to stress-related symptoms. Under high stress, an anxiety condition is likely to develop if we already have the biological sensitivity and anxiety personality ingredients.

Think about endurance competitions, such as triathlons and marathons. These events demonstrate the extraordinary human capacity for handling stress. In fact, training for such athletic events involves developing a tolerance for physical and mental stress. This is possible only with regular recovery to rest, repair, and restore energy. Without adequate recovery, an athlete would experience burnout and a decline in performance. The same requirement applies to all of us in daily life. We need to recover on a regular basis from the stress of life in order to function effectively, without physical and emotional breakdown.

It might be helpful to imagine relaxation as your natural state of equilibrium. Imagine feeling rested, refreshed, and ready for whatever may happen, the way you would want to feel at the beginning of each day. Your body is energized, and yet you are at peace and feel in control of yourself; your outlook is positive. This is your relaxation baseline, or home base. However, throughout each day, you find yourself being pulled away from this inner peace as you deal with the tasks, responsibilities, and stress of life.

In this chapter, you learn a three-step program for recognizing the sources and effects of stress and, most importantly, some methods for reducing the effects of stress. By following the suggestions in this chapter, you can reduce your anxiety as well as prevent future anxiety.

## The Effects of Uncontrolled Stress

The effects of stress accumulate when you do not recover on a regular basis. The signals of stress overload first appear as mild symptoms, such as irritability, headaches, dizziness, lost or increased appetite, sleep difficulty, back pain, difficulty concentrating, and fatigue. If you understand the meaning of such symptoms and have skills and practices for stress recovery, you can counteract stress and return to your relaxation baseline.

A symptom can be viewed as the body's attempt at a cure. That is, a symptom is a signal of stress in a system that is continually trying to restore and maintain healthy equilibrium. If we can recognize the message of stress overload brought by our symptoms and respond accordingly, we can prevent more serious breakdowns or crises. Anxiety is such a crisis, and it is triggered by stress overload in people who are predisposed to the condition as a result of their biological sensitivity and personality traits. In order to prevent stress overload, we must be able to recognize the early warning signals. We must also have a repertoire of self-healing and stress recovery skills.

Incomplete stress recovery also weakens our immune system, making us vulnerable to disease. Prolonged stress appears to be involved in heart disease, diabetes, arthritis, gastrointestinal disorders, chronic fatigue syndrome, and other physical disorders. And uncontrolled stress is a key ingredient in emotional conditions such as anxiety, depression, and eating disorders. Let's look more closely at the relationship between stress and disease.

Disease means *dis-ease,* or *not-at-ease.* When we are not at ease, we are away from home base—from relaxed equilibrium. In an effort to restore that equilibrium, the body resorts to its emergency survival mechanisms. One example is an increase in the body's ability to store glucose (sugar) from carbohydrates. This raises blood-sugar level, providing more energy for the body to use in dealing with stress. It is interesting to note that the most common medical intervention in hospitals is the administration of intravenous glucose—sugar injected into the blood to help the body deal with stress.

The body's emergency responses are helpful in the short run, but harmful in the long run. When stress is prolonged, the same stress hormones that increase energy—by raising blood sugar—inhibit insulin action and *lower* blood sugar. As a result, energy dwindles during prolonged stress. But there are more serious health consequences. The body begins to break down under prolonged stress, because it runs short on energy resources to cope with that stress. During periods of uncontrolled stress, body chemistry changes. Carbohydrate metabolism is replaced by fat production to supply needed energy. And because our energy requirements are so high during prolonged stress, we crave and eat more fats— as much as 30 percent more than normal. The accumulation of fats in the body increases the risk for heart disease, and lower insulin production increases the risk of diabetes. Prolonged, uncontrolled stress also exhausts the immune system, making us more vulnerable to disease.

## Anabolism and Catabolism

The body has two primary metabolic states: anabolism and catabolism. Anabolism refers to the process by which large molecules (such as glycoproteins and lipoproteins) are built-up from smaller molecules (such as fats, sugars, and amino acids). These larger molecules are then used for cellular function, growth, and storing energy. Catabolism is the opposite process, whereby larger molecules are broken down to smaller ones. This process is usually associated with the release of energy.

Periods of anabolism are like economic "good times." We invest in the house, perhaps expanding it or re-doing a kitchen; trade up to a larger or more expensive model of car; purchase stocks. We build up our net worth during economic good times. Stress, on the other hand, represents a period of "economic hardship." We sell stocks, get rid of the second car, and conserve resources in the interest of maintaining financial balance. In terms of biology, stress is usually associated with catabolic processes that are triggered by stress hormones. Our bodies break down larger molecules in order to create the energy resources necessary to meet the increased demands posed by stress.

## The Stages of Stress

Hans Selye, the biologist known for his groundbreaking research on stress, identifies three stages in the body's response to stress. The first stage is the "alarm" stage, during which the fight/flight reaction is triggered to deal with the stress. During this stage, stress hormones activate the body and provide the energy for fight or flight. Anxiety can begin in the alarm stage if a person reacts fearfully to the fight/flight response.

The second, or "resistance," stage involves repair and damage control. Rest and relaxation are crucial to this stage. Regular relaxation and other steps that are recommended later in this and subsequent chapters can stop the stress cycle at this stage and prevent anxiety or other symptoms.

If stress continues, the "exhaustion" stage sets in. Resistance is already weak, so the early warning symptoms intensify into more severe conditions. By stage three, the immune system is unable to produce lymphocytes and natural killer (NK) cells, and we become vulnerable to invading foreign substances. The potential for anxiety, as well as depression, reaches a high point due to loss of control over stress.

## Complete and Incomplete Stress Recovery

We can stop the negative effects of stress in the early stages if we recognize the warning signals and practice stress recovery techniques. To be effective, we must outpace stress and completely restore equilibrium. Because stress occurs daily, we need to practice stress recovery on a daily basis.

Complete stress recovery is illustrated in the first figure on the next page. The diagram shows how we return to relaxed equilibrium as a result of practicing stress recovery techniques on a regular basis. On the other hand, when stress recovery is inconsistent or incomplete, we do not restore equilibrium or return to our relaxation baseline. In that case, stress accumulates and we become vulnerable to stress-related symptoms and anxiety. An illustration of incomplete stress recovery is shown in the second figure on the next page.

## COMPLETE STRESS RECOVERY

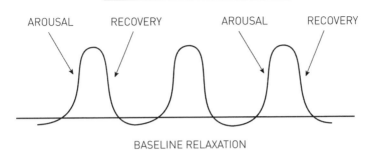

AROUSAL   RECOVERY   AROUSAL   RECOVERY

BASELINE RELAXATION

## INCOMPLETE STRESS RECOVERY

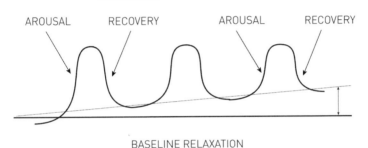

AROUSAL   RECOVERY   AROUSAL   RECOVERY

BASELINE RELAXATION

Stress is a natural part of life and cannot be entirely avoided. Selye suggests that some stress is actually necessary for physical and emotional growth. Events that are generally considered to be positive, such as marriage, pregnancy (if planned or wanted), job promotion, and even a vacation, can be stressful because of the adjustments and effort they require. Of course, negative stress events, such as relationship problems or divorce, loss of a family member or friend, or financial problems, are a threat to health and well-being. Yet stress itself does not have serious health consequences or cause anxiety. In a sense, stress itself is not the problem. The problem is lack of stress recovery.

### The Triple-S Approach to Stress Control

How do you get back to a state of relaxed equilibrium, or home base, if you have reached stress overload? Here are three steps for recognizing and controlling the effects of stress. These steps can be called the *Triple-S Approach to Stress Control.* The three key words in this approach are

SIGNALS —— SOURCES —— SOLUTIONS

**Signals,** the first step, involves recognizing the early warning signals of stress. Some of these are:

The Early
Warning Signs
of Stress

- Increased heart rate

- Cold/sweaty hands

- Stuttering

- Restlessness

- Irritability/moodiness

- Muscle tension/difficulty relaxing

- Fatigue or weakness

- Nervousness/trembling

- Soreness in the jaw from grinding or clenching

- Headaches

- Excessive worry

- Lost or increased appetite

- Back or muscle pain

- Dizziness

- Difficulty concentrating

- Difficulty sleeping

The second step is to identify the **sources** of stress in your life. The Life Change Scale on page 59, also known as The Social Readjustment Rating Scale, can help you identify sources of stress as well as estimate your stress level. You might want to refer back to this stress test to identify the sources of stress in your case, as a step toward creating a personal plan to control stress and move toward a life beyond anxiety.

After you recognize the signals and identify your sources of stress, the third step is to implement the stress **solutions** that are appropriate for you. Select the practices and lifestyle changes likely to create balance and control stress. Ideally, you should have a repertoire of skills, practices, and activities for maintaining your health and equilibrium. You may need to learn some new skills, such as assertiveness, better time management, and relaxation techniques. Or you may need to establish new habits, such as a regular exercise routine or a regular sleep routine to improve the quality of your sleep. Whatever you do, make it a regular and consistent practice. Below I have listed some stress solutions from which you can draw to create a personal plan. We explore some of these stress solutions in the rest of this chapter, while others are addressed in subsequent chapters, such as "Food, Eating and Anxiety," "Don't Just Do Something, Sit There," "Play Is for Adults, Too," and "Feeling Safe with Feelings."

The stress solutions discussed here and in subsequent chapters serve two important functions related to anxiety. One purpose is to reduce the anxiety that arises in biologically sensitive people when they are under stress. The second purpose is anxiety prevention—heading off anxiety before it emerges. It is possible to prevent anxiety symptoms by regularly practicing the following stress solutions:

- Simplify and organize your life

- Eat a healthy and nutritious diet

- Take rest and recovery days

- Manage time and avoid rushing

- Accept what can't be changed

- Develop assertiveness skills

- Identify and express feelings appropriately

- Get enough sleep and rest

- Modify stressful personality traits

- Learn and practice meditation

- Exercise regularly

Solutions for Preventing Stress

- Establish short- and long-term goals

- Set reasonable limits

- Don't feel guilty about taking care of yourself

- Make time for play/fun/recreation

- Practice relaxation techniques

- Find professional help for chronic problems

- Plan ahead (but live in the present)

- Replace worry and negative thinking

- Don't use alcohol/drugs to solve problems

*Simplify and Organize*

One way to control stress is to simplify and organize your life. This is one of the first steps toward creating a life beyond anxiety, and there are dozens of tips and suggestions you can follow. You can easily find books and resources on the topic of simplifying and organizing your life. Two recommended sources are Steven Covey's *Seven Habits of Highly Effective People* and *First Things First,* and Elaine St. James's *Simplify Your Life: 100 Ways to Slow Down and Enjoy the Things that Really Matter* (see Bibliography for complete references).

In many cases, anxiety is experienced as a feeling of being out of control. Usually this feeling is focused internally, on the bodily reactions, thoughts, and feelings associated with anxiety. In this section, I advise developing control in your daily activities and external environment because this can help you feel more in control. Gaining control over your external environment can go a long way toward inner peace and calm.

Here are just a few suggestions to get you started:

- Unclutter your home by disposing of items you don't use or need (old magazines, clothes, defective equipment)

- Develop a filing system for keeping paperwork organized

Suggestions for Gaining Control in Your Daily Activities

- Use one calendar to track all your appointments and commitments

- Manage your money and live within your means (get help with this if necessary)

- Delegate and share chores at home (even young children can be helpful)

- Become more efficient so you can have time to relax and enjoy your favorite activities

- Spend a little time each day staying organized to prevent buildup of stress

- Save time by cooking double amounts and freezing leftovers for other meals

- Sort mail immediately: discard junk mail, place bills in one place, and have a storage spot for mail you want to read later (to reduce junk mail by 75 percent write to the following address and ask to be removed from mailing lists: Mail Preference Service, 11 West 42nd St., New York NY 10163-3861)

- Prepare the night before to avoid morning rushing and stress (pick out clothes, gather items you will need, prepare lunch)

- Keep things in designated places so you can find what you need

### Rest and Recovery Days

Recalling the earlier discussion of complete and incomplete stress recovery, it should now be apparent why virtually all religions observe a weekly rest day. A Sabbath day helps with recovery from a week's worth of accumulated stress, or at least the stress that is not discharged daily even with adequate sleep, proper diet and nutrition, exercise, and other forms of stress recovery. In addition, many traditions observe special holidays, such as Lent, Yom Kippur, and Ramadan, during which rest, meditation, reflection, time with family, and even fasting are advised. Some secular holidays, such as Labor Day, Memorial Day, and Veterans Day, consist of days off from work and school. These special days can be excellent opportunities for controlling the effects of stress and restoring equilibrium.

Rest and recovery days are intentional ways to take time out from the stress of daily life and to induce relaxation and stress recovery. For biologically sensitive people, rest and recovery time is important for counteracting the anxiety aroused by stress or high stimulation.

In keeping with these concepts, I have developed two exercises for recovering from stress, which are described below.

### Exercise: *Recovery Day*

Now that you understand the importance and need for periodic stress recovery, plan a special day off that you will devote to cleansing yourself from accumulated stress. On this day, you will not travel, drive a car, go to work, or have any other agendas. This will be a quiet day, the kind of day you would take for yourself if you were sick and had to stay home. It would be good if you could be alone on this special recovery day.

On this day, do everything slowly, deliberately, consciously. Practice all the recovery skills in your repertoire, such as relaxation, meditation, yoga or stretching, eating properly, and generally taking good care of yourself. Experiment with some new methods. Try spending a period of time or even the entire day in silence—do not talk or communicate with others in person, by telephone, or electronically. Read an inspiring text and savor an uplifting thought you find there, repeating it to yourself. Become quiet inside and conserve energy, doing only activities that are directed toward healing yourself from stress.

Plan several days each year for stress recovery and symptom prevention. You can modify the exercise by periodically taking a half day for this purpose.

### Sleep Well

Sleep is one of the most basic human needs, but a surprisingly high number of people do not get enough sleep. Sixty-seven percent of adults report sleeping problems, and fifty-eight million Americans report day-

**Exercise:** *Catch-Up Day*

More stress is added to your life when you feel you are falling behind in tasks and responsibilities. This exercise is designed to help you feel more in control and less stressed.

Designate a day for catching up during which you are only allowed to work on completing unfinished projects. These can include returning mail-order items, paying bills, sewing or clothes repair, cleaning out a closet, or completing anything you have begun but not finished. Do not begin any new projects.

Imagine that with each completed item you are eliminating a barrier between you and your inner state of peace. As you move through such a day, think about how much better you would feel if you undertook fewer responsibilities. Resolve to take better care of yourself by setting more reasonable limits.

time sleepiness that interferes with their daily activities. The average night's sleep for an adult is 6 hours and 57 minutes, an hour less than the suggested 8 hours. For the anxious or biologically sensitive person, lack of sleep affects not only physical energy but also cognitive functions. Inadequate sleep lowers our ability to control worry, obsessive thinking, and other anxiety triggers.

Sleep disturbance can take a number of forms. Many anxious people have difficulty falling asleep at night. They are unable to turn off their active minds, relax, or fall asleep. In other cases, people fall asleep readily, but wake up in the middle of the night and are unable to fall back asleep. And in some cases, people do sleep through the night, but wake up tired because the quality of their sleep is poor. In most cases of sleep disturbance, the problem is difficulty turning off the mind. An active mind keeps the body in a high state of arousal and interferes with the relaxation necessary to sleep restoratively.

In some cases, sleep problems are caused by biological issues. Sleep quality and quantity can be affected by snoring, sleep apnea, restless leg syndrome, and the hot flashes associated with menopause. Snoring is usually caused by partial blocking of the airway due to throat tissue obstruction. Sleep apnea involves the brain waking up the body when it does not receive enough oxygen, typically due to snoring. In such cases it is advisable to seek professional help. One helpful step is to undergo a sleep study, an assessment that determines the specific nature of the problem and offers suggestions and recommendations for improving sleep.

There are many steps you can take to improve the quality of sleep. Most consist of lifestyle adjustments and establishing good sleep habits, and they should be considered before you seek sleep medication. A list of sleep recommendations is displayed below. Review the following list of sleep recommendations and see if any steps apply to you:

**Recommendations for Improving Your Sleep**

- Create a relaxing ambiance (e.g., dim lighting) at nighttime

- Establish a consistent sleep cycle seven days a week

- Make sleep a priority and avoid the temptation to stay up late

- Do not watch television at least one hour before going to sleep (too stimulating)

- Take a warm (92–97° F) bath or foot bath (also see aromatherapy below)

- Avoid daytime naps if you have difficulty falling asleep at night

- Use your bed only for sleep and intimacy (not paperwork)

- Use a good mattress, one that provides comfort and support

- Exercise regularly (but not within two hours of bedtime)

- Relax or meditate before bedtime

- If you wake up and can't get back to sleep, get up and do something (go to the bathroom, drink water or herb tea, read) until fatigue induces sleep

- Eat "good" foods that are high in tryptophan and induce sleep: milk, bananas, cereal with milk, plain baked potato, tuna, eggs, Horlick's Hot Malted Milk (verified by research)

- Avoid "bad" foods: caffeine (in coffee, black tea, chocolate, many sodas); refined sweets, excessive salt, alcohol, tobacco, MSG, and chemical additives that increase heart rate; and foods with tyramine (sauerkraut, wine, pork, eggplant, spinach, tomatoes)

- Drink herbal teas that have relaxant properties. These include chamomile, passion flower, and peppermint, and consider seeing a health-care professional for other herbal solutions for sleep problems.

- Use aromatherapy: chamomile (6 drops) or lavender oil (6 drops) or blossom (5 drops) added to warm bath. Steep a combination of valerian root, lime blossom, and chamomile in boiling water for 10 minutes and add to warm bath.

- Get a massage: This can be a gentle stroking and kneading of the body or just the feet, using a massage oil with lavender and chamomile.

### Stress Control Without Guilt

During the safety announcements at the beginning of an airplane flight, you hear a variation of the following statement. "In the unlikely event that there is a loss of cabin pressure, oxygen masks will automatically be deployed from the overhead compartment. Simply put the mask over your face and secure it with the safety strap, then breathe normally. *If you are traveling with young children, be sure to put on your own oxygen mask <u>before</u> attempting to help someone else.*" Why do the airlines advise us to take care of our own needs before helping those who depend on us?

As discussed in Chapter 5, anxiety-prone people tend to focus on the needs of others at the expense of their own health and well-being. They may also make too many commitments and approach life in a compulsive or perfectionistic way. As a result, taking time to control their own stress may seem selfish or lead to feelings of guilt.

As a sensitive person, here are some questions you might have asked yourself:

"How can I balance my personal needs with my responsibilities to family, friends, work, and community?"

"What gives me the right to feel stressed when so many people in the world are suffering more profoundly from natural disasters, war, terrorism, and poverty?"

"Is it selfish to take care of myself? Should I feel guilty?"

My answer to these questions is that, if you do not take care of yourself regularly, you will eventually have nothing left to give. You will burn out and have no energy to care for others, to do good work, or to make a difference in the world. If you have an anxiety disorder, you are already paying the price for high stress. You need regular stress recovery in order to prevent your own symptoms from interfering with your ability to give to others. Here, then, is an exercise for overcoming guilt about taking care of yourself. The general idea of this exercise is to balance the scales of giving to others and replenishing yourself so you can continue to give.

### Exercise: *Healing Yourself Without Guilt*

Begin by making a list of all activities that have in the past brought you a sense of renewal. You can also expand the list to include any activities that have in the past or might in the future bring you joy, pleasure, or satisfaction.

For activities that worked for you in the past, note the last time you spent any time doing them. This will give you some idea of how little you give to yourself.

After making the list, you will have a sense of what you can give to yourself. Decide which activities and experiences you want to increase in your life, and begin to nurture yourself—for the sake of humanity!

You can engage in self-care activities periodically or schedule them before or after performing an act of love or caring. Again, the idea is to renew your energy so you can continue to serve others, such as family, friends, or community.

Many religions prescribe loving kindness as a spiritual duty for which no reward should be expected, other than to serve God. In Judaism, for example, a *mitzvoth*, or act of loving kindness toward another person, is the most holy thing you can do. And, as far as I can tell, all branches of Christianity advise loving kindness as the way to be close to God. This spiritual value has sometimes been misunderstood to mean that it is selfish to take care of yourself. I do not believe this is an accurate interpretation. Perhaps we should treat ourselves with the same loving kindness with which we are encouraged to treat others. In fact, the Judeo-Christian Bible makes numerous references to the human body as a temple of the spirit, and advises us to care for ourselves as a spiritual practice.

## Conclusion

When we manage stress, we become less vulnerable to anxiety. As discussed in this chapter, many steps and practices can reduce and even prevent anxiety. The catch is that these solutions must be practiced regularly to have the desired effect.

You can think of stress control as a form of anxiety inoculation. It takes far more stress to activate anxiety in a person who has achieved a state of relaxed equilibrium in daily life than one who has not achieved such balance. This insight should be kept in mind as we turn to the next chapter on learning how to relax.

# CHAPTER 7

# Don't Just Do Something, Sit There

There once was a time when sitting still was necessary for human survival. Before agriculture and the development of long-range weapons, we were hunters who depended on catching prey for food, clothing, and tools. At that point in our history, the only way we could get close enough to throw a rock or spear at living animal targets was to sit quietly and patiently, awaiting their arrival and close proximity. We had to blend into nature to avoid detection by equally cunning prey. Sitting still for many hours was a natural survival mechanism.

Sitting still is as necessary for survival now as it was in prehistoric times, but for very different reasons. In today's high-tech world, we are relieved of many basic survival tasks, which are conveniently performed for us by machines and electronic devices. For most of us, the raw materials for living are readily available, and our food, clothing, tools, and shelters are no longer grown or fabricated by our own hands. Theoretically, we have the luxury of more leisure time, greater control, and less stress.

But how many of us actually take the time for more leisure? How often do we sit still and appreciate what we have? Instead, we have filled our extra time with more tasks, activities, and commitments, and we have increased our speed of living. In spite of modern conveniences and the promise of more free time and an easier life, we are more often rushed and we have more stress. As a society, we are "stressed out" and have difficulty slowing down. Our survival now depends on our ability to cope with stress and minimize the damage it causes.

As discussed previously, the anxiety personality style also contributes to stress overload. Impatience, a desire to please others, difficulty relaxing in spite of a desire for calm, trouble setting reasonable limits or saying "no," and a need to feel in control are some of the traits that create stress. You can think of your anxiety symptoms as warning signals, indicating a need to slow down and reevaluate your thinking and behavior patterns. In this chapter we take another step toward creating a life beyond anxiety.

The challenge is to learn new skills for achieving relaxed equilibrium. In this chapter, I introduce some informal relaxation skills as well as more formal practices, such as inducing the *relaxation response* (described in this chapter) and various forms of meditation. In my view, these skills and practices are essential for creating a life beyond stress and anxiety.

## Resistance to Relaxation

I work with many patients for whom relaxation practice is the most difficult aspect of anxiety recovery. I observe a pattern of resistance to relaxing even in patients who recognize its importance and want to relax. In some cases, the resistance stems from an underlying belief that taking time out from work or household chores to relax means the job won't get done. There is often a compulsive quality to this attitude, and some patients have revealed a fear that relaxing will make them lazy and unproductive. It is important to realize that relaxation actually improves productivity because it restores energy and enhances efficiency.

Resistance to relaxation also stems from difficulty giving up one of the most common defense mechanisms against anxiety: keeping busy. In many cases, "busy-ness" is a form of distraction that serves to avoid anxious thoughts and uncomfortable feelings. By focusing on outside tasks and activities, attention is diverted away from one's inner self, whereas by slowing down or sitting we risk a face-to-face encounter with fearful thoughts and anxious feelings.

Frequent stress and anxiety can cause the body to remain in a state of tension and arousal that is resistant to relaxation. Wilhelm Reich used the term "armor" to describe this pattern. Like the hard shell on some animals, the body molds itself into the patterns of muscular tension associated with chronic stress or anxiety. Reich indicates that an armored person is unable to completely relax. Relaxation can threaten an armored person's protective layers of muscular tension and produce feelings of vulnerability. The survival center picks up on this as a danger signal. This results in an increase in arousal or anxiety—even a strong fight/flight reaction—in response to relaxation.

Another issue is the control need that we discussed in Chapter 4 as an anxiety personality trait. Being in control is associated with psychological vigilance and physical tension. In other words, a strong control need is associated with a frequent or chronic state of arousal. Relaxation, on the other hand, requires letting down your guard, trusting, feeling safe, and opening up.

Relaxation softens the boundaries of separateness and blurs the line between yourself and the world around you. In relaxation, you "open up" to a more permeable and flexible relationship with the world and other people. Relaxing, therefore, is often anxiety arousing for sensitive people with anxiety personality traits, who feel more emotionally and physically vulnerable when relaxed.

You cannot be in a relaxed state and a fight/flight state at the same time. But, for anxious people, the fight/flight state can become chronic and habitual. If you have rigid body armor, a strong need for control, concerns about safety and vulnerability, or strong needs for achievement, you may have to train your body to enjoy the state of relaxation.

To sit still and relax, we must address yet another issue—our own thought patterns. Mind and body are intricately connected, and the body responds in some way to virtually every thought. A worry thought, for example, activates the fight/flight response because the survival instinct interprets it as a danger signal. Although worrying is usually irrational and the "danger" may only be in our mind, we react in a real and physical way. Therefore, relaxation may be difficult because the stimulation and stress caused by our thoughts keep us activated.

We each have between thirty thousand and fifty thousand thoughts every day, an average of approximately one thought per second. Relaxation requires turning off our thoughts, or at least curtailing our reactions to them. In some forms of meditation, the goal is to attain "empty mind," a calm mental state in which there is nothing in the mind. Controlling what we think is a key step in achieving a calm or relaxed state.

On the other hand, pleasant thoughts can have a soothing effect on the body and help to restore a relaxed equilibrium. Once you learn to relax, just the thought of relaxing can have a calming effect.

The power of thoughts to affect us physically can be demonstrated by a simple experiment that you can perform right now. Close your eyes for a few moments and visualize a bright yellow lemon. Picture the lemon being sliced sharply in half, and then squeezed to force the juice out of it. Imagine tasting the juice as you smell its pungent aroma. Most people begin to salivate in response to this thought, making it obvious that the body responds readily to thoughts.

Because the mind and body are intertwined in one organic system, relaxation can be approached from either side of this relationship. It is possible to relax the body by calming the mind, as well as to calm the mind by relaxing the body. Recognizing this, most relaxation instructions include both a physical relaxation procedure, such as *progressive muscle relaxation,* and a mental relaxation procedure, such as *visualization.* Using both forms of relaxation affords a greater chance for acquiring this vitally important skill. In one case, a woman who practiced these skills told me at the end of her therapy, "Whenever I begin to feel tense or anxious, I automatically take a few deep breaths and relax, without even thinking about it." Another patient reported, "I am finding myself using the relaxation techniques when I start to feel anxious. Deep breathing seems second nature now."

We all experience relaxed moments, when our attention is fully engaged in a single activity. Sitting quietly by the fireplace, knitting, reading, or boating on a sunny summer afternoon are examples of activities in which serenity may replace the internal chatter of thoughts. In this state, we are quietly content and the concerns of daily life fade away. However, these activities bring us only temporary peace during the time we are absorbed in them, or perhaps for a short lingering period afterward. Once the mind returns to its normal concerns, our many thoughts are reactivated.

Relaxation can be a growth opportunity. In fact, some relaxation methods, such as meditation, involve processes and goals similar to those of psychotherapy. In order to truly relax and achieve peace of mind, you must face your inner self with all its fears, distorted beliefs, and uncomfortable feelings. In pioneering psychological therapy, Freud asserted that the goal of psychoanalysis was to render the unconscious conscious. That is, freedom would come from conscious awareness of what motivates us and from making choices based on self-understanding. Although psychoanalysis has waned since Freud's time, most therapy approaches still involve facing the inner self as a primary step in healing. This is essential to anxiety recovery, which requires facing our anxiety and learning to handle uncomfortable feelings. When we face anxiety and apply the right self-regulation skills, our self-confidence and courage grow and we can begin to create a life beyond panic and anxiety. Relaxation is the foundation for such skills.

### Relaxed Equilibrium

Inherent in each of us is a natural state of well-being and peace that we can experience when our stress level is low. This inner state has been called "equilibrium" and "homeostasis," terms that imply a state of balance at the core of life. On a day-to-day basis, as well as during the course of a lifetime, our equilibrium is disturbed by various stressors and challenges. If we have the proper skills and use them regularly, we can restore our equilibrium and stay in tune with our inner peace. However, if we do not know how to recover from stress, an accumulation of arousal symptoms can create an emotional or physical health crisis, such as an anxiety disorder.

Restoring relaxed equilibrium is both a biological and psychological necessity. Biologically, the rest and relaxation phase of the stress/relaxation cycle is necessary for recovery and symptom prevention. During relaxation, damaged cells are replaced; the immune system is repowered; and through a variety of other healing processes, organ systems can recover from the effects of stress. As we said earlier in Chapter 6, stress is not necessarily destructive, but lack of stress recovery is. Without relaxation, physical symptoms are sure to develop.

Psychologically, relaxation is necessary for restoring mental efficiency, problem-solving abilities, creativity, peace of mind, and general enjoyment of life. Furthermore, without relaxation the anxious mind remains in turmoil and, in severe anxiety cases, this can lead to a fear of losing control or "going crazy."

Relaxation is necessary to overcome anxiety for a number of other reasons. We have already noted that relaxation and anxiety are incompatible states—the more you relax, the less anxious you will be. By training yourself to relax, you raise the threshold of stress required to activate the fight/flight response. At baseline relaxation it takes more of a truly life-threatening situation to activate a reaction, whereas if you are tense and "up-tight" it takes much less stress to do so. Also, once an anxiety reaction is set in motion, relaxation can help to counteract it, although it still takes time to recover from an adrenaline surge.

### The Relaxation Response

Herbert Benson's extensive research on the healing benefits of relaxation has helped to establish its importance in anxiety recovery. Benson found that the body has an inborn capacity to enter a special state characterized by lowered heart rate, decreased rate of breathing, lowered blood pressure, slower brain waves, and an overall reduction of the speed of metabolism. The changes produced by this relaxation response, notes Benson, counteract the harmful effects and uncomfortable feelings of stress. Furthermore, in this peaceful condition the individual's mental patterns change and "worry cycles" are broken. Relaxation disrupts anxiety and fearful thoughts that, Benson says, "play involuntarily over and over in unproductive grooves."

Benson originally recommended a four-step procedure for eliciting the relaxation response, but recently reports that just two steps are effective. The two steps for eliciting the relaxation response are

1. repetition of a special word, phrase, poem, prayer, or muscular activity (such as knitting, slow walking, dance movement, or yoga posture), synchronized with breathing

2. returning to the repetition when other thoughts intrude

It is advisable to do this practice for a minimum of ten to twenty minutes once or twice each day. The positive effect of this practice is increased if the repetition has special meaning. For example, a person who is soothed by nature could repeat a phrase such as "ocean waves," "beautiful unfolding flower," or "calm water." The repetition could be a

line or two from a meaningful song or poem (" 'Tis a gift to be simple …
'tis a gift to be free") or it could be a positive affirmation ("I feel safe and
empowered").

In his recent research, Benson emphasizes the "faith factor." The
faith factor is a person's deeply held positive beliefs or spiritual convictions, and it can be incorporated into the relaxation response by repeating words that reflect one's faith. These can consist of a personally meaningful biblical passage, psalm, or prayer; a reassuring mantra ("I am one
with the universe" or "let nature take its course"); or an uplifting word
("serenity" or "peaceful").

When combining relaxed breathing with a meaningful thought,
the possibilities for self-healing are almost unlimited. Indeed, Benson
reports an astounding list of physical and emotional disorders that can be
eliminated or significantly reduced using this approach. The list includes
headaches, angina pain, high blood pressure, insomnia, backaches, and
high cholesterol. He reports, for example, that 80 percent of angina pain
can be relieved by relaxation combined with positive belief. Benson also
indicates that most symptoms of anxiety, including panic attacks; anticipatory worry; GI distress (nausea, diarrhea, irritable bowel syndrome,
and constipation); hyperventilation; and irritability can be alleviated with
regular practice of relaxation combined with positive belief.

In addition to practicing Benson's procedure for eliciting the relaxation response, there are countless other approaches to relaxation. For example, you can use recorded relaxation instructions from tapes or CDs
and enhance their benefits by thinking about relaxing while you do
other activities that don't require intense concentration, such as washing dishes, folding laundry, or straightening up your office or home.
Although results achieved this way may not equal the benefits of the
relaxation response, they can still contribute to anxiety reduction.

As an alternative to using tapes or CDs, you can engage in a quiet
and focused activity, such as slow walking, arts and crafts, reading, praying or repeating an inspiring passage, or listening to soothing music.
Other options include learning how to meditate (see the next section)
as a way to calm your mind. You can also experiment with the breathing and yoga postures suggested in subsequent chapters. With all these
practices, be patient and remember that you are learning a new skill and

replacing maladaptive habits. Also, remind yourself that slowing down and relaxing are safe, good, necessary for health, and powerful for counteracting anxiety.

## Meditation

Like the relaxation response, meditation induces relaxation. But meditation leads to more than relaxation because it is directed toward cultivating specific emotional and cognitive qualities, such as mindfulness (awareness without judgment), equanimity (acceptance of things as they are), compassion toward self and others, emotional self-control, and focused attention. All of these qualities can be directly helpful in reducing anxiety.

Two systems of meditation have been shown to be effective in reducing anxiety: transcendental meditation (known as TM) and insight meditation (also known as vipassana). The two systems have similarities and differences, and I address both styles in this section. First, let me describe my own initiation into meditation practice.

As discussed in Chapter 1, I had difficulty controlling anxiety well into adulthood. Fortunately, a door opened for me as a doctoral student in clinical psychology, during my internship year in San Francisco, when I met a friend named John. From the moment we met, John impressed me as a serene and patient person and I envied the peacefulness he exuded. One evening, shortly after we rented a house together, John announced he was going into his room to meditate, and he added, "Don't call me, I'll call you."

I was interested in meditation, but I knew little about the practice, so John offered to be my meditation teacher. He practiced transcendental meditation and taught me the basic principles and instructions. Essentially, the following four steps were advised:

1. Sit quietly in an upright position

2. Begin by breathing deeply and relaxing the muscles

3. Focus on a special word or mental device (a mantra)

4. Adopt a passive attitude toward intrusive thoughts

When I first tried to sit down and meditate, I jumped up within seconds, responding to the call of nature and basic needs, such as thirst. After returning to my chair, I jumped up again quickly with a need to change my clothes and "prepare" myself. This pattern continued and I was unable to sit for even a few minutes without jumping up to do something. So went my first meditation session.

For my next session, I performed all my preparations in advance, but to my dismay, sitting still was again interrupted by a list of things that could not wait to be done. After a few days of such agitated effort, I recognized a pattern of resistance, traceable to my mind's difficulty with letting go. This was frustrating, but John reassured me I would overcome this obstacle with further practice. I stayed with the practice and slowly became comfortable with sitting still. I even began to look forward to my meditation sessions. Within a few months, I experienced a new awareness and inner peace that permeated into other areas of my life. I continued to practice and now I credit meditation with improving my attention and ability to concentrate, energy level, clarity in thinking, patience, compassion, equanimity, emotional self-control, and deepening understanding of the mind.

### Transcendental Meditation (TM)

Transcendental meditation consists of choosing an object to concentrate on and focusing on it while letting all other thoughts dissolve into the background. This meditation style is designed to relieve the mind of thought, and the goal is "awareness without thoughts." Concentration on breath is a common practice, but the focus can be on a chant; an external sound; a specific muscle as it relaxes; or a visual stimulus, such as a candle flame or object of art.

The concept of TM-type meditation is simple, but the practice is difficult, as I personally discovered. What is difficult is the skill of concentration. As mentioned previously, research shows that we have frequent thoughts—approximately one every second—and they all compete for our attention. In addition, we tend to identify with our thoughts, taking them seriously and reacting emotionally to them.

The essence of meditation is learning to let all of these thoughts, which require attention and energy, fade into the background, while you

## *Practicing Transcendental Meditation*

Choose a time when you can be relatively free of outside distractions. The quiet time of dawn and dusk are ideal, but any time that fits your lifestyle is appropriate. Try to set aside approximately twenty minutes for meditation, once or twice each day.

Set up a special place for meditation, such as the corner of a room, where you can build up a peaceful atmosphere to help quiet your mind. Of course, you can meditate anywhere, including a park bench or while waiting in a parked car.

Sit straight but not rigidly, with head, neck, and back in alignment. It is also important to be relaxed, warm, and comfortable in order to mini-mize distraction. If necessary, stretch or exercise before meditation.

Close your eyes and begin with relaxed breathing, pulling in your stomach to fully empty your lungs as you exhale. Establish a natural, deep breathing rhythm, with approximately three seconds each of inhalation and exhalation (for further information on breathing prac-tices, see Chapter 8). The purpose of this step is to slow down your breathing and relax.

Let your mind wander as you begin to regulate your breathing, and then gradually focus on the sensations of breathing. Next, gently bring your attention to the focal point of your choice. This can be a blank screen; a mental picture; a steady sound, such as flowing water; or the rising and falling of your breath. You can also try gazing steadily at an object, such as a candle flame or an inspiring picture.

Hold your concentration on the one focal point, gently returning to it each time your mind is drawn away by passing thoughts. This is the essence of meditation practice. Do not be frustrated by the frequency with which you lose focus. Cultivate an attitude that does not judge your thoughts, but instead detaches gently from them.

For stubborn or compelling thoughts, keep a notebook handy and release such thoughts by jotting them down. Then close your eyes and return to concentration on the focal point or the space between thoughts.

Rise calmly upon completing your session and remain connected to the thin and delicate thread of calm awareness. Carry the serenity of meditation into your daily life and continue your practice on a regular basis.

concentrate on the quiet stillness between them. To do this, you focus on just one thing, such as breathing, to strengthen your ability to concentrate, and then repeatedly let go of extraneous thoughts. With steady practice, you can empty your mind of all thoughts, and as the object of concentration itself fades away, you can experience the quiet peace behind thinking. A suggested procedure for transcendental meditation is located on the previous page.

### Insight Meditation and Mindfulness

Insight meditation differs from TM in that this method does not turn away from thoughts or internal experiences, but rather works with them in a particular way. In this style of meditation, thoughts and sensations are acknowledged, but not judged. In terms of anxiety, insight meditation involves nonjudgmental acceptance of present experience, such as anxious feelings and worry thoughts.

This form of meditation is similar to the exposure technique used in psychotherapy, wherein a client is encouraged to face and experience "phobic situations"—those places or circumstances associated with anxiety. The process of insight meditation involves experiencing anxious feelings with acceptance and realizing such feelings are less frightening than we anticipate.

Insight meditation is known for its emphasis on the skill of *mindfulness*. Mindfulness can be defined as "awareness of present experience with acceptance." Three key elements in this definition are relevant to anxiety. Awareness involves *attentiveness* to early signs and signals of tension or mental unrest and making appropriate adjustments before they become full-blown symptoms. *Present experience* refers to what is happening moment-to-moment, rather than to past or future experience. And *acceptance* means a nonjudgmental attitude toward oneself and others. All three elements are immensely important for managing anxiety.

I apply mindfulness to anxiety reduction by advising my patients to periodically stop and ask, "How am I doing *right now?*" During periods of high anxiety this question can be asked often, on a moment-to-moment basis if necessary, to help the person stay in the present. This counteracts anxiety caused by worrying about what may happen in the future or by regretting what has happened in the past.

Mindfulness can be cultivated through formal meditation as well as through spontaneous exercises. Below I offer instructions in a formal mindfulness meditation, followed by several other suggested exercises. All are designed to help you cultivate full awareness in the present moment, as well as developing such helpful qualities as acceptance without judgment.

---

### Mindfulness Meditation: *Practicing Witnessing*

This practice involves noticing, or "witnessing," an experience that is taking place in the present without judgment.

Begin by sitting comfortably and focusing on your body, with attention to how it feels to be supported by the earth through the chair. Close your eyes if this feels safe.

Allow whatever arises in your awareness—visual images, sounds, physical sensations, feelings, thoughts—to come and go, to move freely.

Next, bring attention to whatever dominates your field of experience. Notice and label the type of mental process occurring, such as feeling, analyzing, judging, remembering, planning, or worrying. See if you can objectively watch, or witness, the activities of your mind. Assume the role of a spectator witnessing a passing parade of experiences.

Take a few slow, deep breaths before ending the session.

---

I now suggest some more structured exercises for developing mindfulness. Use these as a springboard for exercises that you can create spontaneously in everyday life.

---

### Exercise: *Mindful Eating*

Choose a whole fresh or dried fruit, such as an apple, peach, plum, or pear, to use for this five-to-ten-minute mindfulness exercise. Begin by looking at the fruit to observe its color, shape, texture, and other physical qualities. Smell it to experience its odor. Is it fragrant and pleasing? Reflect on how it came to arrive before you now. From where did it come? A tree? Do you know where it grew? What helped it grow: sun,

*(cont'd.)*

water, earth? How did it get from there to here? Take some time to appreciate all that was involved in bringing this piece of fruit to you, as well as the nourishment it will provide.

Slowly take a bite, savoring its flavor and texture in your mouth. Notice the sensations as your tongue presses the fruit against your teeth. Is there a burst of flavor? Take your time to experience the process of eating and nourishing your body with the fruit's latent energy. Notice if you are in a rush to take another bite, and see what happens when you do this. Compare that to chewing slowly, deliberately, mindfully.

You can practice this exercise with virtually any food item. You can also apply this form of full attentiveness to as many daily activities as possible.

### *Mindfulness Exercise:* Cultivating Patience

Select a simple, everyday situation that requires a few minutes of waiting, such as water boiling for tea, hand lotion being absorbed by the skin, food cooking on the stove, standing in line in a store, sitting in traffic, or waiting for someone who is running late. Practice cultivating an attitude of patience by breathing calmly, relaxing, and waiting peacefully. Gracefully accept the situation, allowing it to take its own time, and see if you can enjoy a few minutes of patience and mindful presence.

## Conclusion

The relaxation and meditation practices described in this chapter are important skills for controlling stress and counteracting anxiety. They elicit a calming physical and mental state that replaces high arousal, tension, and anxiety. In addition, these practices counteract the thought patterns that create and maintain anxiety. Such patterns include worrying, obsessive thinking, "shoulding," and judging.

Meditation and the relaxation response have a convincing backing in research as practices that promote mental and physical health. I have personally benefited immeasurably from these practices. If I were limited to only one recommendation for anxiety control, it would be daily relaxation and meditation.

# CHAPTER 8

||||||||||||||||||||||

# *Take a Deep Breath*

B reathing is a matter of life and death, yet many people do not breathe properly and suffer a loss of vitality and health. Breathing is often taken for granted and considered a simple, automatic function that cannot be controlled. How breathing reflects a person's emotional condition and state of mind is also overlooked. However, proper breathing is essential for physical, emotional, and mental self-regulation, and is another key to controlling stress and creating a life beyond anxiety.

Fritz Perls, the founder of Gestalt psychology, pointed to the relationship between breathing and anxiety when he wrote, "Anxiety is excitement without breath." In this chapter, we explore some breathing practices and skills that can reduce anxiety.

### Are You Breathing?

A full breath begins not with an inhalation, but with a complete exhalation that empties the lungs and allows a new supply of air to fill in from the bottom to the top of the lungs. The action of the diaphragm compresses the lungs during exhalation, and releases the pressure as air is drawn into the lungs. The result is full expansion during inhalation, which can be felt in the stomach and chest. In natural breathing, the lungs function like a bellows device, collapsing purposefully to release air, followed by a vacuum effect that sucks in a new supply of air as they expand.

You can evaluate your breathing pattern with the following two simple exercises:

### Assessing Your Breathing

In the first exercise, place one hand on your chest and the other hand on your diaphragm, just above the stomach. As you breathe, notice whether both areas expand and contract or whether one—or both—holds still. In natural breathing, the full participation of the diaphragm and chest is involved, and a maximum amount of air is absorbed and released. Therefore, you should feel movement in both your hands as you observe your breath.

The second exercise involves making a continuous "ahhh..." sound in your normal voice while exhaling. Exhale for as long as you can, and while doing so, time yourself using a watch or clock with a second hand. If you cannot maintain the sound for at least twenty seconds, you are not breathing fully or you have a respiratory problem. You can improve your breathing pattern by increasing the duration of the sound while exhaling.

Should we breathe through our mouth or our nose? Breathing through the nose (nasal breathing) opens more air passages and heightens the senses, especially the sense of smell. Breathing through the nose also warms the air before it reaches the lungs, and the nostril hairs filter particulate matter to protect the lungs. Alertness is also increased through nasal breathing and a person's face looks more alive when breathing nasally, compared to a duller countenance when breathing with the mouth open. However, breathing through the mouth is natural during vigorous exercise because we have an increased need for oxygen. It is advisable to allow your breathing to take its natural form, based on the situation and your body's needs.

### Don't Hold Your Breath

It is common to hold the breath when feeling stressed or anxious. When I am stressed, I feel tension in my chest, neck, shoulders, and back, and my breathing becomes shallow and inhibited. These are the early warning signals of stress overload. Because muscle tension is restricting the spontaneity of my breathing, I respond with a choice of stretches to relieve the tension and restore a deeper and more natural breathing pattern. In addition, I have established some cues for instant relaxation and deep breathing. One cue, for example, is red traffic lights. When I am stopped by a traffic light, I accept it as gift from the universe and pause for a moment to breathe deeply and remember what is important in life. I chose this particular cue because red traffic lights used to frustrate me and cause tension.

To appreciate what a difference even a moment of deep breathing can make, pause for a moment and perform this simple exercise:

**Exercise:** *A Simple Stretch for Deeper Breathing*

Lean back, raise your arms, and breathe deeply several times. Doing this stretches the chest and back muscles, and permits the lungs to expand. With a little practice, you will breathe more deeply.

## The Relationship Between Breathing and Feeling

Babies breathe, cry, and giggle with their whole bodies. There is a deep rhythm noticeable in a baby's abdominal region, where the stomach seems to be involved in these activities. What you cannot see is the flexibility of the abdominal muscles, which expand and contract in tandem with the lungs. Unfortunately, as children mature, chronic tension may replace this natural pattern with a muscle holding pattern that inhibits the release of feeling. Adolescents or adults may consider a flat stomach attractive, but a contracted diaphragm muscle reduces breathing capacity and limits air intake to a fraction of lung capacity. Respiratory movements in this case are limited to the chest, forcing the lungs to expand sideways, rather than downward, when a person tries to take a deep breath. This places a strain on the body because expansion of the thoracic cage requires more effort than expanding the abdominal muscles that are designed for this purpose. Holding the stomach in requires more work to breathe and results in less oxygen for the effort than if you allow the stomach to relax.

To breathe deeply is to feel deeply. The abdominal muscles are normally involved in laughing and crying. We speak of "deep sobbing" or "laughing until your stomach aches." But we can suppress these feelings by tightening our abdominal muscles and reducing our breath to a shallow, constricted pattern. This can serve to cut off painful feelings, but at the same time, we lose our ability to breathe fully and experience positive feelings.

In natural breathing, we inhale and exhale approximately fifteen times per minute. A little arithmetic indicates that this means approximately four seconds for each inhalation-exhalation cycle, or two seconds for each in-breath and each out-breath. Unfortunately, although our lungs have a capacity of about ten pints of air, most people take in much less—one pint per inhalation is not unusual. This pattern deprives the body of potential oxygen and energy, which leads to loss of vitality, strength, and health.

Low oxygen levels can result in fatigue and drowsiness, poor concentration, loss of vitality, headaches, weakness, and other symptoms. Furthermore, shallow breathing results in atrophy of the diaphragm and the chest muscles involved in deep breathing, rendering them inefficient when deep breathing is required. In fact, relearning how to breathe properly can be initially uncomfortable or even painful for those who have lost their natural breathing ability.

Deep breathing, on the other hand, can significantly increase the amount of inhaled air. Deep breathing has a soothing effect on other body systems, such as heart rate and digestion. Furthermore, it has a calming effect on the mind. These benefits speak to the role of natural breathing in anxiety reduction.

Anxiety has an immediate and noticeable effect on breathing, typically increasing the number of breaths per minute and decreasing the amount of air taken into the body. But the fight/flight response calls for maximum oxygen supply to all systems. Two incompatible conditions are created in anxiety: a need for more oxygen and restricted breathing. The result is a pattern of rapid but shallow breathing. In high anxiety episodes, hyperventilation—a rapid, shallow breathing pattern with unpleasant body symptoms—can occur.

The interaction between anxiety and breathing is illustrated in Mary's case. Mary was an anxious forty-five-year-old homemaker and mother of two children who referred herself after hearing my radio show on panic anxiety. She presented with typical symptoms of severe anxiety, such as nervous stomach, shakiness, rapid heartbeat, worrying, and avoidance of situations in which anxiety was anticipated. She also identified an unusual problem with her breathing. Mary described her breathing problem as follows:

> I feel as though my body has turned against me. In the past nine months, I've lost ten pounds, I've been on medication for high blood pressure caused by my anxiety, and I am currently experiencing a breathing problem that my allergist believes would be helped by reducing my stress and anxiety. My panic attacks and resulting agoraphobia and breathing problem have totally sapped my energy and confidence because they started at a time in my life when I was feeling strong and making future plans, despite the fact that my family and I were dealing with a lot of external stress. I feel I cannot proceed with my life until I learn to deal with my anxiety and fears and overcome them.

One of the first steps in my work with Mary was to discuss anxiety and the role of stress, followed by teaching her some appropriate breathing exercises. In her case, I thought breathing exercises would be the most effective approach to relaxation. After approximately eight therapy sessions, Mary said:

> I feel that I have much more control over my panic and my reactions to it. I don't think I'm afraid of my panic anymore. When I'm in a situation in which I feel panic coming, I'm able to flow with it, knowing that it will pass.... When I began therapy, I had a problem with my breathing because I was feeling so much anxiety. I couldn't take even a short walk without feeling anxious and getting a tight feeling in my chest. The relaxation has really helped me with this problem. I am now able to take walks in my neighborhood, and I'm working on increasing their length each time. I have more confidence now that I will be able to get over this condition.

At the same time, Mary also discontinued medication prescribed for her anxiety. At four months into therapy, she remarked, "At this point, I don't even consider things such as driving, going grocery shopping or to malls, or going to restaurants and other places to be fearful situations for me. I can do these things comfortably."

## Hyperventilation

It is estimated that at least 25 percent of the population hyperventilates frequently. Hyperventilation is a form of rapid, shallow breathing that reduces carbon dioxide in the blood and triggers a number of chemical reactions. Whereas carbon dioxide is often thought of simply as a waste product of breathing, this compound keeps the blood's pH, or acid-alkaline level, in healthy balance. In rapid breathing, carbon dioxide is exhaled before it can perform this job. The resulting alkalinity of the blood and other body fluids sets off a chain reaction that alters the calcium balance in muscles and nerves, heightening their sensitivity and producing tension, nervousness, and shakiness. Fingers and toes can feel tingly and cold, and skin can feel warm and flush. Irregularity or sudden alterations in the breathing pattern that are caused by anxiety can be frightening, and secondary anxiety about choking, suffocating, or fainting can develop.

Shallow breathing can reduce oxygen to the brain by as much as 20 percent and add to anxiety in the form of dizziness and headaches. When this pattern persists, the diaphragm and abdominal muscles lose their tone and healthy breathing is reduced. Thereafter, some anxiety symptoms (tension, nervousness, and lightheaded sensations) can occur for no other reason than poor breathing habits.

For further information about hyperventilation, I suggest *Self-Help for Hyperventilation Syndrome*, by Dinah Bradley (see Bibliography).

## Breathing and the Nervous System

Normally, body systems such as the cardiovascular, respiratory, digestive, and glandular systems are regulated by a control center in the brain known as the *autonomic system*. The autonomic system consists of two complimentary nervous systems, the sympathetic and parasympathetic, which as their names imply, work in opposition to each other. The parasympathetic system slows things down and the sympathetic system accelerates them. Heart rate, for example, is regulated by the complementary action of these two systems.

The *vagus nerve* is the main highway of the parasympathetic system. This nerve travels from the brain, down the spinal cord, through the neck and chest, and to the abdomen, where it makes contact with the lungs. The vagus nerve is actually stimulated by the movement of the lungs as they expand and contract. Our breathing pattern influences the action of most other organs through its effect on the parasympathetic nervous system. Slow and deep breathing calms the body, whereas rapid and shallow breathing activates the body. Proper breathing, therefore, allows us to control heart rate, digestive activity, and other involuntary processes. Proper breathing can go a long way toward controlling stress and creating a life without anxiety.

## Breathing Exercises for Anxiety Control

Relaxed breathing is one of the keys to self-regulation and anxiety reduction. Deep and slow breathing is associated with the relaxation response, as discussed in the previous chapter. In the rest of this chapter, I draw from several sources, including bioenergetics, yoga, and exercise physiology in order to describe some techniques for establishing proper breathing habits.

### Bioenergetic Breathing

Alexander Lowen uses the term *bioenergetics* to describe the flow of life force within the body. He observed that, when patients held back a thought or feeling, they also held their breath. Conversely, when patients were instructed to open up their breathing, thoughts and feelings often poured out. After observing this in numerous cases, Lowen began to focus on breathing as the key to unlocking a person's resistance to facing uncomfortable thoughts and feelings. This certainly includes many of the anxiety symptoms we have discussed.

Lowen developed bioenergetics as a system of body education designed to correct emotional problems, such as anxiety and depression.

Clients are taught corrective breathing exercises to help relieve emotional symptoms. The following is a safe breathing exercise in which the voice is used to help deepen breathing:

### Exercise: *Exhalation Practice for Deep Breathing*

In a sitting position, preferably on a hard chair, start with an inhalation, and then make a continuous "ah" sound in your normal voice as you exhale. Measure the length of time with a second hand of a watch or clock. When you reach your limit, you automatically inhale to replace the expired air. Practice this exercise regularly and try to extend the time you can sustain the sound.

Although this exercise is not dangerous, you may feel out of breath and your body may react by breathing intensely to replenish the oxygen in your blood. Such intense breathing mobilizes the tight chest muscles, allowing them to relax. In the process, you may feel an urge to cry, which you should allow yourself to do because crying is a natural mechanism for tension release.

You can also perform this exercise by counting aloud in a steady rhythm as you exhale. Focus on sustaining the expiration. By breathing out more fully, you learn to breathe in more deeply.

### Yoga Breathing Exercises

Yoga offers a set of breathing exercises that are well suited for anxiety recovery purposes. The exercises are known as *pranayama,* or control of *prana.* In yoga philosophy, prana is the universal energy that animates matter. It is the same energy that Lowen calls *bioenergy.* Pranayama exercises are practiced not only for increasing energy, but also for their importance in learning to control the mind. By controlling breathing as well as disciplining the mind, yoga breathing exercises are especially beneficial to the process of overcoming anxiety and fear.

The following pranayama exercises can be practiced by anyone without danger. Through them, lung capacity can be increased, allowing for deeper, slower breathing. This calms the mind, while increasing energy and vitality. Concentration is also likely to improve with the practice of these breathing exercises.

### Exercise: *Yoga Deep Breathing Practice*

Stand firmly in a calm, quiet, and airy place. After breathing in, exhale though your nostrils, keeping the head, neck, and trunk erect. Try to keep the body as still as possible, except for the motion of the stomach and chest muscles involved in deep breathing. Apply the "root lock," by contracting the sphincter muscles of the rectum and pulling them inwards and upwards. This applies pressure to the exhalation and helps evacuate the lungs. The exhalation should be smooth and quiet, without exertion as the air moves through the nostrils. After exhaling, do not pause, but start inhaling deeply through the nostrils. Do this about ten times for one session each day. This exercise can also be done in a sitting position, although standing allows for greater isolation and control of the squeezing muscles.

### Exercise: *Relaxation with Emphasis on Breathing*

Lie down on your back, with a soft pillow under your head. Cover your eyes with a piece of cloth and begin breathing slowly and deeply. Let your mind travel slowly through your body from head to toes, and while focusing on each muscle group, breathe relaxation into each set of muscles. Do this systematically, starting with the forehead, then moving to the facial muscles, neck, shoulders, arms and hands, back, chest, legs, and so on, until you reach your toes. Then, for a moment, breathe relaxation into the entire body—into every muscle and cell simultaneously. Concentrate on an even and deep flow of breath, forming a new habit of deep, slow breathing.

Do not practice this exercise for more than about ten minutes because too much relaxation can lead to loss of control over the muscles. Also, avoid falling asleep during the relaxation exercise.

You can add another phase to this exercise by recreating the tension in the entire body, followed by gradually relaxation of each muscle group, from the head to the toes. Concentrate on an even and deep breathing rhythm.

For those who wish to pursue more advanced yoga breathing exercises, I recommend yoga classes, as well as study of a good book on the subject. One of my favorite yoga books is Lidell's *The Sivananda Companion to Yoga*. In the next chapter, we explore the importance of active play, such as physical exercise and yoga, for improving breathing and managing anxiety.

## Conclusion

There is a strong correlation between emotional state and breathing pattern. Anxiety is associated with shallow, restricted breathing and even with holding the breath. Anxiety also manifests as physical tension and an acceleration of the cardiovascular and other body systems. Most body systems are influenced by our breathing pattern, and we can control ourselves physically and emotionally by regulating our breathing.

The breathing exercises in this chapter are intended to help you gain this control. They can make a difference in anxiety because they reduce stress and tension, regulate the body, and help restore relaxed equilibrium.

# CHAPTER 9

IIIIIIIIIIIIIIIIIIIIIIIII

# *Play Is for Adults, Too*

Virtually all the people with anxiety whom I have seen in my practice have experienced a loss of joy in living. Spontaneity, fun, and playfulness are sacrificed as energy is directed toward emotional survival, managing anxiety, or coping with stress. Furthermore, chronically anxious people tend to become pessimistic and depressed. As a result, they do not participate fully in life and may avoid recreational activities or active body movement.

These feelings are often expressed by patients when they first present themselves for anxiety treatment. Irene, for example, was tense and serious when she came to a free anxiety-screening clinic I hosted during a National Anxiety Screening Day. She was a dedicated budget manager at a sports equipment manufacturing company, but also a workaholic who put in an unreasonable amount of time and energy on the job. She was "all work and no play." However, during her therapy, she discovered this was her way of coping with anxiety. In other words, she threw herself into her work to distract herself from anxiety. Naturally, this pattern created more stress, which intensified her anxiety symptoms. I noted that Irene had a huge, engaging smile that I rarely saw in the early phases of therapy. Irene spoke for many anxiety sufferers on her pre-program evaluation form, when she described what her life was like with an anxiety disorder:

> I am very weary from not feeling in control of myself or my life. As the years go by, I find I worry, stew, and fret over everything—good and bad. About six months ago, I started having panic attacks very early in the morning. I'm not sure if they start after I wake up or if they wake me up. However, I do know that the panic attack sets the pace for the rest of my day. I know that many people don't

like being near me—I am negative, gloomy, and irritable. I want to learn to relax, enjoy life, and HAVE SOME FUN. I do not want to live the rest of my life like this. Anxiety is nobody's friend. I am not sure if therapy can help me or not, but I am willing to try it, even if it adds to my anxiety in the short term.

Irene's joylessness and negativity were further reinforced by the fact that she had seen six mental-health professionals over a period of approximately fifteen years, most of whom she described as "not what I needed" and "not good experiences."

In another example, Christine had been taking medication for anxiety for many years. She was a productive university professor who had published several books, but was unable to enjoy life or feel good about her professional accomplishments. She, too, had a history of prior therapy experiences, which she rated as "somewhat helpful." Christine's biggest fear was that she could not handle the general stress of life without medication, and she therefore became fearful about discontinuing her medication. At the outset of treatment, Christine described her condition as follows: "I feel that I view events and tasks in terms of their stress-producing potential, rather than in terms of positive experiences. My enjoyment of life is affected by my level of anxiety. I am not as free as I would like to be." Christine's straightforward statement about her condition could apply to virtually all anxiety sufferers. Joy and freedom are thwarted when energy is earmarked for the grim task of coping with stress and anxiety.

Playful living can be unimaginable to those who suffer with anxiety, but losing the ability to play is actually one of the reasons anxiety develops. Without play, the anxiety personality traits take over: perfectionism, high achievement with little joy, difficulty setting reasonable limits, needing to please others, fear of rejection, and difficulty relaxing. Life itself is stressful enough, but anxiety is inevitable when these traits are added to the mix.

## The Purpose of Play

Why do children play, and what role does play have in adult life and anxiety recovery? Children play for the same reasons animals play.

The young in most species play in order to learn social skills; for mock combat, hunting, and evasion; and to experiment with sexuality and mating before reaching maturity. Even domesticated animals, such as cats and dogs, reveal their survival programming when they play exciting games of stalking and hunting: holding still, waiting, pouncing, dodging, nipping, and rough-and-tumble mock fighting. Play is part of nature's plan for survival. Play is practice and preparation for life.

Play is one of the primary outlets for stress and tension, not only for children but also for adults. In his book, *The Hurried Child*, psychologist David Elkind discusses play as an "antidote to hurrying." "Hurried children" are pushed into adulthood by schools, media, and their highly stressed parents, and are deprived of developmentally appropriate play. As a result, hurried children show symptoms of anxiety and stress. Adults with anxiety disorders also tend to be hurried, even if they were not rushed into adulthood. Their personality traits almost guarantee a stressful life.

A.S. Neil takes a similar but more radical position on the subject of play. In *Summerhill*, Neil's book about a school in England that is based on a philosophy of freedom and governed by the students themselves, he asserts that children are often "hothoused" into adulthood by being deprived of adequate time for play. The agents responsible for this "adulteration" of children are usually their own anxious parents, concerned about their children's future, as measured by their grades in school, achievement test scores, and ability to compete for college acceptance and financial aid.

Yet another observer, Neil Postman, declares childhood to be endangered if not already extinct. In *The Disappearance of Childhood*, Postman points out that traditional games and imaginary play have been replaced by busy lifestyles involving competitive sports and multiple extracurricular activities. Indeed, a parent recently told me that, on the way home from soccer practice, her children asked, "Will we have time to play when we get home?" The children were apparently not experiencing soccer as fun or as play.

It is apparent to me that anxiety develops when children are deprived of childhood and expected to function like adults before they are mature enough to assume adult responsibilities. I also find it ironic that, after children are "hurried" prematurely into adulthood, they must then learn as adults how to play, be spontaneous, and live "in the moment."

Play is an opportunity to reconnect with the spontaneity, fun, and joy that have been usurped by anxiety. Play is recreation in the truest sense of the term, an opportunity for re-creation, for creating oneself anew. Play is a healing retreat from the stress, anxiety, and seriousness of life. Soothing to the mind and spirit, play is like taking off a too-tight shoe. It is a break from the work of life, and a way of enjoying the fruits of our labors.

What happens when the balance between work and play is lost? Too much work and too little play disrupts the stress and recovery cycle. Although the human body can handle enormous stress on a short-term basis, recovery from stress is necessary to rebuild and replenish the resources depleted during stress. As discussed in previous chapters, high or prolonged stress not only depletes energy resources, but also keeps the body in a high arousal state. The first signs of stress overload occur as mild symptoms that signal a need for time out—for rest, relaxation, or play. Ignored, these signals become louder, in the form of more intense body reactions. Finally, organ systems break down and disease processes are initiated. At any stage in the sequence, anxiety can be triggered in sensitive people who react strongly, or with fear, to their body reactions.

Play, however, releases the survival focus and allows for natural stress recovery processes to take place. In this sense, play is therapeutic, serving a healing or regenerative function. Play can be healing when it is soft, involving quiet rest and relaxation. Play can also be healing when it is hard, involving tension release and discharge of pent-up frustration or other feelings.

Laughter is associated with play and having fun. Although not all play activities involve laughter, even a smile or the pleasant feelings elicited by recreation and fun can have a healing effect similar to that of laughter. In fact, studies have shown that movement of the facial muscles involved in smiling and laughing activates the "feel-good" hormones that make us feel alive, joyful, and happy. We can even make ourselves feel better by pretending to smile or laugh. Clearly, smiling and laughing can counteract stress and anxiety.

## Overcoming Obstacles to Playfulness

When the time comes and you are looking back at the course of your life, what do you want to feel? My guess is you want to feel your life was fulfilling, that you succeeded in reaching important personal goals, and that you found time to play and enjoy living. What we yearn for most is not more work, but more play.

Is play selfish? Is there time for play, when so much needs to be done? Many anxious people, accustomed to stress, negative thinking, and worry, do not have energy for or interest in play. Others with anxiety personality traits—such as concern about what others think, difficulty relaxing, perfectionism, and high achievement needs—view play as self-indulgent or irresponsible. And some highly sensitive people, who are attuned to human suffering, ask, "How can I play amidst so much suffering? Is it moral, or even possible, to ignore those in need and take time for play?"

In my opinion, play is not selfish. Play is necessary to revitalize ourselves in order to return with renewed energy and commitment to our social roles at work, home, and in our communities. Mother Teresa, considered by many to be an example of piety and selflessness, says, "She gives most who gives with joy.... The best way to show our gratitude to God ... is to accept everything with joy. A joyful heart is the normal result of heart burning with love." In other words, when we are fulfilled and joyful, we are more likely to transmit love and hope to others. A related view has been expressed by Thich Nhat Hanh, the Vietnamese Buddhist monk who has won the hearts of many through his books and retreats. He says, "If you are happy, all of us will profit from it. All living beings will profit from it."

Here we begin to recognize the important benefits of play in anxiety recovery. Play helps us to let go of irrational thoughts, worries, and negative expectations. We play to have fun, rather than to control what might happen. In order to play, in fact, we must let go of outcomes and be less attached to what will happen. Play is spontaneous and concerned primarily with the present moment, the here-and-now. As such, play is a good antidote to the future focus of worry and anxiety. Play is also relaxing—if not during the activity, then at least as a result of it.

## Making Room for Play

There are many forms of play. Children's play, of course, varies with age and encompasses a wide range of activities. Solo games, artwork, sports, and hobbies all qualify as play. With adults, the range of play is just as wide and includes recreational activities, crafts, exercise, dancing—anything that involves joy, pleasure, or satisfaction. My favorite forms of play consist of skiing, bicycling, kayaking, hiking, being with nature, photography, landscape gardening, exercise, socializing with friends, writing, woodworking, listening to music, riding my motorcycle, and sitting quietly. I try to live life playfully, as a dance to enjoy, but also as a source of learning and personal enrichment.

Friends can help us play. When we play with friends, a deeper level of contact is attained because we interact more spontaneously and authentically. Playing with friends creates community and a social support system, important ingredients in health and anxiety recovery.

When I play, I feel free. I "let go" when I am skiing, diving off a boat into the lake, walking through the woods, singing a song, riding my bicycle or my motorcycle, and dancing to music. Time stops, and I am fully engaged in the activity. Past and future fade out of consciousness, and I am in the present moment. I may have to plan for play time, but when it's here, it's the only thing that matters. And when I am playing, I think, "This is it! There is nothing else I would rather do." When I play, I am dancing with life.

Is there room for play in your life? Try the exercise on page 129 to assess the fun factor in your case, and to help direct your attention to how you can increase it.

If you want to increase the joy in your life, you can use the information gained from the preceding exercise to initiate more fun. You can add any new or unfamiliar activities you think might be fun. Decide which activities you want to increase in your life, and make a personal commitment to allow more playfulness into your life.

## "Flow" Activities

Psychologist Mihaly Csikszentmihalyi has studied human happiness and concludes that the secret is to be in "flow." In *Flow: The Psychology*

**Exercise:** *Playful Living*

Sit down and relax, with your eyes closed. Take a few minutes to breathe deeply and elicit the relaxation response. Scan your body from head to toes, and release any tension as you exhale.

Now begin to review the happiest moments in your life. Visualize enjoying yourself, having fun, experiencing pleasure, feeling satisfied. Take mental notes on these images, in preparation for the next part of the exercise.

Open your eyes and make a list of all the things you can think of that have given you joy, pleasure, or satisfaction. This is your activity list for playful living.

Next, go over the list and note in the margin the last two or three times you engaged in each activity. This will give you some idea of how much joy, pleasure, and satisfaction is in your life—how often you play.

You may find that activities you previously enjoyed, such as socializing, physical exercise, or travel, are no longer part of your life because they have become associated with anxiety. It is important to find ways to resume such activities as part of your anxiety recovery process. The desensitization procedure described in Chapter 12 can be helpful for this purpose.

*of Optimal Experience,* he defines the flow experience as one of being engaged in a meaningful activity to such an extent that you lose your sense of self. In the state of flow, time seems to disappear as you focus fully on the activity. Many activities can lead to the feeling of flow, including composing or playing music, reading, gardening, sports, and creative involvements. As far as I am concerned, these are all forms of play, and such activities can reduce anxiety. In fact, any personally meaningful activity that takes you outside of your self is anxiety reducing. When you are engaged in something outside of your self, there is no self to feel anxious.

The flow experience is so important to me that I plan for it. I make a point to carve out some time each week, usually several hours on weekends, when I can disregard time and engage fully in a favorite activity. This allows me to relax into the desired activity, without time pressure, and to engage in it to the point at which everything else temporarily fades into the background or disappears entirely. I find this to be healing, anxiety reducing, and regenerative. I can experience flow while engaging in any of a wide range of activities, including hiking with my camera in hand; skiing; bicycling; writing; listening to music; and even certain chores, such as washing and waxing my car or motorcycle, trimming shrubs around the house, or cooking. When I am in flow, life is play.

The following is a suggested approach to identifying ways you can experience flow:

> As in the playful living exercise described in the preceding section, sit quietly for a few minutes and elicit the relaxation response. Then review your life for experiences in which you were fully engaged in a positive activity, to the point at which you lost your self in it. Note those occasions when you felt "at one" with the activity and came away feeling renewed or refreshed. Make a mental or written list of such activities because these are some of the ways you can intentionally plan to experience the anxiety-reducing state of flow.

### The Importance of Physical Exercise

Most people recognize the importance of physical exercise for overall health, yet many people do not enjoy exercise or they avoid it altogether. For some people with panic disorder, exercise can even be anxiety arousing because it is similar to the arousal state in anxiety. However, anxiety recovery is unlikely to be successful without some form of regular movement or exercise. My own anxiety recovery process would not have been possible without the benefits of physical exercise. In this section, I provide information and suggestions for creating an exercise program that works for you. My hope is that you will experiment with the suggested exercise options so you can experience reduced anxiety as well as more energy and improved health.

A complete exercise program has three components:

1. Aerobic exercise

2. Flexibility training (such as yoga)

3. Strength training

Ideally, readers are encouraged to incorporate these three components into a personal plan for health and anxiety recovery. Some readers
may want to add the missing components to their current fitness activities. For those with no current exercise activities, I encourage starting
with just one component and adding to it gradually.

*Aerobic Exercise*

Many of my patients have reported a reduction in anxiety after they began to exercise regularly. In one case, a mother of four young children
who came to therapy with generalized anxiety disorder, told me that
running three or four times a week was key to her anxiety reduction.
Although it was difficult for her to arrange the time, she found that
exercise increased her energy and positive outlook, while reducing her
stress and worry.

It is common knowledge that aerobic exercise promotes health by
conditioning the heart, lungs, and vascular system. Aerobic exercise is
generally defined as a minimum of twenty minutes of sustained, rhythmic exercise, with heart rate between 60 and 90 percent of maximum,
depending on fitness level. You can use a simple method for determining maximum heart rate by subtracting your age from the number 220.
For example, a forty year old would have a maximum heart rate of 180,
and a training heart rate between 108 and 162.

Exercise is referred to as aerobic or cardiovascular only if it is continuous. Some excellent examples of aerobic exercise are running, bicycling,
cross-country skiing, dance aerobics, jumping rope, and vigorous walking, as well as use of exercise machines, such as a step machine, rowing
machine, elliptical trainer, and stationary bicycle. Stop and go exercises,
such as tennis, downhill skiing, golf, basketball, baseball, or football, are
not considered to be aerobic, although that does not mean they are without health benefits.

New studies indicate that vigorous exercise has greater health benefits than does moderate exercise. And for those interested in weight loss
or weight control, the latest guidelines call for one hour of aerobic exercise every day. The health benefits of exercise include lower blood pressure, release of muscle tension, improved circulation, improved digestion
and metabolism, and a stronger immune system.

Exercise helps in anxiety reduction for many reasons, one of which is that it releases muscle tension. Tension is stored in the body's muscles, and aerobic exercise releases it. The heart itself is a muscle, and exercise is beneficial to the cardiovascular system through its conditioning effect on this vital organ. A heart that is accustomed to stimulation from exercise can handle more stress and is less likely to develop palpitations or accelerate wildly when a person feels anxious.

Exercise also has important psychological benefits. Exercise stimulates the body's production of endorphins, the feel-good brain chemicals that improve mood, self-esteem, and feelings of well-being. Breathing stimulated by vigorous exercise supercharges the blood with oxygen and improves alertness, vitality, mental clarity, and memory. By discharging tension, exercise results not only in physical relaxation, but also in feelings of peacefulness. Yet another psychological benefit of exercise is that it focuses attention away from stress and toward an empowering, health-promoting activity. All these psychological benefits are helpful for stress and anxiety control.

Whatever your age or fitness level, implementing a regular exercise program is essential for overcoming anxiety and managing the stress that triggers it. There may be many reasons or excuses for avoiding exercise, including fear of anxiety arousal in some cases, but these must be addressed if you are to succeed in anxiety recovery. "I don't have time," "I'm too out of shape," "I'm too old," or "Exercise is boring" are some common explanations for avoiding exercise. For those who say, "I don't have time," consider a recent study showing that men could gain an average of two years of life by expending 2,000 calories a week on aerobic exercise. Perhaps it is more a question of priorities, than a shortage of time.

For those who say they are "too out of shape to exercise," I suggest a gentle start or consultation with a physician for advice. Your fitness level determines the appropriate intensity of exercise. Monitor your pulse and stay within 60 percent of maximum heart rate at the outset—a level that might be reached by a simple walk around the block.

And for those who claim they are "too old," think about the many marathon runners who did not even begin to exercise until their fifties or sixties. Finally, for those who feel exercise is "boring," have you really experimented with a variety of exercise options?

If aerobic exercise turns you off, consider starting with some gentle stretching or yoga. Let's consider the role of yoga for stress and anxiety control.

### Flexibility Training Using Yoga

In this section I discuss yoga as a system of flexibility training. There are other exercise systems that improve flexibility, such as t'ai chi, but I have chosen to emphasize the system that has been central to my anxiety recovery and overall health.

Yoga is an ancient spiritual and health practice that originated in India. Although it may seem gentle compared with aerobic exercise, it is a powerful practice with many health benefits. The yoga system has eight different branches, the most familiar being hatha yoga—the physical branch that is usually referred to simply as *yoga*. Yoga consists of a series of *asanas,* or postures, that are practiced with steadiness and concentration. Research has shown that this practice lowers heart rate and respiration, resulting in a calming effect on the nervous system. Yoga postures also have a positive effect on the endocrine glands, one of the body's regulatory systems involved in hormone production. Yoga, then, is a form of self-regulation in which emotions, body, and mind are brought under control. By improving the healthy functioning of the body, calming the mind, and controlling the emotions, yoga offers a potent approach to stress reduction and anxiety recovery.

#### Anita

*Anita was a single woman with several anxiety disorders, including social phobia, emetophobia (fear of vomiting, which developed into an eating disorder), and panic disorder. She expressed an interest in yoga, but the idea of attending a class raised her anxiety. I encouraged her to participate in group therapy, and as she became more comfortable in this structured social situation, she took the step of trying a yoga class. Anita reported feeling more relaxed after learning yoga than at any other point in her life.*

Each yoga posture has specific health benefits. The plough, for example, corrects spine deviations, eliminates fatigue, cures headaches, and rejuvenates the digestive organs, sexual glands, and kidneys. The corpse pose has been shown to lower blood pressure. And the headstand calms the nervous system by providing a rich supply of arterial blood to the brain, cranial nerves, pituitary gland, and pineal gland. The headstand is also known for its ability to alleviate digestive distress and varicose veins.

As a whole, yoga has been found to have a positive effect on many aspects of health, such as lung capacity for deeper breathing, controlling body weight, stress resistance, lower cholesterol, and stable blood sugar. On the other hand, there are some contraindications for yoga. For example, it is inadvisable to perform the plough posture during menstruation or pregnancy, or if suffering from high blood pressure, asthma, or neck injury. For those with any health issues, I suggest consulting with a physician or certified yoga teacher for guidance. Some additional recommendations are discussed in the rest of this section.

As mentioned earlier, yoga was at the core of my personal recovery program. Yoga helped me relax and discover a deep inner peace as I worked tension out of my body. Even after some thirty years of practice, I stay in control with the help of yoga practice. Although I can spend less time now with my practice, not a day goes by without at least a few asanas to straighten out my posture and relieve tension and stress. I sometimes take a short break between appointments at my office to release accumulated stress and restore my energy. If I ignore my need for this, I lose concentration and develop stress symptoms.

One of the appealing features of yoga practice is that it requires no special equipment and it can be practiced virtually anywhere. However, it is advisable to obtain proper instructions, preferably from a teacher who can observe and correct your postures. It is beyond the scope of this book to provide proper instruction in yoga. Therefore, I recommend that you read a guidebook on yoga, and consider taking a class at your local recreation center, YMCA, health club, or other community venue. Check with health food stores for information on yoga classes, and for copies of *Yoga Journal,* a monthly magazine devoted to yoga.

To give you an idea of what a yoga session involves and to get you started with a few safe and simple yoga postures, try the three steps on page 137.

## THE PLOUGH POSE

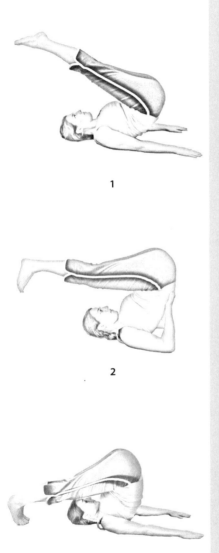

1

2

3

### Beginner Asana: The Plough Pose

This in one of my favorite asanas because it corrects my posture and relieves tension in my neck and back. The plough is also a good foundation for some more advanced, inverted postures, in which the head is lower than the trunk of the body. The flow of blood into the head is refreshing and improves mental clarity.

Lie comfortably, with your back on the floor, and place your arms at your sides. Gently raise your legs up together, then lower them and raise them again one at a time. Also, try pulling your knees up toward your chest. Perform all movements slowly and do not strain. You can then try the plough, which is an extension of the leg raises you just did. Bring your legs back over your head, toward the floor behind your head. If you are overweight, go only as far as your current flexibility permits. Hold the posture for as long as comfortable and then slowly return your legs to the prone position. You are now in position to end your yoga session with the corpse pose (see the figure on page 138).

**THE SUN SALUTATION**

10

11

12

9

8

7

## *The Sun Salutation*

This is a series of stretches that begins in the standing position (see above and on the next page). Move slowly and mindfully through the sequence of stretches. This exercise warms and prepares the muscles for additional asanas, but the sun salutation in and of itself can be an excellent yoga session.

1. Warm up with the sun salutation. Start with figure 1 above and continue clockwise through figure 12.

2. Perform some beginner asanas (see page 135 for one my favorites, the plough)

3. End your yoga session with the corpse pose (described on page 138)

**THE CORPSE POSE**

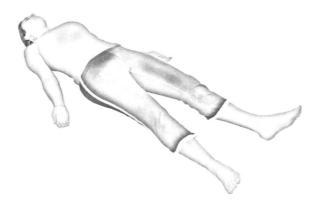

KALI FOXMAN AND CHRIS OWENS

### The Corpse Pose

Lie on your back on the floor, with your feet slightly apart and your arms out from your sides. Allow gravity to gently pull your back flat onto the floor, while at the same time allowing the earth to support you. Let go of tension by breathing relaxation into all parts of your body. Place your palms over your eyes and press gently, as you give your eyes a rest. Let your mind calm down by releasing thoughts as you exhale. Rest peacefully. Be sure to rise slowly, and try to carry the calm feeling into your next activity.

### Strength Training

The third exercise component I recommend for stress and anxiety control is strength training. Strength training contributed immeasurably to my own anxiety recovery and is a regular part of my exercise routines. What is strength training, and how can it be helpful for our purposes?

When strength training you use weights or resistance to strengthen and develop the muscles that are typically underused or underdeveloped. Sometimes called body building or weight lifting, strength training should not be confused with the grotesque development of muscles as seen on the covers of muscle magazines, and often with which steroid drugs are possibly involved. The benefits of strength training include increasing muscle tone, strength, and endurance; improving posture and range of motion; enhancing athletic performance; allowing greater ease in carrying and lifting; reduction of muscle tension following training sessions; and preventing injuries to the body. However, the psychological benefits of strength training, which include self-confidence and feelings of personal power, are equally important.

In my case, the emotional benefits were unexpected because my original reason for experimenting with strength training was to build up my lean body. Within a few short months after beginning a program of strength training, however, I noticed a change in my attitude as well as increases in physical strength and muscle mass. I felt stronger and more powerful as a person and became more assertive in my interactions with other people. In addition, my posture improved, and I walked taller and more confidently.

These benefits reduced my anxiety, as I gained a more positive body image and more confidence in social interactions. Increased physical strength made me feel safer in conflict situations, in which other people might become upset with me. In addition, physical strength translated into emotional strength and an increase in ability to handle myself confidently in most situations. In short, being stronger translated into less fear and anxiety.

A typical strength-training session begins with warming up by stretching or engaging in a brief aerobic activity. Serious weight lifters alternate strength-training days with aerobic workouts. After warming up, a sequence of controlled movements is performed using weights

### Strength-Training Tips

You can take a step toward creating a strength-training program by doing several sets of push-ups each day in the comfort of your own home. Also consider purchasing a set of inexpensive latex Thera-Bands (available at sporting goods stores) that you can use to perform a wide variety of muscle strengthening exercises based on the instructions that come in the package.

or other form of resistance. The American Academy of Sports Medicine recommends using the amount of weight required to perform six to twelve repetitions. This is called a *set,* and after a brief rest, the set may be repeated a second and third time to get the maximum benefit. Generally speaking, there should be a minimum period of 48 hours set aside for recovery between strength-training sessions. This can be translated to mean that you should not work the same muscles on two consecutive days.

Guidebooks on strength training are readily available. I have used Pearl and Moran's *Getting Stronger,* which includes instructions for both men and women. There are even guidebooks specifically for seniors, such as *Strength Training for Seniors* by Michael Fekete. It is also advisable to consult with a personal trainer to create an individualized program.

The body adapts to stress by improving its ability to handle stress. This is what happens as a result of strength training. Although muscles are fatigued and stressed by working against resistance, they adapt by increasing their strength and power.

There is little in the psychology literature about the use of strength training for anxiety reduction. However, it is obvious to me that this exercise component is helpful for several reasons: muscles become relaxed as well as stronger, deep breathing is stimulated (to supply extra oxygen needed during this form of exercise), self-confidence is improved, and emotional strength is acquired.

### Conclusion

In this chapter, I have made the case for play as an important part of anxiety reduction. Play reduces stress, and in this sense, it can also prevent and protect against anxiety. Some people have difficulty with playfulness, and I have addressed some of the obstacles to play and offered suggestions for making room for play activities.

Play comes in many forms. These include any activities that result in "flow," as well as recreation outlets and several forms of exercise. All of these forms of play can reduce stress and anxiety.

In a sense, play can be considered a goal of life. Although you may need to work to support yourself and to provide for basic needs, such as food, shelter, clothing, and transportation, what other goals do you have in your life? I suspect you'll want to find ways to enjoy the process of living, and perhaps have some fun.

# CHAPTER 10

||||||||||||||||||||||||||

# *Food, Eating, and Anxiety*

Why do we eat? Normally, we eat to provide energy and regularly rebuild our physical body. However, sometimes we eat for emotional nourishment, rather than to meet our body's requirements. This, of course, is part of the joy of eating, but sometimes it conflicts with health. Eating to cope with feelings such as boredom, anger, anxiety, or depression can result in eating too much or consuming addictive substances, such as alcohol, sugar, and caffeine. Furthermore, anxiety about gaining weight is the basis of some eating disorders, such as anorexia and bulimia.

The most obvious consequences of unhealthy eating are physical: obesity, heart disease, low energy, poor skin and hair condition, and other signs of health deterioration. In addition, there are emotional consequences, such as depression, poor self-image, and shame.

Many aspects of food, eating, and nutrition can produce anxiety symptoms and strong emotional reactions in sensitive people. To understand the relationship between food and anxiety, recall that sensitive people react strongly to external and internal stimuli. This includes what, when, and how much a person eats. Anxiety level is influenced by these factors, so we may need to modify eating patterns as part of anxiety recovery.

As we consider some nutritional approaches to controlling stress and anxiety, we discuss how certain foods stimulate anxiety, as well as how eating habits can affect anxiety. We end with some dietary guidelines, or what could be called the "antianxiety diet."

## Blood Sugar and Anxiety

One of the most basic food-related issues you face on a daily basis is fluctuations in your blood-sugar level. Blood sugar is a factor in determining your energy level, and it is influenced largely by the timing of your meals and the type of foods you eat. Sharp rises in blood sugar, resulting from intake of simple carbohydrates such as white bread and heavily sugared candy, cakes, and cookies are associated with increases in adrenaline—the activating hormone in anxiety symptoms. On the other hand, low blood sugar, resulting from missed meals or eating large amounts of simple carbohydrates, produces symptoms such as fatigue, irritability, headaches, blurry vision, mental confusion, and weak or "strung-out" feelings. These symptoms are also commonly associated with anxiety.

Ironically, both high and low blood-sugar levels can be caused by a diet that is high in sugar and simple carbohydrates. Such foods cause the pancreas to release larger amounts of insulin, the blood-sugar regulator, to ensure that sugar level doesn't get too high. But often the amount of insulin released exceeds what is really needed to lower the blood sugar. When this occurs, glycogen is released by the liver to increase the blood-sugar level. Such fluctuations in blood sugar can cause a host of physical, emotional, and mental symptoms.

Low blood-sugar level can also result from an inconsistent eating schedule. Therefore, it is important to eat regularly, and perhaps more frequently (four to six small meals per day), to maintain a consistent blood-sugar level.

Sugar can affect sensitive people as though it were a drug. In fact, reliance on sugared foods for energy can lead to sugar addiction, and its long-term use can weaken the organs involved in sugar regulation. When your body cannot properly regulate blood-sugar level, you are likely to experience sugar fluctuations as irritability, lethargy, headaches, mood changes, mental confusion, impaired attention and concentration, and visual problems. These symptoms put you at risk for anxiety due to body and mood changes that occur for no apparent reason. Excess sugar on a continual basis also puts you at risk for disease, such as adult-onset diabetes.

The best solution for maintaining steady blood-sugar levels is to eat complex carbohydrates from natural sources, such as grains (breads, cereals, and pasta), vegetables, and fruits. Foods high in protein, such as beans and legumes, also help regulate sugar level in the blood. These foods contain plenty of fiber, which helps the digestive system break down foods slowly and absorb sugar gradually.

## Other Food Issues and Anxiety

Consider how you react to the taste, smell, texture, temperature, and immediate biological effect of foods. Hot and spicy foods, for example, can raise body temperature and cause flushing, which are anxiety symptoms in some people. Stimulants, such as caffeine in coffee, chocolate, and many sodas "rev up" your body, another typical symptom of anxiety. Depressants, such as alcohol in wine, beer, and liquor, have mood-altering effects that can trigger anxiety in sensitive people. Caffeine and alcohol, of course, are drugs with the potential for addiction and other pitfalls for the biologically sensitive person. Therefore, it may be necessary for you to avoid certain foods and drinks as part of your anxiety recovery.

Our response to food begins even before it enters the body. How and under what conditions we eat are the first considerations. For example, our mental state and degree of physical relaxation at the time of eating have a significant influence on our response to food. If rushed or pressured while eating, for example, our energy may not be available for the task of food metabolism. In this case, eating is not enjoyable and digestion is less efficient. In some instances, when we eat by the clock or when it is simply convenient, we may not even be hungry. In other instances, we may be hungry but unaware of it because we are too stressed or busy. These conditions can trigger anxiety, and eating under stress is likely to reinforce the stress-anxiety cycle.

Our reaction to food is likely to be affected by our past experiences. Just the thought of certain foods can make us nauseous or weak, while the thought of other foods can give us energy, strength, or a relaxed feeling. As with anxiety, conditioning plays a central role in our physical and emotional responses to food. Our feelings about most foods are based on past experiences with them, including childhood experiences. Therefore, changing what and how we eat requires experimentation, patience, and new learning.

Some medical conditions affect diet and create anxiety. For example, any condition that requires a gluten-free diet (such as celiac disease or allergic reactions to wheat) can be stressful with respect to finding nutritious foods without wheat products. It can also raise anxiety about social activities where food may be served. Similar anxiety issues can occur with other food allergies. A peanut allergy can create anxiety because many foods contain hidden traces of peanuts and can have severe medical consequences. Some people experience mysterious and troubling symptoms as a result of food allergies that have not been identified. Their anxiety may be stimulated by uncertainty about the basis of their health problems.

Another issue is our beliefs and expectations about food. A vegetarian may avoid animal foods, based on health concerns or moral convictions, while a meat-eater might delight in the same fare. At a conference I attended some years ago, a panel of experts was asked their opinion on taking vitamin supplements. The response of the panel's physician emphasized the powerful role of belief in diet and nutrition: "If you believe you need vitamin supplements and don't take them, you'll probably develop symptoms of vitamin deficiency. On the other hand, if you believe you do not need them, you'll probably show no deficiency symptoms without them."

I believe proper nutrition and eating habits are a form of preventive medicine and that they can have healing powers. We can become and stay healthy through healthful food and eating choices. And we can significantly enhance our anxiety recovery process with proper nutrition and eating habits. The guidelines and recommendations offered later in this chapter are based on this belief.

### Control Issues, Food, and Anxiety

One of the most important issues for the anxious person is control. Anxiety almost invariably develops when a person feels out of control, whether it is about losing control over eating behavior, emotions, or health. Therefore, as long as we are not in control of our diet or eating behavior, we are at risk for developing anxiety symptoms. In the case of drugs and alcohol, the problem with control is easily recognized.

However, we can develop similar control problems with foods. For example, it is possible to develop an addiction to particular foods, such as chocolate, potato chips, or candy, in which case a person becomes controlled by a need or desire for such foods. This can leave the person with subtle feelings of powerlessness or weakness, sometimes coupled with shame or guilt about "giving in" to impulses or hurting his or her own health. On the other hand, this does not mean we must never indulge in treats. The issue is control: Are we in control of our eating or is our eating in control of us?

## Anxiety and Eating Disorders

Anxiety can be associated with eating disorders, such as anorexia, bulimia, and binge eating. These are serious physical-emotional disorders that can affect health and can even have life-threatening consequences. Anorexia and bulimia are commonly associated with fear regarding weight gain and body image, while compulsive or binge eating is often a coping response to difficult emotions. These complex eating disorders may involve other issues, including shame, rebellion, and low self-esteem.

Compulsive eating, overeating, and binge eating are driven by emotional pain. Sources of emotional pain include anxiety; feelings of loneliness, emptiness, or rejection; lack of interest in work; unexpressed anger; loss; and disappointment in some aspect of life. To cope with these unpleasant emotions, some people use food as a tranquilizer. Even normal eating is tranquilizing due to blood being temporarily withdrawn from the brain and other extremities during digestion. This produces a pleasant and relaxed feeling. However, emotional eating can become chronic overeating, with resulting weight gain or obesity. Weight problems, of course, can create additional health risks, such as heart disease, back and joint disease, diabetes, cancer, lowered stamina, and breathing difficulties. For the anxious person, fear of illness, death, and dying is intensified by symptoms of poor health. In addition, being overweight often lowers self-esteem and creates social anxiety. Anxiety, therefore, can both *cause* overeating and *result from* overeating.

### Alice

*One of my patients, Alice, had a long history of anxiety resulting from sexual abuse within her family. She exhibited several anxiety disorders, including post-traumatic stress disorder, panic anxiety, and social anxiety. When I asked her to consider how her life would be different without anxiety, Alice made a long list entitled "My Life without Anxiety." One item on the list was "I would not be overindulgent with food and drinking."*

Another eating pattern is under-eating due to body image issues or a wish to lose weight. Intentional under-eating in order to lose weight is common among people whose eating behavior or life circumstances are out of control. Usually, this is done in the form of dieting. Dieting is reinforced by the social stigma of being overweight, as well as the cultural value placed on being thin. For others who are not overweight, especially many women, problems with distorted self-perception of body size and shape, as well as low self-esteem and concerns about social acceptance, can lead to under-eating. Women who see themselves as overweight—even if they are within a normal weight range as determined medically—may resort to habitual under-eating in order to "correct" their "deficiency." Another pattern is purging after eating, an eating disorder known as *bulimia*.

Although under-eating and bulimia can result from anxiety, these eating patterns can also increase the risk for anxiety in a number of ways. First, blood-sugar level decreases when eating is inconsistent or insufficient. Low blood-sugar level is experienced as weakness, irritability, visual fluctuations, impaired attention and concentration, headaches, and fatigue, which are typical signals for an anxiety reaction in the sensitized person. Problems with the menstrual cycle can also be caused by restricted eating. Second, the shame, frustration, guilt, and other feelings typically associated with under-eating and bulimia can create an anxiety state. Such feelings are unpleasant or anxiety arousing, and they raise the need for defense mechanisms, such as denial. Third, these eating patterns are often compulsive and involve anxiety about not being in control.

## Cher

*Cher was a single, professional woman struggling with social anxiety and an eating disorder. Her central issue appeared to be a fear of emotions, and she used many rituals to prevent herself from feeling. She developed an excessively controlled approach to life, with rigid rules about diet and exercise. Due to her fear of losing control, she restricted herself to a few "safe" foods and counted calories obsessively. In addition, she exercised excessively, despite symptoms of exhaustion and warnings by her physician that she was underweight and thus jeopardizing her health. Although she tried to manage her anxiety through this over-controlled lifestyle, her anxiety actually increased whenever she was unable to follow her rules.*

*I viewed Cher's compulsive eating and behavior patterns as a fear of emotions. We approached emotions using a desensitization process (see Chapter 12). In addition, I advised a mindfulness practice, especially the aspect of accepting emotional experiences without judgment. In a breakthrough moment, Cher said, "I realize I have been avoiding emotions by obsessively following my rules and avoiding relationships with people. I've been stuck in this box. I need to face my emotions and not be afraid of them." With this insight, she introduced more variety into her diet, became more flexible about exercise, and began to participate in social activities.*

### Fasting and Breaking Fast

Related to under-eating is a less frequent but intriguing issue related to anxiety, namely fasting. Fasting, or intentionally abstaining from food, can have powerful therapeutic effects. Fasting is cleansing and rejuvenating to the body, and is usually associated with increased mental clarity and feeling "high." Many spiritual texts espouse the benefits of periodic fasting, and some religious holidays, such as Lent, Yom Kippur, and Ramadan, involve food abstinence. You should, in fact, fast every day for approximately ten hours between your evening and morning meals (individuals with a tendency toward low blood sugar should consult their doctor for advice on intervals between meals). Indeed, the morning meal, breakfast, literally means *breaking fast,* or ending the fast. During this daily fast, your body detoxifies itself and your digestive system has an opportunity for rest and recovery. It is important to "break fast" properly, and resupply your body with food. Skipping breakfast is a set-up for anxiety due to the likelihood of low blood sugar later in the day. I believe the best way to start your day is with herbal tea, fruit juice, or fresh fruit. After an assimilation period of thirty to sixty minutes, eat an energy-packed, whole-grain breakfast, such as hot or cold cereal or toast.

I have personally used more extended fasting for both health benefits and spiritual enhancement. Obviously, fasting involves some risks, particularly in terms of its immediate impact on blood-sugar level. I have had to be careful with this practice because my total body fat is low, leaving me with little stored energy reserves. An excellent alternative to total abstinence is a juice fast, a period of time during which you drink only diluted fruit and vegetable juices. This approach helps to maintain blood-sugar level and energy, while providing the benefits of fasting. Fasting is best done within a contemplative time and place, away from strenuous activities or work. If you are interested in the benefits of fasting, I recommend that you learn more through reading and seek guidance from a nutritionist for fasting longer than one day.

## Dehydration and Anxiety

There is yet another food-related issue to be addressed, in spite of its being almost too obvious to mention. Our body cells are primarily composed of water, and water is required for almost every biological process, including blood and lymph flow, hormone production, digestion, and excretion. When our water level drops too low, we experience signals of dehydration in the form of thirst; loss of concentration and attention span; and in later stages, headaches, fatigue, and weakness. These signals are virtually identical to some common symptoms of anxiety. Therefore, dehydration can be confused with anxiety symptoms, such as weakness, low energy, mild disorientation, and cognitive inefficiency. It is important to drink an adequate supply of pure water throughout the day, preferably between meals. Water can also be supplied by other drinks, such as juice and tea. My suggestion is to be attentive to signs of dehydration (urine should be close to clear in color), and hydrate yourself accordingly. Most people need to drink more water than they do.

## Proper Nutrition and Anxiety Control

A number of writers over the years influenced my diet and attitudes toward food. Francis Moore Lappe, for example, impressed me in *Diet for a Small Planet* with a discussion about the politics and ecology of food. In *The Book of Tofu,* Bill Shurtleff and Ikiko Aoyogi helped me recognize the potential for a vegetarian solution to world hunger. I became interested in the diets of people known for their health and longevity, such as the Seventh Day Adventists and the Hunzas. I discovered that a vegetarian diet was known to be the most healthful way to eat, long before the U.S. Department of Agriculture was willing to acknowledge it. I must also mention the impact of my many visits to "The Farm," a spiritual community in Tennessee, where up to twelve hundred people lived a vegan (no-animal-products) lifestyle, from food to clothes. The Farm diet is based on soybeans, a virtually complete protein source. I am still fond of The Farm's "Ice Bean" products, which are sold today in health-food stores as a soy-based alternative to ice cream.

My own diet evolved toward vegetarianism about thirty years ago. I found that a vegetarian diet was more suitable to my digestive system, as well as more compatible with my beliefs and environmental awareness. For example, I was sensitive to world hunger, and discovered through reading that it took approximately five pounds of beans and grains fed to cattle to yield one pound of meat, and that those foods could instead efficiently serve the nutritional needs of more people. I also knew that, although meat is a source of complete protein, it is higher in fat than a grain-based diet is. I was attracted to a healthy lifestyle with ecological benefits.

For a number of years I was somewhat rigid and moralistic about my diet, denying my occasional desires for meat and sweets. However, after moving from the warm climate of southern California to the cold and long winters of Vermont, I found it necessary to include some meat and fish in my diet. Perhaps a flexible diet that takes into account climate, seasonal changes, stress level, lifestyle, and locally available foods is the best approach to a healthy diet.

My typical daily eating pattern begins with fresh fruit or diluted fruit juice, followed by a carbohydrate breakfast. I eat again about mid-morning, having a carbohydrate snack of bread, muffin, bagel, or banana and dried fruit. A light lunch at mid-day might consist of a salad, sandwich, or leftovers from the previous night's dinner. In the afternoon, I snack on crackers and cheese, more leftovers, or fruit (fresh or dried, depending on the season). My main meal is dinner, for which I emphasize grains, beans, and vegetables. I generally keep a supply of food at my office and carry healthy snacks when I travel, so that I can maintain my blood-sugar level and energy wherever I am.

### Food Guidelines for Creating a Life Beyond Panic and Anxiety

Each of us is physically and emotionally unique, and our individual nutritional needs vary from day to day, based on activities and stress level. Therefore, in making recommendations about nutrition and eating patterns, I prefer to avoid rigid rules and formulas. Instead, I offer the following guidelines and encourage you to experiment with what works best for you. Consultation with a nutritionist is also a good idea to help individualize what you learn. Here, then, are my food guidelines for creating a life beyond panic and anxiety:

- Eat smaller meals four to six times a day

- Allow a daily fast period of eight to twelve hours between dinner and breakfast

> **Food Guidelines for Reducing Anxiety**

- Drink an adequate supply of fresh water to avoid dehydration

- Eat primarily fresh, minimally processed foods

- Read and understand food-packaging labels to avoid chemicals such as preservatives, artificial flavors, and artificial dyes

- Avoid caffeine (including caffeinated sodas) and discover alternatives to coffee, such as herbal teas and grain-based brews (e.g., Caffix, Pero, Roma, Inka)

- Eliminate refined and sugared food products that have little nutritional value

- Use the U. S. Department of Agriculture's "Food Guide Pyramid" as a nutritional guideline (go to www.mypyramid.gov to obtain a personalized breakdown of what your diet should contain)

- Learn the creative art of cooking and develop some favorite healthful recipes

- Avoid excess oils in cooking by using steaming and pressure-cooking methods

- If you are making a transition to vegetarianism, eat a variety of foods each day to ensure adequate nutrition

- Read, learn, experiment, and expand your awareness of diet and nutrition

- Remember that exercise aids digestion and food assimilation

- Relax before and during eating, and eat in peaceful surroundings

- Be flexible in your diet to account for activity level, stress, seasonal changes, and other factors

- Chew thoroughly and liquefy foods in your mouth

- Develop an attitude of thankfulness and reverence toward food

- Discover sources of emotional nourishment other than food

### Conclusion

Many aspects of diet and eating correlate with anxiety, including the type and quality of food, eating frequency and schedule, chemical additives, water intake, anxiety about weight gain, food allergies, and use of food as a coping mechanism for dealing with anxiety and other unpleasant emotions.

Anxiety recovery can be enhanced by making changes in your diet and eating habits. Taking the steps recommended in this chapter will not only reduce anxiety, but also improve your energy and overall health.

# CHAPTER 11

|||||||||||||||||||||||||||||

# *What If?*

W ithin the past twenty-five years, a new approach to therapy has emerged based on a simple but powerful idea—that how we feel and behave is determined largely by how we think. This idea has given rise to "cognitive-behavioral therapy," or simply CBT. In this chapter, we discuss this approach to changing the cognitive habits and patterns that produce anxiety. To create a life beyond anxiety we need to literally change our minds—to replace old cognitive habits and patterns with new alternatives. Let's begin by understanding the power of the mind, and then discuss how to reduce anxiety by changing five key thought patterns.

## Mind, Emotions, and Wellness

We now know that the brain and body communicate using chemical messengers that connect to receptors on the surface membranes of our cells. The chemical messengers are mobile protein molecules called *neuropeptides* or *neurotransmitters*. Our thoughts, moods, and attitudes have a significant impact on which neurotransmitters are sent and how they are received. These messengers have been called the *biochemical units of emotion* because their activity is directly dependent on a person's state of mind. Neurotransmitters translate every thought—whether conscious or unconscious—as well as feelings, into physiological changes. They are found not just in the brain, but in the immune and endocrine systems, heart, lungs, intestines—everywhere in the body. We are an integrated mind-body entity with a complex communication network that spreads thoughts and emotions throughout the entire body.

The mind can heal because the brain and immune system are in constant dialogue via nerve fibers going from the brain to virtually every immune system organ. In other words, our brain is in direct contact with our immune system cells. The effectiveness of the immune system is influenced by how we react to the stress of everyday life and how we perceive ourselves in relation to outside events.

What's more, viruses use the same receptor sites in cells as do neurotransmitters, and the two types of molecules appear to compete for cell contact. Therefore, the more neurotransmitters in the vicinity of cell receptors, the less likely viruses are to make cell contact. This means our cognitive and emotional states can influence whether we get sick from exposure to a virus or not.

The importance of thoughts and emotions at the onset of viral diseases is underscored by the fact that most microbes infecting humans are already in our bodies and instigate a disease only when extra stress lowers our immunity. What determines who gets ill and who does not may well be a matter of thoughts, emotions, and attitudes.

Stress, like germs, is often considered a cause of disease. However, psychoneuroimmunology research indicates that it is not stress itself that causes symptoms; rather, how we think about and react to stress determines what effect it will have. A real-life study illustrates this. Conducted in 1984 by two psychologists (Maddi and Kobasa), the study tracked two hundred business managers at Illinois Bell Telephone Company during a court-ordered company reorganization to see how they handled stress. It was known that jobs would change or be eliminated, and there were many uncertainties. The researchers found that some managers viewed the company breakup as inevitable and as an opportunity for growth, rather than as a threat to security. They were the "stress-hardy" managers and they used a coping strategy involving three elements:

1. Optimism

2. A proactive rather than passive response

3. Personal stress management (e.g., exercise, relaxation)

These three familiar steps minimized the effects of stress. The stress-hardy executives with these personal resources showed less than a 10 percent rate of stress symptoms or illness. In contrast, high-stress managers who lacked these resources showed more than a 90 percent rate of stress symptoms or severe illness.

Emotions and attitude have a lot to do with a person's health status. For example, anger, cynicism, and a hostile attitude contribute to a higher than average rate of heart attacks due to atherosclerosis and blockage of coronary arteries. A twenty-five-year longitudinal study of 255 physicians who took a battery of psychological tests while they were medical students found that those with high hostility scores had four times as many cases of heart disease and six times as many cases of death than did those with low hostility scores.

On the positive side, attitude can also enhance healing from physical illness. For example, it has been found that certain attitudes contribute to death or survival from life-threatening diseases, such as cancer. Positive attitudes, such as love, faith, confidence, and peace of mind, can heal or at least significantly influence recovery.

### The Placebo Effect

When we worry or expect to experience anxiety in a particular situation, we are actually creating that anxiety. This can be understood in terms of the *placebo effect,* which refers to the power of expectation.

Technically, the placebo effect is a reaction to a benign substance having no known effects. Here is a research example: A group of medical students were told they would be personally testing the effectiveness of two drugs—a stimulant and a depressant. They were informed about the expected side effects but were not told that both drugs were actually placebos. In response to the placebos, more than half the students exhibited either the "expected" benefits, including lower pulse and decreased arterial pressure, or many of the "expected" side effects, such as dizziness, abdominal distress, and watery eyes.

If thoughts and expectations can influence the body's reaction so powerfully, we should be able to reduce anxiety by changing the way we think. This has, in fact, been demonstrated in research on anxiety. At an obsessive-compulsive disorder research program at the University of California, a simple cognitive-behavioral technique was shown to change brain chemistry. Subjects in the research were asked to re-label their anxiety, refocus their attention, and relax. This changed the brain chemistry in the caudate nucleus, the brain structure associated with OCD. What's more, the psychological technique changed brain chemistry as much as medication did. Similarly, if we replace worry and anticipatory anxiety with positive thinking and trust that things will work out favorably, we are likely to change the hormones that determine how we feel.

The power that belief and expectation have to influence health is also reflected in the fact that newly released drugs are initially more effective than existing drugs. The fanfare with which a new drug is marketed stimulates enthusiasm among physicians, which is transmitted to patients and helps create a positive effect. After an initial high-expectation period, however, when the actual patient response and side effects are reported, the doctor-patient community becomes more skeptical and the drug becomes less effective.

### Positive Thoughts and Health

Positive thoughts and feelings, such as love, compassion, peace, courage, faith, and hope, can change body chemistry and improve health status. Positive thoughts produce positive feelings, and dozens of studies have shown that positive feelings have health-promoting powers. Research has shown that positive feelings can have the following effects:

- Increased immune function
- Increased resilience to adversity
- Increased happiness
- Lowered cortisol (stress hormone) levels
- Reduced pain
- Increased resistance to viral infection
- Reduced incidence of stroke
- Increased longevity
- Enhanced creativity
- Enhanced intuition

The Positive Health Effects of Positive Feelings

Two names are associated with the idea that positive thinking is powerful. Norman Vincent Peale is known for his writings about *prayer power* and numerous cases of individuals who were able to solve difficult life problems using this power. Norman Cousins is known for his recovery from congestive heart failure by using positive thinking and changes in lifestyle. He used positive thinking, diet changes, meditation, and exercise—all steps recommended for anxiety recovery. Peale and Cousins translated into practical skills what research is now verifying about the power of the mind. Positive thinking combined with a few fundamental health practices can improve and maintain health, and this approach can help create a life beyond panic and anxiety.

## Change Your Mind and Reduce Your Anxiety

The mind is primarily responsible for creating anxiety, but we can also harness its power to help create a life beyond anxiety. In this section, we discuss steps for changing the cognitive patterns that contribute to stress and anxiety. In Chapter 2, I identified five key thought patterns that need to be addressed. The five thought patterns are:

1. Worrying

2. Shoulds

3. Perfectionistic thinking

4. Negative thinking

5. All-or-nothing thinking

Cognitive
Patterns
That Increase
Anxiety

Each of these patterns needs to be replaced with more productive thinking styles that send positive messages to the mind-body system, and practiced until they become new habits.

### Worrying

Worrying is the most pervasive pattern of thinking in anxiety. Although excessive worry is the hallmark of generalized anxiety disorder, it is found in virtually all anxiety disorders, including panic disorder, OCD, social anxiety, and phobias. What is worry?

Worry is anticipatory concern or preoccupation with what might happen in the near or distant future. Most people worry as part of an effort to feel in control. The mistaken assumption is that worrying about things will somehow help them feel more prepared. Of course, worry has no effect on what actually happens in life, except to the extent that it motivates people to take productive action. Worrying about doing well on a test or exam, for example, might motivate a person to study, but it is the study that makes a difference, not the worrying. If you care about how you perform on a test, why not just study and skip the worry?

Keep in mind that worrying is harmful to your health. It is often said that some people "worry themselves sick," or "worry to death." There is much truth to these commonplace expressions.

A worry thought is easy to identify because it invariably begins with the two words: what if? Some examples are:

"What if I make a bad impression or say something foolish in the interview?"

"What if the lab results show a life-threatening illness?"

"What if I have another panic attack?"

"What if the plane goes down while I am on it?"

"What if I left the toaster on?"

"What if I catch some germs and get sick or die?"

"What if I get stuck in traffic and show up late for the appointment?"

All worry thoughts seem to fall into one of two categories, which I have labeled *harmless* and *tragic*. By this I mean that, if the worried outcome were to occur, the consequences would be either harmless or tragic. For example, the consequences of being late for an appointment are likely to be harmless, whereas the consequences of having a life-threatening illness or being in a plane crash would be tragic. Look again at the worry examples above and see if you can distinguish between the harmless and tragic worries. I make this distinction because there are some differences in techniques to address each.

One step for replacing worry is to change the "what if" thoughts into their opposites. Do this by adding the word "so" before "what if" so you end up with "so what if." This works for harmless worries only. For example, you could replace "What if I get stuck in traffic and show up late for the appointment?" with "So what if I get stuck in traffic and show up late for the appointment. It would be better if I am on time, but it will not be tragic if I am late." Playing out the worry in your mind will help you gain perspective and stop reacting as though the situation were life-threatening. Apply this technique to any worries that fit into the "harmless" category.

For a tragic worry, I recommend acknowledging its *possibility* but also evaluating its *probability*. In reality, most tragic worries are highly unlikely to occur. For example, it is possible an airplane will crash while you or a loved one is on board, but the probability is so low that worrying about it is irrational and inappropriate. This step introduces rational thinking into the thought process.

Another technique for controlling worry is to schedule a regular time for worrying. This may sound silly, but it has worked for many worriers. Schedule five to thirty minutes for worry anytime except just before bed. Focus on your worries during this dedicated time. However, there is one important qualification. If a worry thought arises at any other time, say, "Not now," and state the time at which you will be available. Think of this technique in terms of hospital visiting hours. You will only "visit" with your worries during a specified time period.

Similarly, you can try writing your key worries down, one worry per sheet of paper. Neatly fold each worry paper in half and then again several times, until it is approximately the size of a business card. Then make an agreement with yourself that you will only allow yourself to think about a worry if the paper is unfolded in your hands. That means you will need to keep the folded worry accessible so you can retrieve it when you have the urge to worry. The goal of this exercise is to begin regulating the amount of time you devote to worrying.

Finally, do not confuse planning with worry. It is prudent to plan for the future, but you can only live in the present. Planning is productive, worrying is not.

To summarize the steps you can take to control worrying, review this list of techniques:

- Change "what ifs" to "so what ifs" (for harmless worries)

- Acknowledge the worry but evaluate its probability or likelihood (for "tragic" worries)

- Schedule a regular "worry time"

- Write down your key worries (one per page) and worry only with the paper unfolded in your hands

You can practice some or all of these steps if you are a frequent worrier. The goal is to develop confidence in your ability to handle whatever might happen, so that you do not have to worry so much and waste energy that could be better used for productive action.

Another suggested alternative to worry takes the form of an affirmation. Notice that the affirmation below contains some key words that represent alternatives to worry, such as trust, faith, and living in the present.

### An Affirmation for Creating a Life Beyond Anxiety

I do not worry in advance about what might happen. Instead, I live each day, take care of myself, and take things as they come. I plan for the future, but live in the present. I know anxiety is a normal part of life and is not life-threatening. I have faith in myself and trust I can handle whatever may happen. Beyond that, whatever happens was meant to be.

### Shoulds

The next thought pattern we need to address is our "shoulds." Related to perfectionistic thinking, shoulds are rigid, internalized rules or standards, often rooted in parental expectations from early in life. I include shoulds as thought patterns because, in many cases, people spend more time thinking about them than actually obeying them.

Shoulds are associated with our beliefs about how to be a good, worthy, or productive person. Shoulds contribute to anxiety through the stress they create, and the negative feelings that arise when we do not live up to them. Feelings, such as regret, self-hate, frustration, and guilt tend to arise when people do not perform their shoulds. Shoulds are reinforced by personality traits and values, such as a sense of duty, strong work ethic, responsibility, and dependability. Pleasure is not usually associated with these self-imposed obligations, although temporary satisfaction may come from completing a should.

In one of my anxiety therapy groups, I asked everyone to make a list of their shoulds. Their responses illustrate some common patterns but show that shoulds are a highly individual matter. What serves as a should for one person can actually be a "shouldn't" for someone else. Here is one person's list of shoulds:

- I should read the newspaper more often to keep up with world news.

- I should exercise more and eat better.

- I should call my sister more often to keep in touch.

- I should always look presentable.

Another member's list contained some opposite shoulds, but they had the same results in terms of stress and frustration. Her list included the following self-statements:

- I shouldn't waste so much time reading the newspaper, so I can get more work done.

- I shouldn't be so compulsive about my exercise and eating; I should loosen up about them.

- I shouldn't spend so much time and money on the phone with my sister in California.

- I should be less concerned with what other people think.

In my anxiety therapy groups, we sometimes joke that people with anxiety "should on themselves" too much.

The first step in addressing your shoulds is to identify them and increase your awareness of when they occur. It can help to make a list of your should thoughts. Next, create an appropriate replacement for each should thought by substituting "I should..." with "It would be preferable if..." or "I could choose to...." Practicing these alternatives can help reduce stress, anxiety, and negative feelings. Here is an example: "I could choose to spend more time reading the newspaper." After you have identified your key shoulds and their replacement thoughts, mentally substitute the replacement thought every time you catch your self "shoulding." The goal with this step is to make sure your behavior is based on *choices* rather than on shoulds. With practice, you can free yourself from shoulds and take a giant step forward in creating a life beyond anxiety.

## *Perfectionistic Thinking*

The next pattern to address is perfectionistic thinking. This is a cognitive and behavioral pattern in the anxiety disorders, and it is one of the sources of anxiety in people who attempt to meet unreasonably high standards and expectations.

Anxiety is generated when a person cannot be satisfied with a "good enough" performance, or even excellence. Perfectionism creates enormous stress, as well as frequent dissatisfaction and disappointment. In addition, low self-esteem and other negative feelings are associated with failure, as defined by imperfection in some aspect of work or family life. Perfection is related to a need to be in control, which is invariably frustrated by reality. Furthermore, perfectionism makes it impossible to relax or take pleasure in accomplishments that do not meet the unreasonably high standards.

Is perfection possible? The Greek philosopher, Plato, asserted that the world is an imperfect reflection of ideals that cannot exist in physical form. If he was correct, then perfection is impossible. We may be capable of perfection sometimes, but it is not realistic to expect perfection all the time because the very conditions under which we live and work are imperfect.

I have a tendency toward perfectionism, and I take pride in high-quality work. However, because perfection is impossible to attain in all situations, I have learned instead to strive for excellence. Excellence is achieved when I do my best, given the time constraints and conditions—which are usually less than perfect—within which I have to work. I can feel good about whatever I do, if I do my best in each situation. This includes a need to balance my many responsibilities and commitments.

Another step in taking control of perfectionism is to accept our human condition. Being human means living in the real world and acknowledging the fact that you have limited resources, skills, and control. Being human also means making mistakes and learning from them. Allow yourself to be less than perfect, so you can learn and grow. Also, establish realistic goals and set reasonable limits on what can be accomplished in a particular situation.

In addition, counteract perfectionism by focusing on both the *process* of doing and the *outcome* of doing. Enjoy the day-to-day process of living as well as your accomplishments.

## Negative Thinking

Negative thinking and pessimism contribute to anxiety by projecting disability rather than capability, or what psychologists have termed *learned helplessness*. This thought pattern also reflects low self-esteem, which is the root of social anxiety, generalized anxiety disorder, and other forms of anxiety. And negative thinking fosters the dark feelings of depression. All these consequences add to the cycle of anxiety.

Biologically, negative thinking produces a type of neurotransmitter that sends despair messages throughout the body. Negative expectations also activate the fight/flight mechanism, while sapping the energy needed to drive it. The body is much more vulnerable to stress and less able to recover from its effects when there is a high concentration of negative thoughts.

Negative thinking makes you feel like a victim with little control. With negative thinking there is a lower probability of health and happiness. Negative thinking seduces you into giving up. And when we are depressed, we lose perspective and negative thinking takes over. We project bad events and outcomes into the future, and this feeds into worry and anxiety.

Negative thinking comes in many forms. Here are some examples:

- Assuming the worst

- Projecting "bad" events into the future

- Comparing yourself to others and not measuring up

- Being judgmental

- Seeing the down side of things

- Having hostile or hateful thoughts

- Not believing in yourself

Examples
of Negative
Thinking

One of my anxiety patients, an intelligent and creative artist with two adolescent children, became aware of her negative thoughts and wrote them down as part of her recovery process. These were some of her negative thoughts:

- I'm a bad mother because by daughter is bored this summer.

- When my boss goes on her leave of absence, I hope I don't have too many responsibilities or stress, otherwise I'll go crazy or my anxiety will spike out of control.

- I have to get all this work done today or else it will all pile up and I will never get it done.

- Things are going too smoothly.

- My friend's mother has a heart problem—maybe I have one, too.

- I'm never going to be able to do all these things—it's too hard.

- I feel overwhelmed—the anxiety will surely get out of control this week.

- We are having trouble with our teenage son ... it must be my fault.

Imagine the messages sent by these negative thoughts to the heart, immune system, and other organs in this individual.

One way to correct negative thinking is deceptively simple: Replace negative thoughts with positive thoughts. To do this, convert each negative thought into its opposite. If the negative thought is "I feel overwhelmed, I'll never get all this work done," it could be replaced with the positive alternative, "I'll do the best I can, and in time the work will get done." Here are some other examples:

### Replacing Negative Thoughts with Positive Ones

| NEGATIVE THOUGHT | POSITIVE ALTERNATIVE |
| --- | --- |
| I woke up feeling tired. I'm going to have a miserable day. | I woke up feeling tired, but I'll pace myself and my energy will return. This could be a great day. |
| I wish I had as much money as he seems to have. Then I'd be happier. | Happiness does not come from having more money. I will focus on enjoying the process of living in the present, rather than waiting for something to happen before I am happy. |
| If something does not come easily, it means I'll never be good at it. | Most learning involves trial and error, as well as mistakes. This is the feedback mechanism that helps learning. I could be good at something if I practice it. |

Another way to develop a habit of thinking positively is to practice affirmations and focusing intentionally on positive, uplifting thoughts. An affirmation is a positive statement that can improve mood and, some believe, increase the probability of having positive experiences and outcomes. An affirmation seems to be most effective when it is a self-statement that consists of a complete sentence that has the following four components or qualities:

1. Is in the present tense

2. Uses an action verb

3. Starts with "I"

4. Has a positive meaning

Here are some samples I have collected from my patients over the years:

I enjoy being free of worry, fear, and anxiety.

I like knowing I have a choice about the way I live.

I am actively changing and growing, and I enjoy the process.

I feel good about myself, and I enjoy each and every day.

I am getting better and I will get over this.

I create plenty of room in my life for joy.

**Affirmations for Developing Positive Thinking**

I let go of suffering, drama, and negative thinking.

I choose the way I live.

I am living happily in the here and now.

I care for myself by eating healthy food and exercising regularly.

I accept my mistakes as an inevitable part of learning.

I enjoy the challenge of practicing new behaviors.

I regard myself with dignity, loyalty, and benevolence.

I feel at home wherever I am.

The theory behind the power of positive affirmations is that, when we repeatedly make statements that are not yet true but could become true, we create an internal tension that has a natural tendency to seek resolution. One of two possibilities will occur to reconcile that tension. One is simply that we will stop saying the affirmation. The second possibility is that if we continue to repeat the positive affirmation, we will begin to think of ways to make it become reality. Consistent repetition often results in changes that can actualize the affirmed statement.

Jack Canfield, principal author of the best-selling *Chicken Soup for the Soul* book series, credits positive affirmations for his success. Twenty-five years ago he was a schoolteacher with a limited income who wanted to improve his financial status. A visit to any bookstore suggests Canfield has achieved this goal. He recommends we repeat a positive affirmation at least fifty times each day.

Be aware that negative thinking is a habit, and thus likely resistant to change. Therefore, a consistent effort is necessary to establish new habits of positive thinking. I sometimes point out to my patients that negative thinking is like telling yourself a story about the future. Because you cannot truly predict the future, at least let the story be positive until you find out what really happens.

### All-or-Nothing Thinking

One final pattern in many anxiety cases is "all-or-nothing" thinking. This habit consists of judging things as good or bad, right or wrong. All-or-nothing thinking provides only two categories in which to put all experiences. It reflects discomfort with uncertainty and open-ended situations. It is a distortion of the instinctual need to evaluate what is safe and what is not. All-or-nothing thinking is limiting because it over-generalizes and ignores the multiple shades of meaning and possibilities in life. Here are some real-life examples of all-or-nothing thinking I recall hearing from some of my patients:

> "If I don't understand something, it means I'm stupid or it's too complicated."

> "If I make a mistake, it means I'm no good."

> "If I don't like one aspect of something, I can't like any of it."

> "If I start feeling anxious, it means a full-blown panic attack is coming and I'll be out of control."

> "If someone hurts my feelings, I can't like that person anymore."

Some years ago, I published a study of all-or-nothing thinking, which I referred to as "low tolerance for ambiguity." I was interested in what personality traits go along with an all-or-nothing style of thinking. Using psychological tests, thirty-six subjects were classified as relatively high or low in self-actualization (positive self-esteem, as measured by the Tennessee Self-Concept Scale), with equal numbers of males and females in each group. All subjects then performed on a test of tolerance for ambiguity. I found that, regardless of gender, the high self-actualization group showed higher tolerance for ambiguity than did the low self-actualization group. When confronted with an unstructured task, for which there were no rules or guidelines, or right or wrong answers, the high self-actualization group felt free to "play" with multiple possibilities. There were no signs of anxiety in high self-actualized subjects under these conditions. In contrast, the low self-actualization group was uncomfortable with the unstructured situation and judged their responses negatively. These findings suggest that people with positive mental health are more tolerant of ambiguity and less likely to engage in all-or-nothing thinking.

To eliminate all-or-nothing thinking, begin by accepting that, being human, you cannot know everything. Refrain from judging things as good or bad, and resist putting everything into a category. Instead, learn to "let things be." Mindfulness meditation (see Chapter 7) can help, because this practice leads to an attitude of acceptance without judgment.

In addition, recognize that there is usually more than one way to do something, and more than one way to interpret the meaning of things. Distinguish between facts and opinions, and keep in mind that most of what people say is an expression of their beliefs and opinions. No one can be wrong in their opinion, so give yourself and others the right to hold differing points of view. It would also be helpful to allow other people to be different, and refrain from imposing your standards or values on others. Finally, rejoice in the many possibilities life offers, as well as in your choices about how to live your life. These include the possibility of creating a life without anxiety, and fulfilling your purpose in life.

## Conclusion

The central idea behind cognitive-behavioral approaches to anxiety is that how we feel is determined primarily by how and what we think. Contemporary research has verified this mind-body connection and has demonstrated that the chemistry involved in anxiety can be altered by changing the way we think.

Five key "anxious" thought patterns were identified in this chapter and suggestions were made for replacing them with appropriate alternatives. The anxiety-arousing thought patterns are worry, shoulds, perfectionism, negative thinking, and all-or-nothing thinking. Practicing the alternative cognitive patterns is an essential step toward creating a life beyond anxiety.

# CHAPTER 12

||||||||||||||||||||||||||

# Facing Your Fears and Phobias

Most people dealing with an anxiety disorder avoid certain situations associated with uncomfortable or anxious feelings. Whatever they are—crowds, being alone, stress, relaxing, public speaking, driving, bridges, airplanes, elevators, darkness, exercise, meetings, conflict, strong feelings—they must eventually be faced in order to overcome the anxiety associated with them.

Facing our fear is the way to convert a phobic situation from an ordeal into "no big deal." Much of the information contained in this book is designed to help accomplish this one essential step. Without facing our fears, all the insights, understanding, and information in the world will be insufficient for anxiety recovery. We must face and directly experience anxiety in a new way in order to overcome it—to create a life beyond fear. How do we face our fears so we move forward in recovery, and why is this necessary?

## How Phobias Develop

We develop fears about certain situations as a result of a learning process known as *classical conditioning*. When a negative internal experience (a panic attack, anxiety reaction, or response to trauma) occurs in a particular situation, the emotional response and that particular situation become linked. As a result, we may then perceive those situations as threatening or dangerous. In other words, based on a past experience, we learn to anticipate a reoccurrence of the negative emotional reaction in specific situations. Furthermore, the linkage between the emotional experience and a particular situation generalizes in many cases to similar situations that share a common element. In one of my patients, for example, a panic attack that occurred while watching a movie generalized to anxiety in other situations involving crowds of people or enclosed spaces, including concerts, subways, and shopping malls.

We can use the term *phobic situations* to refer to such situations. To manage the associated anxiety, we may instinctively avoid those situations when possible or, if avoidance is not possible, we may simply dread them and suffer through them.

### James

*The learning, or conditioning, process is illustrated by a patient named James, a perfectionistic man who worked in a government agency. The staff in his department rotated the responsibility for presenting at weekly meetings to update each other on the latest government regulations and policy changes. While presenting at one of these meetings, James became nervous and his mind went blank. Because James had many of the anxiety personality traits, such as perfectionism, need to please others, strong need to feel in control, and high concern for how others viewed him, the incident was traumatic. Self-conscious and embarrassed, he excused himself from the meeting room, which drew additional attention from others. From that moment forward, James dreaded meetings and began to avoid them. When he was scheduled to present, he agonized for days in advance. Furthermore, his worrying and negative thinking about meetings generalized to other social situations. James contacted me for help because his public speaking phobia was spiraling out of control and interfering with his sleep, appetite, social life, and effectiveness on the job.*

### The Two Stages in Sensitization

Claire Weekes, a pioneering psychiatrist known for her work with agoraphobia, used the term *sensitization* to explain how these learned patterns of fear and avoidance develop. She points out that the initial reaction to stress or trauma is usually normal, but that sensitive people tend to react strongly to or fear those reactions. A vicious cycle then develops in which the person sensitizes to his or her reactions. The person becomes more concerned about the reactions or symptoms than the situations giving rise to them. This is the basis of the expression "fear of fear." Weekes's explanation of "sensitization" was discussed in Chapter 2. I have found this explanation to fit many of my anxiety patients whose biggest fear is of having anxiety. I attribute this tendency to the biological sensitivity and personality traits discussed in Chapter 4.

This two-stage pattern is most evident in panic disorder, in which physical symptoms (heart palpitations, difficulty breathing, sweating, shaking, and so on) are pronounced and distressing. The first stage is the anxiety reaction. The second stage is fear of the reaction. This fear is recognizable by heightened arousal and "what-if" thinking: "What if this is a heart attack? What if this is the beginning of a major panic attack? What if something terrible is wrong with me? Could this be a life-threatening illness? What if I can't control it, what will happen next?"

We have little control over our immediate reactions to stress or danger. Such reactions are part of our survival instinct; that is, the fight/flight response to danger, which is something we would not want to eliminate even if we could. However, it is possible—and desirable—to eliminate fear of our immediate reactions. This important step is accomplished in part by changing our inner dialogue about the initial body reactions. We can begin to change our inner dialogue about the fight/flight reaction by reassuring ourselves it is merely an instinctive adrenaline reaction, is not life-threatening, and will subside in time. Substituting such thoughts and thinking positively help to modify the second fear, interrupt the anxiety cycle, and make it possible to face feared situations.

Avoiding situations that cause us to feel anxious does bring some relief. However, there are several problems with this way of coping with anxiety. First, some situations are unavoidable, such as the weekly staff meetings dreaded by James. Other situations, such as car travel for some commuters, grocery shopping, being alone, or social situations, are also difficult to avoid because they are built into daily life for most people. On the other hand, infrequently occurring situations, such as air travel or taking vacations far from home, can be avoided without significant disruption to daily life. But the biggest problem with avoidance is that it does not address the underlying fear of fear. As long as we remain fearful of our reaction to any phobic situations, we are not free and are unable to live without anxiety.

## Group Therapy for Social Anxiety

Naturally, no one would feel comfortable facing his or her fears without preparation and some new skills. Even when equipped with new skills, there is often a hesitation to face a feared situation. This hesitation is poignantly illustrated by Paula, an attractive, youthful-looking woman with five young children. In spite of an engaging smile and bright brown eyes, Paula was passive and uncomfortable around other people, particularly those seemingly in positions of authority, such as her children's teachers, school principal, doctors, and even store clerks. Paula knew she was intimidated by most people and was keenly aware of her social avoidance behavior.

Recognizing the limitations her anxiety was placing on her, Paula came to me for help. After she began to see me for therapy, we identified her underlying issue as a fear of rejection—a common fear shared by people suffering from social anxiety. Although Paula was instructed in assertiveness skills and knew what she needed to do to overcome her fear of rejection, she continued to avoid the moment of truth when speaking up was the right thing to do. Paula recognized the times when assertiveness was necessary and appropriate, but inevitably backed down and missed the opportunity to grow and overcome her fear of rejection. Her self-esteem suffered deeply, but her fear of facing the fear was greater.

I encouraged Paula to participate in group therapy, which she did with initial reluctance and high anxiety. By meeting and becoming comfortable with other people who understood her anxiety, Paula began to interact verbally with others and express her feelings. Her progress in the group helped her to speak up for herself in other situations. One instance was a meeting with one of her children's teachers, who, in Paula's opinion, was not meeting her child's needs and also was not responding to Paula's phone calls. Another success took place when Paula, who had a nursing background, was asked by a pregnant friend to support her during her hospital childbirth. Paula had a positive experience advocating on behalf of her friend to the hospital staff. By joining the therapy group, Paula faced her fear of dealing with people and gradually developed assertive communication skills and self-confidence in social situations.

## Fear of Anxiety

Another case illustrates how fear of anxiety can persist well beyond the point at which actual anxiety symptoms subside. Elaine, a vivacious and verbally expressive woman, came to one of her therapy appointments and declared, "Dr. Foxman, I haven't had a panic attack now in about six weeks and I'm worried about it." When I inquired about this, Elaine explained she did not trust the fact that her anxiety symptoms had subsided. "I almost feel I am getting away with something, as though I'm supposed to have a certain amount of anxiety, and I am due for a really big one," she reasoned. In addition, Elaine revealed she was afraid of feeling anxious and had a high level of anticipatory anxiety—fear of the fear. I pointed out to Elaine that, although she had made progress, she was not anxiety-free because she had not yet faced her biggest phobic situation. In her case, being alone was the biggest fear. She needed to face and experience her fear in order to realize she could handle it. It was evident that, although Elaine's avoidance of this phobic situation helped manage her anxiety, she had not completed her recovery. As long as she remained fearful of an anxiety reaction, Elaine could not be free.

Most people with an anxiety disorder, especially those who have experienced panic attacks, know an episode of severe anxiety always passes, but the fear of it taking over does not allow an open, accepting attitude toward it. There is a tendency to fear that the anxiety will not end or that it will become a permanent state. In fact, we can identify a third fear in many cases—fear of what will happen if the anxiety does not let up. I note three categories of such fear: fear of "going crazy," fear of losing control in public, and fear of dying. These associated fears magnify anxiety. The only way to overcome these associated fears is to face and go through the anxiety experience. This is where true recovery lies.

Many people cope with their anxiety with a determined effort to "not give in." The need for control is often so strong that the person forces himself or herself to endure phobic situations, feeling that running away would mean weakness or failure. In one case, a determined man who could not tolerate the thought of appearing weak, said at the outset of treatment, "I'm going to fight this thing! I'm going to beat it!" Unfortunately, fighting only prolongs the anxiety.

Another example was a woman who called in to my radio program and said, "I thought I was facing my fears by going on wilderness camping trips by myself. I can handle the challenge of taking care of myself in a wilderness environment, but it doesn't seem to help. On some days, I can't even go to the mailbox by myself without extreme anxiety. Why?" In responding to this question, I asked what she experienced on her wilderness challenges, and she replied, "They're sheer torture!" There was the answer to her question: She was not benefiting from facing her fears because they were not positive experiences and she was not developing confidence in her ability to face her fear. Instead, she was forcing herself to face her fear without applying the appropriate skills to convert the experience from an ordeal to "no big deal." Her approach could be called *counterphobic*—an attempt to prove she was not afraid by jumping in with grit and determination. She was actually fighting her fear, rather than facing it.

Are there any effective alternatives?

## Techniques for Facing Phobic Situations

There are several recommended techniques and procedures for facing feared situations and overcoming the associated anxiety. All are designed to help unlearn the phobia reaction and take a step toward living without anxiety. We will look at the floating technique, distraction techniques, and exposure and desensitization.

### *The Floating Technique*

The floating technique is specifically designed to address the anxious feelings that arise when you face, rather than avoid, a phobic situation. There are four steps to this technique, which are explained below.

*Facing* refers to avoiding avoidance. That is, facing a fear requires a willingness to meet the fear on its own turf. Instead of running away, using distraction, or trying to forget about it, facing a fear literally means standing squarely in the face of it.

The second step, *accepting*, is the opposite of fighting against fear. Accepting a fear is an attitude that allows anxious or uncomfortable feelings to occur. In accepting, you surrender to anxiety and receive it as an opportunity to make progress.

## THE FLOATING TECHNIQUE

FACE

ACCEPT

FLOAT

LET TIME PASS

This is followed by *floating,* which goes beyond acceptance by directly experiencing the fear without resistance or tension. Floating means relaxing through fear or anxiety and openly working with it. Think of floating as floating on gently undulating water. Another analogy is what is taught in childbirth preparation classes: breathing though contractions rather than tensing up in anticipation of pain. Floating is counterintuitive. This step requires an ability to relax in the face of fear, which is possible only as a result of practicing relaxation skills.

The fourth step is *letting time pass,* which has two meanings. Letting time pass addresses the problem of impatience or the need to see immediate results. It is important to trust that an anxiety episode will always pass in time. Letting time pass also means leaving the past behind and facing fear with a new attitude. Instead of focusing on how long it will take to overcome anxiety, or how long it has been since you have suffered from it, view facing fear as a practice opportunity.

Using the four-step process of facing, accepting, floating, and letting time pass, fear can be experienced as a mind-body wave that approaches, passes through, and then leaves. As Claire Weekes puts it, "To recover, you must know how to face, accept, and go through anxiety until it no longer matters. This is the only way to permanent cure."

### Distraction Techniques

In the process of facing their fear, some people find it helpful to distract themselves rather than concentrate on relaxing or floating through the anxiety. This can be effective if it is done in the spirit of facing and accepting anxiety, and as a temporary measure to cope with it. However, distraction does not contribute to recovery if it is used to deny the fear or to run away from it. Here are some simple distraction techniques that can be used in this way:

- Count backwards from 100 by 3s or 7s

- Count objects, such as letters on signs or cars of a specific make or color

Techniques to Distract Yourself from Fear

- Repeat a reassuring affirmation, such as "These feelings are not life-threatening and I can handle them" or "It's only a matter of time before these feelings subside and I can make it until then"

- Say the words to a song or poem

- Make a list (wish list, gift list, grocery list)

- Write down your thoughts

- Visualize a place you like and imagine the scene in detail

- Focus on the details of things around you

- Make physical contact with things around you (touch a tree, piece of furniture, item of clothing; manipulate the buttons on an electronic device; rub a rock or other object between your fingers or in your hand)

In my own anxiety recovery process, I knew the difference between avoiding and facing my phobic situations. Although it brought temporary relief, I also knew avoiding was only postponing the moment of truth when facing my fear would be necessary for recovery. My most troubling phobic situation was being alone. I worked hard to avoid it by planning social activities whenever I was not at my office. My anxiety level went up whenever I had no plan for the unstructured time in my schedule. Travel alone far from home was even more frightening and I only traveled with a companion. As I gradually faced these phobic situations and learned to relax through them, I was able to overcome my fear.

One specific experience stands out as a significant step in facing my deepest fear. I accepted an opportunity to further my professional training that required me to move from San Francisco to Nashville. I had to separate from my friends, and because my girlfriend was not prepared to uproot herself, I had to go alone. Tennessee was completely unfamiliar to me, and I did not know anyone there before I relocated. Although extremely anxious about the move, I knew I had a higher purpose for facing this challenge. As it turned out, I did not simply survive, but thrived socially and professionally. I developed many friendships and received a lot of support for my work. This experience is an example of "exposure" to phobic situations, a method to be discussed in the next section of this chapter.

In our hearts, we know when we are avoiding and when we are facing our fears. In the end, we must come face-to-face with our fears to develop confidence about our ability to handle them. This is the only way to fully recover from an anxiety disorder.

### Exposure and Desensitization

So far, we have addressed the importance of facing and experiencing our fear in order to overcome it. This approach helps to reverse the sensitization process. Facing the fear helps to separate the fear reaction—the body's normal alarm reaction to stress or trauma—from the phobic situation. Facing the fear or intentionally entering a phobic situation in order to reduce anxiety is known as *exposure.*

The process by which anxiety is reduced is called *desensitization.* Desensitization occurs as a person learns to relax in phobic situations and realize they are not as threatening or uncomfortable as anticipated. This is a reversal of the sensitization process, through which anxiety becomes linked to specific situations.

Relaxation is a foundation skill for desensitization. By combining relaxation with exposure to a phobic situation, a new pattern is formed, which dramatically alters our attitude toward the situation and our reaction to it.

The first step in desensitization is to practice relaxation while thinking about or imagining the phobic situation. In my office, I sometimes ask my patients to make a list of situations that are uncomfortable or anxiety arousing, and rank them from least to most distressing. A person's most feared situation will have the highest number. I then provide the following instructions: "Beginning with the least uncomfortable situation, create a detailed mental movie of yourself going through the situation. Elicit the relaxation response and visualize yourself going through the situation step-by-step until you can complete the entire sequence for each situation on the list. You may initially find yourself reacting anxiously to the imagined situation and unable to remain relaxed. Stop there, take a break, and return to relaxation practice. After relaxing again, start the visualization from the beginning. You will probably be able to visualize a little further into the situation each time. Repeat the process until you can complete an entire phobic situation while remaining relaxed and calm. At that point, it is time to enter the situation—to face the fear in real life."

In real life, it is best to enter a feared situation gradually. Using a sequence similar to the imagined situation, start with small steps and build on them until you can experience the full situation. Let's take fear of driving as an example. A person who has experienced a panic attack in a car, or a traumatic automobile accident, may develop a fear of driving and may become tense and anxious at the thought of being in a car. The first step in facing this situation is to practice relaxation without driving or being in a car. Then practice relaxation while imagining or visualizing getting into a car, checking out the controls, starting the car, driving around the block, driving in traffic, and so on. Once this can be done mentally, these steps can be repeated in real life. Many patients have overcome their fear of driving, and many other types of phobic situations, using this procedure.

Here is a summary of the steps involved in the exposure process:

**The Steps of the Exposure Process**

- Make a list of your phobic situations.
- Number the list from least to most troubling.
- Elicit your relaxation response.
- Starting with the least troubling situation, visualize yourself going through it while remaining relaxed and open.
- Stop the process whenever you feel anxious or tense and return to relaxation.

- Start again from the beginning of the phobic situation and practice until you can relax throughout the complete visualization.

- At that point, begin to face the situation in real life using relaxation and positive thinking.

- View this gradual process as an opportunity to overcome anxiety and be satisfied with small, progressive steps.

The exposure process can apply to virtually any situation you fear. Public speaking, parties and social events, being alone, shopping, traveling, crowded places, and interpersonal conflict—all can be approached through the process of combining relaxation with gradually facing the situation. However, it is important to not move too quickly or directly into exposure. A setback (return to a prior level of anxiety or phobic avoidance) is more likely to occur if too big a step is taken or if the relaxation skills have not been practiced sufficiently.

## Conclusion

Anxiety recovery can be defined as having the skills and confidence to handle anxiety or fear to the point at which it no longer matters. Facing the fear or phobic situation is the way to develop such confidence. When it no longer matters, there is no need to worry about it or waste energy anticipating it. When it no longer matters, the chances of experiencing anxiety decrease dramatically. When it no longer matters, you can dance gracefully through fear.

# CHAPTER 13

||||||||||||||||||||||||||

# *Feeling Safe with Feelings*

eelings are associated with anxiety for many people. Anxiety is an emotional state, but it is by no means the only feeling that makes people uncomfortable. Anger, hurt, guilt, ambivalence, and even excitement may be "unsafe" and anxiety arousing. In this chapter, we explore the relationship between feelings and anxiety, and discuss ways to deal safely and effectively with feelings.

## Defense Mechanisms

The majority of people who develop anxiety disorders grew up in families with dysfunctional patterns of dealing with feelings. As a result, feelings may be experienced as uncomfortable and anxiety arousing. In some cases, people never learn how to express their feelings in appropriate or effective ways. Their poor regulation of feelings may be evident in losing control or acting out, rather than in skilled verbal communication. At the other end of the spectrum are people who are not in touch with their feelings. They may use a variety of defense mechanisms to manage their feelings.

### Avoidance

Avoidance of situations that evoke uncomfortable feelings is the most common defense mechanism found in anxiety disorders. People who are fearful of conflict, for example, may avoid expressing feelings honestly or directly, even when it is in their best interest to do so. For those who are anxious or uncomfortable in social situations, avoidance of people, parties, or other social events is a likely defense mechanism. Any situation associated with feelings of anxiety or vulnerability can be managed by avoidance. Avoiding an anxiety-arousing situation can be helpful in preventing unpleasant feelings, but it comes at a high price. Avoidance limits freedom and spontaneity, and often creates dependency on others in order to feel safe in certain situations. Depression also tends to develop from excessive avoiding as our comfort zone shrinks, particularly if social withdrawal occurs.

### Intellectualization

Intellectualization involves separating and distancing thoughts from feelings. We can spot intellectualization by its emphasis on words, abstract knowledge, logic, and retreat from emotions and interpersonal relationships. Intellectualization also allows an objective focus on theoretical issues, rather than feelings. With this mechanism, people may say they are "probably" angry, sad, afraid, hurt, or depressed without actually experiencing these feelings. Intellectualization removes us from the experience of feelings, while enabling us to talk about the feelings.

Intellectualization can be advantageous in coping with anxiety, but it is not selective—all feelings are blocked by this defense mechanism. Therefore, the price paid for use of intellectualization is a loss of positive as well as negative feelings. Joy, pleasure, passion, love, and empathy are not available to the person who relies on intellectualization. In addition, excessive reliance on intellectualization interferes with intimacy and warmth in relationships.

### Repression

Repression consists of unconsciously shutting unpleasant feelings out of awareness, resulting in an inability to identify feelings. Repression is also responsible for losing memory of painful experiences or trauma. This defense mechanism can develop in families in which emotional expression is prohibited or even punished. Repression can be adaptive because it keeps uncomfortable or painful feelings out of conscious experience, but repression can make it difficult to have any feelings. To varying degrees, repression is the result of all defense mechanisms.

## Suppression

A variation of repression is a defense mechanism known as suppression, which consists of consciously ignoring feelings. In this case, people realize they are "stuffing and storing" feelings, rather than facing them. Some reliance on defense mechanisms is necessary for daily functioning, and suppression is useful for this purpose. It can also be helpful in anxiety recovery. For example, suppression can be adaptive if it enables us to ignore anxiety while facing a phobic situation.

## Denial

Denial consists of unconscious censorship of feelings, along with an effort to hide them from others. Denial hides our feelings from ourselves as well as others. One purpose of this defense mechanism is to maintain emotional control, but if used extensively, it occurs at the expense of emotional awareness.

## Projection

Projection is another mechanism through which we try to control our feelings. Projection involves attributing negative feelings to other people, instead of recognizing them as our own feelings. Projection is the basis of judgmental or critical attitudes toward others, who may be perceived as inadequate, imperfect, "stupid," or defective in some way. For example, a self-critical woman may perceive other people as critical as a way of denying it in herself.

We may also project our anxiety or fear onto objects in the environment. This happens in virtually all anxiety disorders. The internal sensations of fear are attributed to places or situations that are assumed to be responsible for the anxiety. However, it is not the situation or place that causes anxiety. It is the anticipation of having anxious feelings in those settings and the prospect of losing control under those conditions that causes the anxiety.

## Reaction Formation

To achieve emotional control, it is common for people with anxiety disorders to use reaction formation. A variation of denial, this interesting mechanism involves disguising feelings behind their opposites. An angry person, for example, may act "nice" or "friendly." A depressed or sad person may smile. A person who feels inadequate may emphasize his or her competencies. A person who feels insecure may project self-confidence. And when a person feels anxious, he or she may appear to be strong and in control.

There are some pitfalls in the use of reaction formation as a defense against anxiety. The first is increased pressure to keep up the image or appearance of being in control. As the discrepancy increases between what we feel inside and what we portray on the outside, anxiety is likely to increase. Furthermore, when we hide our anxiety behind an appearance of having it all together, others are less likely to offer help and support.

*Sublimation*

One final mechanism deserves a brief mention. Sublimation consists of channeling an uncomfortable feeling into an activity—drawing attention away from the troublesome feeling, but at the same time giving expression to it. There are often elements of reaction formation and denial involved in sublimation. For example, people with the anxiety personality may sublimate their fear of rejection and criticism by engaging in efforts to please others.

## The Problem with Defense Mechanisms

Feelings can be thought of as emotionally charged energy. When feelings are blocked by defense mechanisms, their emotional charge builds up. When that emotional pressure reaches a critical threshold, there are two options for restoring emotional balance. The first is a gradual implosion of feelings in the form of physical ailments. The more successful we are at avoiding feelings, the more likely we are to develop such physical symptoms. In many cases, there is no apparent cause for the symptoms because we may not see the connection to unexpressed feelings.

The second option is a loss of emotional control. This usually takes the form of an unregulated emotional energy release, in which the expression of feelings is likely to be out of proportion to the situation in which this occurs. Explosiveness, moodiness, irritability, anxiety, depression, and impatience can result from this pattern.

Fear of losing of control, of course, is a core issue in anxiety disorders. The prospect of losing control is what makes us feel vulnerable, anxious or fearful, and in need of self-protection.

We try to maintain emotional self-control in two ways. One is to try to control our feelings and behavior. This is the primary role of the defense mechanisms. The second consists of attempts to control other people and the world around us, in order to feel in control of ourselves. For example, if we feel anxious or uncomfortable when things are disorganized, we may demand that everyone else pick up the house. We might even becoming angry or withdraw when others do not do what we want. There is a hidden desperation in our attempt to control others.

Anxiety personality traits play into our control efforts. For example, if we fear rejection and disapproval, we may control our feelings or say what we think others want to hear so no one will be upset with us. In short, we strive to be in control at all times. But too much control restricts our quality of life. With too much control, we sacrifice growth and development as we try to avoid conflict or rejection.

### Blocked Feelings and Psychosomatic Symptoms

Psychosomatic symptoms are physical symptoms caused or influenced by psychological pressures, such as stress and pent-up feelings. Headaches, ulcers, high blood pressure, and asthma are common psychosomatic symptoms associated with unexpressed feelings. Feelings are a form of energy, and that energy accumulates if it is not released. Like a pressure cooker, unexpressed feelings accumulate within the body, creating an internal pressure that affects health.

Muscle tension is another psychosomatic symptom of unexpressed feelings. Blocked feelings create a form of muscle tension known as *armor*. There is some evidence that blocked feelings are associated with tension in specific muscle groups. Anger and frustration, for example, are associated with tension in the neck and shoulders. Grief and sadness are often held in by tightening the chest and eye muscles. Fear is commonly held in by tension in the stomach and diaphragm muscles, which, in turn, restrict breathing. Blocked sexual feelings are often indicated by muscle tension in the pelvic region. These correlations may not be precise, but the idea that bottled-up feelings are associated with muscle tension is widely accepted, and you can verify this from personal experience.

Once a pattern of muscular armor is established as a result of holding feelings in, the tension itself makes it difficult to be in touch with feelings. Therefore, although some therapeutic approaches advocate tuning into feelings, this is difficult to do if we have extensive muscular armor. Relaxation training and softening of the muscular system, using massage, stretching, and other interventions, may be necessary in order to feel. In addition, shifting out of our minds and into our bodies can help.

## What We Should Know about Feelings

Feelings are natural, normal, and safe. What is unsafe is the behavior associated with some feelings. For example, feeling anger is safe, but violence, aggression, and other out-of-control behaviors are not safe. One of the first lessons to be learned about feelings is that we have choices about how we express our feelings, and there are appropriate and inappropriate ways of doing this. Anxiety surrounds feelings when we have not learned to distinguish between feelings and behavior, and when we lack the skills for managing feelings appropriately and effectively.

We should also recognize that the source of most our feelings is our own thoughts. As discussed in Chapter 11, this is the basis of the cognitive-behavior therapy approach. Depression, for example, is considered to be the result of negative or depressing thoughts, and anxiety is considered to be the result of worrying or obsessive thinking about bad things happening. From this viewpoint, we can regulate our feelings by controlling our thoughts. Some effective techniques for accomplishing this were discussed in Chapter 11.

Although thoughts can be responsible for our feelings, the reverse is also true: our feelings can influence our thinking. Once a feeling is activated, we tend to focus on thoughts that are linked to that feeling. When we feel depressed, for example, our thoughts about the past, present, and future are all filtered through the lens of depression. We are likely to remember things that caused us to feel depressed in the past and to project negative outcomes into the future. Likewise, when we feel anxious, we tend to worry and ruminate. We are likely to think about losing control, going crazy, having another panic attack, and so on. This is called *state-dependent thinking,* meaning that our thinking can be influenced by our emotional state.

Feelings involve both mind and body. Feelings are controlled by both the brain's limbic system and the body's autonomic nervous system (which controls the hormones responsible for the physical aspect of feelings). In many cases, the body's reactions to strong feelings (increased heart rate, perspiration, shallow/rapid breathing, trembling, and so on) are identical to the fight/flight response, but the mind determines *how* we will react to these body reactions. Without the mind's ability to distinguish between the fight/flight response and strong feelings, all feelings are likely to trigger fear and anxiety in sensitive people.

It is also important to understand the basic pattern of feelings. Feelings follow a natural course, involving a waxing phase, a peak, and a waning phase. The course of feelings can be compared to ocean waves that approach, reach a crescendo, and then wash away from shore. Happiness, sadness, anger, grief, and fear all follow this pattern. If we understand this, we will be more effective at handling feelings. There are more options for handling a feeling if it is recognized at an early, waxing stage. Once a feeling reaches a peak in intensity, it is more difficult to control because rational thinking is outweighed by strong emotional arousal.

There are no "wrong" feelings. A feeling is an emotional reaction to something—usually our thoughts or perceptions. Although the underlying thoughts and perceptions may be distorted, it is not quite accurate to say that the corresponding feelings are "wrong." Indeed, it could be said that feelings are always "right" in relation to their triggering thoughts or perceptions (even if those thoughts or perceptions are distorted or not based in reality). In communicating feelings, the most appropriate attitude is to allow each person to have his or her feelings, and focus instead on the thoughts, perceptions, and assumptions underlying the feelings. It is also important to recognize that all people have a right to their feelings, just as they have a right to their opinions.

*Distinction Between Venting and Expressing Feelings*

A useful distinction can be drawn between venting and communicating feelings. Venting one's feelings usually includes a raw release or discharge of frustration or pent-up emotional energy. In a relationship, it is more productive to communicate feelings, which means to *verbally discuss* feelings, with the goal of resolving them. However, discussing feelings is not productive during a state of high emotional arousal, when rational thinking is compromised. It is sometimes necessary to release the emotional charge associated with a feeling before discussing that feeling. This may require a separate release activity, such as creativity, exercise, art, humor, insight, or simply doing something, while a feeling moves through its cycle and enters the resolution stage. Once self-control is reestablished, productive emotional communication is possible. On the other hand, this does not mean becoming intellectual or losing touch with our feelings. Later in this chapter, some guidelines are offered for communicating feelings.

## Emotional Skills for Anxiety Reduction

Anxiety, in many cases, involves deficiencies in emotional communication skills. This is most evident in social anxiety disorder, in which a self-conscious person feels anxious about opening up with others or expects to be judged negatively or rejected when being assertive about feelings or opinions. For many post-traumatic stress disorder patients who were victims of sexual or physical abuse, trust and intimate communication can be anxiety arousing. In some specific phobias, such as public speaking phobia, anxiety is associated with communicating, especially when it involves feelings or personal information.

The psychologist Daniel Goleman is credited with popularizing the idea of *emotional intelligence*. Emotional intelligence refers to the ability to understand feelings and emotions, and to use this knowledge to communicate and interact effectively with people. Goleman asserted that successful people tend to have higher emotional intelligence rather than better education or technical skills.

Anxiety can be reduced by learning and applying emotional regulation and communication skills. In this section, we will discuss some of the skills that have helped many of my anxious patients. They include accepting the right to have feelings, developing a feelings vocabulary, recognizing feelings as they occur, discharging emotional tension appropriately, and developing specific emotional communication skills, such as assertiveness and anger management.

### Working with Irrational Beliefs

One step toward managing our anxiety is to work with the beliefs that underlie our feelings. This is similar to the cognitive-behavioral approach discussed in Chapter 11, where we focused on changing the thought patterns that create anxiety. However, beliefs are related to values and the way we understand the world, particularly relationships. For example, the belief that love and approval from others is necessary for personal happiness can lead to anxiety about expressing opinions, needs, and feelings, especially when it is anticipated that other people will disapprove. This belief can motivate a person to fear and avoid honesty or to adopt a passive role in relationships.

A useful approach to this issue is to identify and change irrational beliefs to more rational alternatives. In the example above, the alternative belief would be "I would like to be loved by everyone, but I don't need this to be happy. It is not reasonable to expect everyone to like me or to please everyone all the time. There will be times when people won't love me, just as I don't love everyone I meet. Even if someone doesn't love me, I know other people who do love me."

This approach is drawn from a system of psychotherapy known as *rational-emotive therapy (RET)*. Like cognitive-behavior therapy, this system assumes that feelings are determined primarily by underlying cognitions and that we can manage our feelings by controlling what we think and believe.

I have observed another common irrational belief underlying anxiety: "I must be good at everything I do. I cannot make mistakes." This belief is the basis of perfectionism, anxiety, frustration, and feelings of low self-esteem. Once such irrational beliefs are replaced by rational beliefs, the corresponding behavior and feelings tend to change.

Let's translate this discussion into an experiment you can perform that might reduce anxiety. Next time you feel anxious, see if you can pinpoint an underlying irrational belief. Write it down and then replace it in writing with a more rational belief.

## Acquiring a Feelings Vocabulary

In order to identify feelings, it is important to have a "feelings vocabulary." A feelings vocabulary is a repertoire of words that we can use as constructs or labels for our emotional experiences. It is the language necessary for knowing feelings.

If a young child is asked, "How do you feel right now?" just two possible answers are likely: "good" or "bad." This is because young children have not learned the words necessary to describe the many different feelings they can experience. Eskimos are known for having a large vocabulary for describing snow because, in their environment, they are tuned into the subtle variations in snow quality (crusty snow with soft snow below, dry snow, wet snow, and so on) that are not apparent to people in other locations who have less familiarity with snow.

## Tuning In to Your Feelings

Equipped with a wider vocabulary for feelings, the next step consists of "tuning in" to your feelings. When we use expressions such as "pain in the neck," "heart-broken," "scared stiff," "so mad I could cry," and "gut-level feeling," we acknowledge that feelings are often located in our bodies. Therefore, by tuning into our bodies, we are more likely to become aware of our feelings. Anxiety usually decreases when we become more aware and accepting of our feelings. Here are four steps to help tune in to your feelings:

1. **Relax.** Spend five or ten minutes in meditation, yoga, visualization, or a muscle relaxation procedure. This will help you focus on your body.

2. **Ask yourself,** "What am I feeling right now?"

3. **Attune** to the place in your body where you feel emotional sensations. Use your feelings vocabulary as you scan your body for the location of feelings, and name them as they become apparent.

## Exercise: *Feelings Vocabulary*

Below is a list of feelings I created to enhance your feelings vocabulary. The goal is to develop a vocabulary for identifying feelings, which can then be used for more effective emotional communication (see subsequent sections in this chapter).

Review this list a few times and then begin to record your feelings. You can go through the list at the end of each day and check those feelings you experienced during that day. The alphabetized list of feelings has columns for recording feelings for ten days. There are a few blank rows at the bottom of the list for you to add your own feeling words. After completing the exercise, try to name your feelings as you experience them. You may copy the list as necessary to repeat this exercise.

| DAYS FEELINGS | 1 | 2 | 3 | 4 | 5 | 6 | 7 | 8 | 9 | 10 |
|---|---|---|---|---|---|---|---|---|---|---|
| Alienated | ☐ | ☐ | ☐ | ☐ | ☐ | ☐ | ☐ | ☐ | ☐ | ☐ |
| Ambivalent | ☐ | ☐ | ☐ | ☐ | ☐ | ☐ | ☐ | ☐ | ☐ | ☐ |
| Angry | ☐ | ☐ | ☐ | ☐ | ☐ | ☐ | ☐ | ☐ | ☐ | ☐ |
| Annoyed | ☐ | ☐ | ☐ | ☐ | ☐ | ☐ | ☐ | ☐ | ☐ | ☐ |
| Anxious | ☐ | ☐ | ☐ | ☐ | ☐ | ☐ | ☐ | ☐ | ☐ | ☐ |
| Apathetic | ☐ | ☐ | ☐ | ☐ | ☐ | ☐ | ☐ | ☐ | ☐ | ☐ |
| Bored | ☐ | ☐ | ☐ | ☐ | ☐ | ☐ | ☐ | ☐ | ☐ | ☐ |
| Concerned | ☐ | ☐ | ☐ | ☐ | ☐ | ☐ | ☐ | ☐ | ☐ | ☐ |
| Confident | ☐ | ☐ | ☐ | ☐ | ☐ | ☐ | ☐ | ☐ | ☐ | ☐ |
| Confused/ puzzled | ☐ | ☐ | ☐ | ☐ | ☐ | ☐ | ☐ | ☐ | ☐ | ☐ |
| Curious | ☐ | ☐ | ☐ | ☐ | ☐ | ☐ | ☐ | ☐ | ☐ | ☐ |
| Depressed | ☐ | ☐ | ☐ | ☐ | ☐ | ☐ | ☐ | ☐ | ☐ | ☐ |
| Disappointed | ☐ | ☐ | ☐ | ☐ | ☐ | ☐ | ☐ | ☐ | ☐ | ☐ |
| Discouraged | ☐ | ☐ | ☐ | ☐ | ☐ | ☐ | ☐ | ☐ | ☐ | ☐ |
| Disgusted | ☐ | ☐ | ☐ | ☐ | ☐ | ☐ | ☐ | ☐ | ☐ | ☐ |

*(cont'd.)*

| DAYS FEELINGS | 1 | 2 | 3 | 4 | 5 | 6 | 7 | 8 | 9 | 10 |
|---|---|---|---|---|---|---|---|---|---|---|
| Lonely | ☐ | ☐ | ☐ | ☐ | ☐ | ☐ | ☐ | ☐ | ☐ | ☐ |
| Loved | ☐ | ☐ | ☐ | ☐ | ☐ | ☐ | ☐ | ☐ | ☐ | ☐ |
| Miserable ✓ | ☐ | ☐ | ☐ | ☐ | ☐ | ☐ | ☐ | ☐ | ☐ | ☐ |
| Negative ✓ | ☐ | ☐ | ☐ | ☐ | ☐ | ☐ | ☐ | ☐ | ☐ | ☐ |
| Nervous ✓ | ☐ | ☐ | ☐ | ☐ | ☐ | ☐ | ☐ | ☐ | ☐ | ☐ |
| Optimistic | ☐ | ☐ | ☐ | ☐ | ☐ | ☐ | ☐ | ☐ | ☐ | ☐ |
| Overwhelmed ✓ | ☐ | ☐ | ☐ | ☐ | ☐ | ☐ | ☐ | ☐ | ☐ | ☐ |
| Peaceful | ☐ | ☐ | ☐ | ☐ | ☐ | ☐ | ☐ | ☐ | ☐ | ☐ |
| Pessimistic ✓ | ☐ | ☐ | ☐ | ☐ | ☐ | ☐ | ☐ | ☐ | ☐ | ☐ |
| Positive | ☐ | ☐ | ☐ | ☐ | ☐ | ☐ | ☐ | ☐ | ☐ | ☐ |
| Proud | ☐ | ☐ | ☐ | ☐ | ☐ | ☐ | ☐ | ☐ | ☐ | ☐ |
| Rejected | ☐ | ☐ | ☐ | ☐ | ☐ | ☐ | ☐ | ☐ | ☐ | ☐ |
| Relieved | ☐ | ☐ | ☐ | ☐ | ☐ | ☐ | ☐ | ☐ | ☐ | ☐ |
| Remorseful | ☐ | ☐ | ☐ | ☐ | ☐ | ☐ | ☐ | ☐ | ☐ | ☐ |
| Restless | ☐ | ☐ | ☐ | ☐ | ☐ | ☐ | ☐ | ☐ | ☐ | ☐ |
| Sad ✓ | ☐ | ☐ | ☐ | ☐ | ☐ | ☐ | ☐ | ☐ | ☐ | ☐ |
| Satisfied | ☐ | ☐ | ☐ | ☐ | ☐ | ☐ | ☐ | ☐ | ☐ | ☐ |
| Scared/fearful | ☐ | ☐ | ☐ | ☐ | ☐ | ☐ | ☐ | ☐ | ☐ | ☐ |
| Shamed | ☐ | ☐ | ☐ | ☐ | ☐ | ☐ | ☐ | ☐ | ☐ | ☐ |
| Shy ✓ | ☐ | ☐ | ☐ | ☐ | ☐ | ☐ | ☐ | ☐ | ☐ | ☐ |
| Stubborn | ☐ | ☐ | ☐ | ☐ | ☐ | ☐ | ☐ | ☐ | ☐ | ☐ |
| Surprised/ ✓ shocked ✓ | ☐ | ☐ | ☐ | ☐ | ☐ | ☐ | ☐ | ☐ | ☐ | ☐ |
| Suspicious ✓ | ☐ | ☐ | ☐ | ☐ | ☐ | ☐ | ☐ | ☐ | ☐ | ☐ |
| Tired | ☐ | ☐ | ☐ | ☐ | ☐ | ☐ | ☐ | ☐ | ☐ | ☐ |
| Withdrawn | ☐ | ☐ | ☐ | ☐ | ☐ | ☐ | ☐ | ☐ | ☐ | ☐ |

4. **Wait and listen.** Be a patient observer and allow your senses to pick up on the place in your body where you have a feeling. When you get a general sense of what you are feeling, ask the following questions to further identify your feelings:

   — Where in my body is this feeling?

   — What is the shape of this feeling?

   — What is the size of this feeling?

   — If this feeling had a color, what would it be?

*Being with Your Feelings*

Fear of feelings decreases if we can simply *be* with our feelings and suspend negative judgments about them. Thoughts such as "I shouldn't feel this way," "He'll be upset with me if I tell him how I feel," and "I won't be able to handle my feelings" are all based on a judgmental attitude toward negative feelings. Replace this with the truth about feelings:

- We have a right to our feelings.

- Feelings are not inherently dangerous.

- Feelings and behavior are two different things.

- We have a choice about how we express our feelings.

- Feelings are like waves and always subside with time.

- We can learn how to communicate our feelings effectively.

It is helpful to cultivate an accepting and nonjudgmental attitude toward feelings, much the same way as we treated thoughts when discussing mindfulness meditation in Chapter 7. This approach to anxiety is also similar to the floating technique, discussed in Chapter 12, which involves the steps of facing, accepting, floating through, and letting time pass. Here are some specific guidelines for sitting intentionally and nonjudgmentally with anxiety:

- In this meditation, be reminded that feelings—including anxiety—are safe.

- Allow yourself to face anxiety objectively by asking these questions: "Where is the sensation strongest? In the chest, the muscles, the belly? What additional images arise along with the fear? Where does the fear linger?

- Simply watch and investigate anxiety, making peace with the sensations that arise.

- Resist the urge to protect yourself.

- As you move gently through the emotional experience, what other sensations or impulses arise?

- Let anxiety simply exist as images in the mind and sensations in the body.

- Feel safe with anxiety and let it pass, without the usual disturbances and secondary reactions.

We already discussed the important distinction between feelings and behavior. Keeping this distinction in mind can prove helpful in cultivating emotional equanimity and in accepting feelings without judgment or fear. Knowing you can simply be with your feelings, without responding to any impulses to act them out or behave in a programmed way, can help lower your anxiety. In this sense, being with your feelings is a quiet and private process that allows you to move through emotional sensations without taking action. If action is necessary and appropriate, it is best done with skillfulness, as described in the next section.

### Taking Appropriate Action

Feelings sometimes do require action. For example, it may be helpful to discharge the energy or tension associated with a feeling by engaging in physical activity or exercise (see Chapter 9 for a discussion about exercise). Some other release mechanisms include talking about your feelings with someone you trust, writing your feelings in a diary or journal, or writing a letter (that does not necessarily need to be mailed). For anger, there are some additional methods to release the emotional charge, discussed later in this chapter. These are all methods for letting off emotional steam. In the next section, we consider some steps for verbally communicating feelings.

By far the most difficult action is to verbally discuss your feelings with other people, especially those who may have behaved in ways that hurt you or with whom conflict is likely to emerge. These are people with whom you may have unresolved issues. In such relationships, it is important to use assertive communication skills.

I personally had great difficulty with assertive communication. I feared that if I expressed my feelings to other people, they would become angry or upset with me. I intellectualized my feelings and avoided assertive communication by telling myself that conflict was negative and the world needed more peace. Like most people with anxiety disorders, I was concerned about rejection, and this led me to please other people and avoid conflict. I was sometimes passive and compliant, even when it was not in my best interest. I was frequently unable to be honest about my feelings. In addition, I feared my own feelings when they were intense, and assumed I would be unable to control them. Anger, sadness, and guilt were particularly difficult for me to handle.

I was able to overcome this problem, but not without practice. One helpful tool was a simple but powerful formula I learned from Ann Seagrave and Faison Covington's book, *Free from Fears* (no longer in print). In it, the authors provide a three-step formula for expressing feelings assertively. I added a fourth step to make the technique more complete and successful, and these four steps are given on page 196. This formula can be used for most interpersonal situations, when there is potential conflict or a difficult issue that needs to be resolved. Here are some sample situations in which assertive communication is appropriate:

- Saying no to a request from a friend

- Returning a defective product for a refund

- Asking your boss or supervisor for a raise

- Addressing a problem with a coworker or friend

- Discussing an emotionally loaded issue (money, sex, household responsibilities) with your spouse

- Setting limits with your children

## *Four Steps for Expressing Feelings Assertively*

### 1. Make a sensitivity statement

Start by showing sensitivity toward or appreciation for the other person. This reduces defensiveness on the part of the listener. With a sensitivity, or empathy, statement, such as "I know you are very busy, but I need to speak with you about something important," you show the other person you understand his or her position, and that you are sensitive to his or her needs and feelings. An empathy statement is a signal that you are "safe" to talk to and are in control of yourself.

### 2. State your feelings or needs

When stating your feelings or needs, be sure to use "I" statements rather than "you" statements. For example, say, "I felt hurt when you said...," rather than "You hurt me when you said...." Another example is, "I am disappointed in the way this product works, and I want to return it for a refund."

### 3. Propose an outcome or solution (if one is needed)

This step is frequently overlooked by people when they state their feelings. Without a clear idea of your desired outcome, you are unlikely to get it. The desired outcome or solution is usually the answer to the question you should first ask yourself: "What do I want to have happen as a result of this communication? What is the purpose of this communication?"

### 4. Make an agreement

People are more likely to follow through if they make an agreement. You can seek an agreement by simply asking the other person if he or she is agreeable to the proposed solution. An agreement is a commitment. If someone makes an agreement with you, but fails to follow through with it, you then have a solid basis for your next assertive communication. In that case, you can remind the person that an agreement was made, and communicate your feelings—such as disappointment or frustration—about their lack of follow-through.

## Anger

Of all the feelings we have discussed so far in this chapter, anger is the most anxiety arousing. Why does anger create so much anxiety?

For many people, anger has been associated with violence, abuse, or out-of-control behavior. Children are particularly vulnerable to adult anger, and parents do not always realize how angry they are or how frightening anger can be to their children. Naturally, if you have been the target for someone else's anger or a victim of abuse in which violence (or threat of harm) was involved, you probably developed a fear of anger. Perhaps you lost control of your own anger and that was frightening. Finally, witnessing a heated argument between other people can be enough to trigger anxiety about this emotion.

Feeling anger within ourselves can be anxiety arousing because of intense physical reactions, such as rapid heart rate, shortness of breath, muscular tension, hot flush, and overall arousal due to increased adrenaline. These physical reactions can make us feel we could lose control. For all of these reasons, we tend to avoid anger both in other people and in ourselves. We do this by using the defense mechanisms discussed earlier in this chapter.

### Passive-Aggressiveness

One defense mechanism that seems to be unique to anger was not addressed earlier. It is passive-aggressive behavior, which involves denial and repression, while providing for a release of anger. Passive-aggressive behavior is an indirect or disguised expression of anger. Coming late for meetings, "forgetting" things, and procrastinating are forms of passive-aggressive behavior. Typically, the person is unaware of both the anger and passive-aggressive behavior, and therefore does not take responsibility for either.

Research shows that anger can damage our health, especially if it is not properly managed. For example, a study of 1,877 men found that those who scored high on a hostility scale were one and a half times more likely to have a heart attack than men who had lower hostility scores. Another study, involving 255 medical students, found those who scored high on hostility were six times more likely to develop coronary heart disease twenty-five years later than were those who scored lower on hostility. In a third study, 424 patients who were referred for coronary angiography were assessed for hostility. Those who scored higher on hostility had more serious atherosclerosis than those who scored lower. These findings suggest that chronic anger can damage the cardiovascular system and increase the likelihood of heart attacks.

### Anger and Depression

Depression is another sign of anger that is sometimes not appropriately expressed. Psychoanalytic theory suggests that when anger is held in, it can turn against the self. If you find yourself being self-critical along with feeling depressed, anger turned inward may be the underlying source.

### How to Express Anger Appropriately

More than any other emotion, it is important to separate the negative aspects of anger-driven *behavior* from the underlying angry *feeling*. Violence, destructiveness, verbal abuse, withdrawal, and aggression are behaviors, and it is not necessary to express angry feelings in these ways. However, the most appropriate option for expressing anger is the one least likely to be used by most people: verbal discussion with the person toward whom angry feelings are directed.

The biggest obstacle to appropriate verbal expression of angry feelings is the physical tension associated with them. Anger is typically associated with intense neuromuscular activation, which gives anger a highly charged quality. This muscular tension is often responsible for the sudden and explosive release of anger in the form of violence and aggressive behavior. In order to be in control of angry feelings and to engage in appropriate verbal discussion, one must first release this physical tension.

There are a number of methods for discharging the physical tension associated with anger. Vigorous exercise, hitting a pillow or mattress, progressive muscle relaxation, and other tension-releasing activities can help to lower the charge and explosive potential of anger. Just taking time out and focusing on another activity can allow muscle tension to subside. Here is a safe, simple, and effective way to discharge the physical tension associated with anger:

**Exercise:** *Tension Release for Anger Control*

In private, take a hand towel and fold it in half lengthwise and then fold a second time. After that, fold the towel in half the other way. Twist the towel between your two hands and hold.

Close your eyes and think about the situation that has aroused your anger. Allow yourself to imagine vividly the situation or person toward whom your anger is directed. As you mentally focus on the anger, begin to twist the towel with everything you have. As you wring the towel, repeat out loud, "I'm angry, I'm angry, I'm angry."

Do this ten or twelve times, each time allowing the intensity of the feeling and the energy put into the towel wringing to increase. You will have successfully discharged your physical tension if your body feels limp—like cooked spaghetti. You will then be more in control and able to discuss your anger appropriately.

Discharging tension associated with anger in exercises such as the one described above should be a private, safe, and constructive activity. Keep in mind that venting anger toward others is destructive. Furthermore, acting out anger can increase rather than decrease this feeling.

Anger is safer to feel and discuss after you have discharged the physical tension. Try to stay with the feelings associated with anger and begin to consider what you want to do with them. Most likely, you will need to talk with someone toward whom the feelings are directed. You may still feel anxious about the anger, based on years of conditioning, but remember that anger is simply a feeling and not necessarily linked to any particular behavior. You can decide what to do with the feelings.

In order to discuss anger with another person, you must be in control of yourself and you must feel safe (and so should the other person). The exercise on the next page is a method for creating personal safety when discussing anger with another person in a tense or charged situation.

After you establish a safety shield, you can express angry feelings appropriately using the assertiveness skills described earlier in this chapter. Remember to focus on your own feelings, without criticizing, blaming, or demoralizing the other person. Start with empathy and make

---

**Exercise:** *Invisible Safety Shield*

To help you feel safe, draw an imaginary boundary or safety zone around yourself. Consider yourself physically and emotionally safe as long as the other person does not intrude into your safety zone. Draw the boundary line wherever you need—the line may differ from person to person. Under some circumstances in which safety is a significant issue, you may want to tell the other person where your boundaries lie and what you need in order to feel safe when discussing your feelings. Normally, it may be sufficient to privately define your safety zone and determine in advance what steps you will take if you feel threatened. Your safety zone is behind this invisible shield of protection. Speak from inside this safety shield and practice relaxing and feeling safe in the presence of angry feelings.

---

"I" statements. After expressing your feelings, offer a solution or ask for what you need. For example, you may need an apology, or perhaps a commitment by the other person to change a particular behavior pattern. Always keep in mind that anger is not dangerous unless there is loss of control or it is expressed destructively. You want to experience your anger while regulating the physical tension associated with it. You want to learn to verbally express your angry feelings in a constructive mode with a positive outcome.

## Conclusion

A great deal of fear and anxiety could be prevented if we learned that feelings are safe, that feelings and behavior are two different things, that feelings are a form of energy that needs to be released, that feelings follow a natural and predictable course, and that it is healthy to communicate feelings. It would also help reduce fear and anxiety if we practice the skills necessary for identifying, expressing, communicating, and otherwise dealing with feelings.

Anger seems to be the most anxiety-arousing feeling because, for many people, it has been associated with violence. Some specific skills can be learned to reduce the anxiety associated with anger. Ideally, emotional skills should be learned in childhood, when we are forming our personality and behavior patterns. However, it is never too late to acquire the information and skills to change our feelings about feelings.

# CHAPTER 14

||||||||||||||||||||||||||

# *Anxiety and Relationships*

Anxiety sufferers are involved in multiple relationships—with parents, spouse or partner, children, peers and friends, or people at work. Anxiety invariably exists in a social context, being affected by others and affecting others. Even professional help for anxiety is an interpersonal process, not only in terms of the therapeutic relationship between therapist and patient, but also in terms of how change in the recovering person affects the lives of others in his or her life.

In this chapter, we explore the interaction between anxiety and relationships. We see that relationships can be a source of anxiety for those who have been hurt or disappointed in the past, as well as one of the most powerful opportunities for anxiety recovery and emotional healing.

## Relationships as Self-Regulating Systems

Every relationship is a self-regulating system that seeks to survive stress and strains while maintaining stability. In a relationship system, behavior and feelings in one person affect the *field* of others who are influenced to respond or adjust. This is sometimes called a *mutual reaction process,* implying simply that, in any relationship, the behavior of each party affects the behavior of the other.

The systems view of relationships forms the foundation of most approaches to family therapy. Although strategies vary within family therapy approaches, one principle unites them all; namely, that symptoms often serve an equilibrium-maintaining function within a family. Often, a *symptom bearer*—the symptomatic person—is the stress release valve in a family. In an alcoholic family, for example, one child may develop a behavior problem that diverts attention away from an impaired parent. Another child, often the oldest, may become a high achiever whose accomplishments serve to mask the family's dysfunction.

When family stress is high, one member may develop an anxiety disorder. This usually occurs in the person whose personality fits the profile described in Chapter 4. Although the anxious person may absorb the family stress, the anxiety disorder puts pressure on other members to provide support and reassurance. If the anxiety is incapacitating, other family members are required to fill in the gaps by providing transportation, doing extra household chores, and taking on other responsibilities. As roles shift, additional stress is created and another family member, such as a spouse, may also become symptomatic.

Sometimes the ego needs of a spouse or significant other are satisfied by the anxiety sufferer's dependency or incapacity, but in an unhealthy way. If a partner has strong needs for control, for example, serving as a caretaker or support person can seem natural, even if resentment accompanies this role.

### Ethel

*The dependent relationship pattern was evident in one of my patients. Ethel was an insecure and highly dependent woman whose husband called to make an initial appointment and brought her in for help. On the surface, the husband resented his wife's dependency, complaining he had to drive her everywhere "like a taxi." He also became angry if she left something off the grocery shopping list and needed to make a second trip to the supermarket within the same week. However, beneath his complaints and resentment, the husband felt more comfortable having the upper hand. When Ethel complained about his demanding and critical parenting style with their children, he agreed to talk about it—but only on the condition that she overcome her anxiety disorder first. Approximately a month later, when she was showing signs of greater risk-taking and independence, Ethel called to cancel her next appointment and to indicate she would not be continuing. When I telephoned Ethel to discuss this decision, she told me her husband did not think therapy was helping and wanted her to stop. It was apparent, however, that her husband wanted her to stop because the therapy was working, which meant the balance of power in the relationship was beginning to shift.*

Generally speaking, as we saw in Chapter 4, people who develop anxiety disorders have many strengths and competencies. They are hard working, dependable, perfectionistic, high achieving, and eager to please. The anxiety personality also has a strong need to be in control, as well as difficulty asking for help. Feeling out of control and being dependent on others runs against the grain of this personality style. It is often the anxious person who keeps relationships running efficiently; when this role is reversed, the relationship can go into crisis.

Intimacy can be a special challenge for the person with anxiety personality traits. The need to please others, fear of rejection, and sensitivity to criticism tend to make this type of person highly reactive to any kind of negative feedback. This anxious person can react strongly to the slightest indication of displeasure, rejection, or criticism by a partner. To maintain relationships, the anxious partner then tries even harder to please, creating more stress and anxiety.

A number of ideas from family therapy and systems theory can be helpful in understanding the impact of anxiety on relationships. One idea is that a relationship must periodically reorganize in order to survive. Reorganization can be precipitated by a crisis, such as a major illness, life stress, or a family member undergoing change. An obvious example is the impact of an adolescent maturing into an adult who asks for increased responsibility and freedom. If the family does not adapt to the changing needs of the adolescent, the adolescent may emotionally act out or reject the family in order to continue growing. Any relationship that is incapable of adapting to internal or outside changes is unlikely to survive as a unit.

This concept pertains to anxiety disorders in several ways. First, an anxiety disorder sometimes develops in response to a relationship problem. For example, a marriage that is not going well can precipitate anxiety about a possible separation or divorce. Or a passive person can develop anxiety about greater independence because this is likely to involve some loss of security. Conversely, one partner can become more anxious if the other partner shows signs of increasing independence or autonomy.

Another family therapy idea is that, when one family member undergoes therapy for anxiety, the other family members must adapt. If the person in therapy becomes stronger, more assertive, or more independent, the spouse and other family members need to accommodate these changes. Unfortunately, in the case described earlier in this chapter, the husband was unable to accommodate the positive changes in his wife when she developed new skills and showed signs of increasing strength and independence. And she, not wanting to jeopardize the security of her marriage, was unable to go forward and complete her anxiety treatment. In effect, the husband wanted his wife to overcome her anxiety without changing anything else within the marriage, and the wife wanted to change without rocking the boat.

### Working with Couples

When I work directly with couples, I keep in mind that there are four stages in the development of an intimate relationship. The first is *symbiosis,* a stage of mutual dependence in which there is little separateness or individuality. An undifferentiated togetherness is characteristic of this stage, and couples speak predominantly about "us" and "we." In the symbiotic stage, the identity of each partner is defined in terms of the relationship. This is normal in the early stages of a relationship, when a couple first falls in love and wants to spend all their time together.

The second stage is *rapprochement,* the French term for leaving-and-returning, in which couples experiment with separation and individuation. In this stage, partners strive for balance between meeting their individual needs, while preserving and protecting the relationship. A common issue in the rapprochement stage is the extent to which each partner is permitted to have separate friends, have personal space, or spend time doing things outside the relationship. This stage often precipitates anxiety and brings couples into therapy.

The third stage is *independence,* in which one partner may emotionally separate from the relationship, or even physically leave, in the process of "finding himself or herself." Although necessary for the next and final stage of development, a need for independence in one or both partners can be confusing and mistaken for incompatibility. This stage can also precipitate an anxiety crisis.

Finally, the fourth and most mature stage is *mutual interdependence,* in which a couple can accommodate the independence of each partner, while allowing reciprocal dependency on each other. In other words, in mutual interdependence, each partner is acknowledged to be separate and mutual dependency can take place without symbiosis.

The potential for anxiety is high at any stage in the development of a relationship, especially for those with anxiety personality traits. During the symbiotic stage, for example, when the members of a couple are getting to know each other, there is always the possibility the relationship will not work out. Therefore, the potential is high for anxiety about rejection, trust, abandonment, and being alone if love turns sour. These concerns continue during rapprochement and independence. If a relationship makes it to the stage of mutual interdependence, there is usually sufficient security and trust to counteract anxiety.

In the case of most couples who seek professional help, the two partners are not at the same stage at the same time. While one partner may be experimenting with independence, the other partner may feel threatened and fearful about losing the relationship. In such cases, the anxious partner can have difficulty letting go and supporting the growth of the other partner. In turn, the partner seeking greater independence can experience anxiety about functioning more independently or relying more on his or her self.

When an anxiety disorder or anxiety symptoms emerge, it is common to become temporarily dependent on another person for support. I see this often in cases of panic disorder with agoraphobia. Typically, the support person is a spouse, family member, or close friend. Feeling weak, helpless, or out of control, the anxious person regresses emotionally, sometimes with feelings of shame about the anxiety. A sensitive partner recognizes this as a temporary condition, but a less understanding partner becomes impatient or resentful.

## Communication in Relationships

Many people with anxiety disorders have problems with interpersonal communication. In some cases, this is due to lack of communication skills, but more often this reflects fears of rejection, conflict, or criticism. People with the anxiety personality style hesitate to be honest and open about their feelings or needs and tend to say what they think others want to hear. If this has been a long-standing pattern, the anxious person may be out of touch with feelings.

People in successful relationships are capable of sharing power, making decisions and plans, expressing feelings, and resolving conflict. The basis for these abilities is effective communication.

Effective communication is *congruent*. Congruent communication is honest and above-board, rather than disguised or indirect. There is congruence between *what* is said and *how* it is expressed. Tone of voice and body language matches the content of communication. Congruent communication is open, with eye contact between two people who acknowledge their real feelings and listen to each other. The more congruent the communication, the more emotional contact is made.

## The Healing Power of Intimate Love Relationships

A love relationship can be an opportunity for healing from an anxiety disorder. By offering a person unconditional love and support, for example, a love relationship can counteract insecurity, low self-esteem, and separation anxiety. A love relationship can also provide a safe atmosphere for a person with an anxiety disorder to be involved in therapy or other personal work to learn new skills to help overcome anxiety.

Unfortunately, many people recreate their dysfunctional family relationships in their adult love relationship. They may be attracted to and marry a partner who has characteristics similar to a parent toward whom conflict or negative feelings exist. In most relationships, these recreated patterns are mutual. That is, partners are attracted to each other to unconsciously recreate and attempt to change damaging family patterns. On the positive side, this creates opportunities for resolving problem relationships. It is reasonable to think there is a higher purpose to relationships; namely, an opportunity to grow emotionally by creating new patterns of communication and emotional contact.

A love relationship is an emotional and spiritual growth opportunity. This view of love relationships is explored by Joyce and Barry Vissell in their book about couples, *The Shared Heart*. A husband-and-wife therapy team, they tell us that the deeper we go emotionally with another person, the more we learn about ourselves. But a deep relationship involves trials and tribulations that can threaten our sense of emotional safety and security. Our longing for love and security, however, combined with a commitment to growth, enables us to benefit from a love relationship. As the Vissells put it, "The deeper the relationship, the more imperfection is brought to the surface. The deeper our longing for love, the more light floods our being, and the dark shadows of fear, doubt, pride, anger, jealously, greed (and many others) emerge for their last stand. They are exposed by our desire for truth, and then transfigured by the light of love."

Relationships, then, can be both a source of anxiety and an anxiety-recovery opportunity. Intimate relationships require trust, commitment, openness, and love. Intimacy can raise anxiety for those who have been hurt, disappointed, or deprived in previous relationships. To protect ourselves, we have a tendency to hold back and keep some doors closed, but this limits growth for both the individual and the relationship.

### Guidelines for Friends and Family

Living with someone who has an anxiety disorder can be stressful. Family and friends can have a variety of reactions and feelings, which they may have difficulty keeping under control. This section addresses the needs of friends and family. We begin by considering some of their common reactions and feelings (see the box on the facing page), and then move to some suggestions and guidelines.

Here are some guidelines for friends and family members who are dealing with an anxious person:

- Educate yourself about anxiety
- Show understanding and empathy

- Avoid talking about symptoms

- Encourage independence

- Refrain from critical or condescending remarks

- Do not "micromanage" the person's efforts to overcome anxiety

---

### Common Reactions of Friends and Family

**Confusion:** "How can this possibly be just anxiety? I don't understand why everything is such a big ordeal."

**Fear:** "What if he stays this way? What if the doctors missed something? Maybe he is going crazy or having a serious illness."

**Depression:** "We don't have fun anymore. We're never happy."

**Anger:** "This is not the person I married. What's wrong with her? I can't do it all by myself. Why can't she just get it together?"

**Guilt:** "Maybe it's my fault he is like this. Why can't I help better? What am I doing wrong? Is there something wrong with our marriage?"

**Loneliness:** "If I tell her what I'm feeling, that would be a burden. I can't tell other people what we're going through."

**Resentment:** "What about *my* feelings and needs? She is trying to control me! She must be exaggerating. This is taking over—I have no freedom."

---

Finally, based on information discussed in previous chapters (Chapters 7, 8, 11, and 12), here are some examples of statements that would be helpful to an anxious person:

"Tell me what you need now."

"Go ahead and feel the anxiety—I'm here for you."

Statements That are Helpful to an Anxious Person

"Stay in the here-and-now. Don't anticipate the future."

"Don't 'what if.' "

"Don't add the second fear."

"Face the fear and it will slowly disappear."

"It's not the place, it's the thought."

"Don't fight it. Float through it."

"Breathe slow and low."

"I'm proud of you. You're courageous."

"I love you no matter what."

## Conclusion

Anxiety can be the cause of a relationship problem as well as the result of a relationship problem. In either case, an anxiety disorder can be a disguised opportunity for growth and freedom—not only for the anxiety sufferer, but also for those in relationships with that person.

The family systems view of relationships offers an explanation for how one person's behavior can affect a family or marriage, as well as how a family or marriage can affect an individual. We discussed these as they relate to anxiety, and considered suggestions about how the anxious person's family and loved ones can be helpful to the anxiety recovery process.

A relationship is most receptive to change during a crisis, when the equilibrium of that system is most out of balance. The crisis can be an anxiety disorder, and when it leads to learning new skills and making positive changes, everyone involved benefits. The skills learned during anxiety recovery often lead to more independence, self-confidence, assertiveness, and interest in pursuing new activities. Such growth and change usually causes a positive shift in relationship dynamics.

On the other hand, sometimes a partner or family member feels threatened by positive changes in the person. In such cases, there is work to be done within the relationship system, and couples or family counseling may be advisable.

# CHAPTER 15

||||||||||||||||||||||||||||

# *Sex and Anxiety*

I n this chapter, we turn to the relationship between sexuality and anxiety, recognizing that sexual issues can both cause anxiety and result from anxiety. Sexual abuse, for example, is the most traumatic disruption to psychosexual development and it can create fear of sexual intimacy, problems with trust, and anxiety about sexual pleasure. In many families, just talking about sex is anxiety arousing, and as a result many people who develop anxiety are lacking in accurate sex education. However, even when anxiety occurs for other reasons, it can interfere with a healthy sexual life. And yet sexuality can be a healing experience for those with anxiety. Sex is not only a source of pleasure, but also one of nature's mechanisms for releasing tension and stress.

We begin by discussing sexuality as an energy system, followed by considering the ways sexuality can lead to anxiety and sexual disorders. The chapter provides suggestions for reducing anxiety by improving sexual function and creating a healthy sex life.

## Our Sexual Energy System

Sexual energy is a form of life force. Throughout history, many names have been suggested for this concept, such as "vital force" (Paracelsus), "orgone energy" (Reich), "prana" (yoga tradition), "chi" (Chinese medicine), and "electromagnetic energy" (Galvani). Early scientists found that life energy has a natural rhythm and flow. In 1791, Galvani proposed—and we now know this to be true—that life force flows through our bodies by a process of expansion and contraction, the same expansions and contractions found in all somatic structures, including the pulsations of the cardiovascular, digestive, and muscular systems. The

211

flow of life force seems to be a universal pattern in nature, reflected in the way nutrients move through plants and trees, as well as in the ebb and flow of the oceans.

The flow of life energy in each of us needs to be regulated in order to maintain biological equilibrium, and nature provides a number of means for accomplishing this. Relaxation, rest, and sleep, for example, are necessary for recovery from effort or energy output. Food, which provides fuel for energy, also contributes to the recovery effort and helps to stock up for future energy expenditure. Exercise, on the other hand, is important for releasing energy that is pent-up in the form of muscular tension. Changes in breathing are another mechanism for regulating energy, accomplished by adjusting the oxygen supply to meet energy requirements. Some of these mechanisms were addressed earlier in this book as part of regulating anxiety (see Chapters 7, 8, 9, and 10).

Sex is another one of nature's mechanisms for regulating energy, and it is the most pleasurable. Like exercise, sex has a tension-releasing function. Sexual release is a way to renew the body's energy, by virtue of the deep peace and relaxation it produces. The mind, which is temporarily "lost" in complete sexual release, is also refreshed by sex.

Sexual drive, like other life energy patterns, flows in pulsations that build up to a state of sexual tension. Periodically, as the sexual tension accumulates, there is a natural need for release or discharge. Sexual tension and release are nature's way of maintaining a state of biological balance or equilibrium. Although the time period involved in this cycle seems to vary from person to person—there are no rules about what is normal—most people do experience a periodic need for sexual release. An insufficient discharge of sexual energy or a block in its natural flow leaves a person in a state of accumulated tension, which is responsible for many emotional symptoms. Anxiety can be one of the symptoms of sexual frustration.

## Sexual Disorders and Anxiety

Wilhelm Reich, a student of Freud, took an interest in sexuality in an attempt to understand psychological disorders and concluded that sexual repression is the basis of anxiety. As he put it, "It became more and more clear that the overloading of the vasovegetative system with undischarged sexual excitation is the central mechanism of anxiety." While Freud believed anxiety causes sexual repression, Reich believed sexual repression causes anxiety.

Reich also believed blocks in the flow of feelings and sexuality develop in children to avoid punishment or rejection by parents. These blocks consist of muscle tension that interferes with feeling and sexuality. Clinically, Reich noted a relationship between the ability to flow emotionally and the discharge of feeling during sex. People with muscular blocks, or *armor* as he calls it, are unable to achieve orgasm. In addition, those who are raised with a negative attitude toward sex tend to develop what is known as "pleasure anxiety," which is anchored in chronic muscle tension. These observations and concepts led Reich to a theory about sexual orgasm and its relationship to anxiety, as well as illness and health in a broader sense.

In Chapter 8, we discussed a breathing exercise derived from bioenergetic therapy and designed to help reduce tension. This is one of many exercises developed by Reich and those he trained. Besides breathing exercises, the approach emphasizes sexual release for counteracting anxiety and a healthy emotional life. Reich's formula for the relationship between sexual tension and anxiety seems almost too simple, but certainly reasonable:

$$\text{tension} \longrightarrow \text{bioelectric charge} \longrightarrow \text{bioelectric}$$
$$\text{discharge through orgasm} \longrightarrow \text{relaxation}$$

At the time Reich studied the function of orgasm, it had already been discovered by Galvani that the human body is a bioelectric organism. We can measure the electricity in muscles with a simple device called an *electromyelogram (EMG),* which is used today in neurofeedback and relaxation training. Reich's idea was that when tension builds up in the body, an electric charge—a *stasis,* as he calls it—also builds up. An accumulation of excess charge overloads the autonomic nervous system and causes anxiety.

Reich notes that sexuality and anxiety can have opposite effects. Sexual pleasure is relaxing and expansive, while anxiety contracts us, causing tension and pulling us inward toward separateness and self-protectiveness.

To maintain biological and psychological equilibrium Reich advises three thousand to four thousand orgasms in a lifetime—approximately once per week, assuming an active sexual life of fifty to sixty years. He presumes orgasms at this rate would counteract a buildup of tension and frustration, as well as the tendency for repressed feelings to harden into muscular armor. If accumulated tension can lead to anxiety, it follows that an active sexual life can reduce anxiety.

Orgasmic release is not limited to the pelvis, although the genitals are located there. Orgasm releases feelings and tension throughout the body and, therefore, Reich considered orgasm a therapeutic answer to many emotional disorders. In addition, even when feelings become blocked in childhood as a coping response in an emotionally repressed family, orgasms in adulthood can help release those blocks and return a person to a tension-free life.

On the other hand, the same fears that might be triggered by feelings can interfere with attaining orgasm. In fact, sexual arousal is a strong emotional state, as well as a time of intense physical activation. The physical aspects of sexual arousal, such as elevated heart rate, rapid breathing, increased body temperature, heightened muscle tension, and sweating, are virtually identical to the fight/flight reaction triggered by any situation involving danger. Because sexual arousal involves intense feeling, it can arouse anxiety in people who are uncomfortable with feelings.

### Sara

*This was the case with Sara, a young woman with panic disorder who talked with me about a sexual problem. Sara had been sexually abused as a girl by an uncle. She had a live-in boyfriend and two preschool children. In one of her therapy sessions, Sara said, "This is embarrassing, but I was having sexual relations with my boyfriend, and as I became aroused and my breathing became erratic, I had a panic attack. Why did it happen, when I didn't want it to?"*

*In addressing her question, I pointed out that sexual arousal has many qualities in common with anxiety. Sexual arousal involves activation of the vascular, respiratory, glandular, and other organ systems, and physically resembles the fight/flight reaction in anxiety. Although sexual arousal is normally associated with pleasure, in Sara's case there were at least two obvious complications. One was her anxiety disorder, in which panic attacks and severe anxiety were associated with body arousal. She was, at that point in therapy, still "fearful of fear." She was afraid of physical arousal because it was so similar to the frightening symptoms of panic anxiety. In fact, Sara's "erratic" breathing seemed to be a trigger for her anxiety attack. It is also likely that the gasping breaths during sexual arousal activated memories of the hyperventilation she experienced during previous anxiety episodes.*

*In addition, Sara was a victim of childhood sexual abuse, which meant some anxiety was associated with sexuality. While it did not occur consistently, Sara had problems with trust and relaxation during sexual activity with her partner. She reported she had to be "in the mood" for sex, which in her case meant feeling in control of any sexual interaction. Because orgasm and the progressive excitation leading up to it involve a surrendering to powerful feelings, as well as a loss of normal consciousness and control, Sara could not easily "give in."*

*Sara's body language also revealed her issues with sexuality. I noted she had a tendency to wear tight clothes in bright colors, with lace and exaggerated styles, and walked and behaved in a coy, seductive manner. On the surface, she appeared to be sexually potent and free. However, her seductive behavior belied her sexual anxiety and insecurity. As a victim of sexual abuse, Sara was uncomfortable with her sexuality. Assuming sex was the basis of any man's interest in her, Sara emphasized her sexuality to attract attention and bolster her self-esteem. But she needed to be in control of men, and "played" with them in a teasing way. Developmentally, her playfulness seemed to correspond to the age at which she was sexually abused. In this way, Sara was acting out some of the issues emanating from her history as a victim of sexual abuse, including her anxiety about sex. Her need to be in control was a way of handling the anxiety.*

Most, if not all, sexual problems involve anxiety. Two kinds of anxiety have been identified in sexual disorders: pleasure anxiety and performance anxiety. In the past, all male sexual disorders were called *impotence* and all female sexual disorders were called *frigidity*. Based on the work of Masters and Johnson, Kaplan, and others, it is now recognized that many sexual problems involve problems with feelings, such as inhibited desire, anxiety about pleasure or performance, and pain (not due to a medical condition). Premature ejaculation, for example, reflects anxiety about sustaining pleasure. Inorgasmia is viewed as an inhibition of the orgasm reflex due to fear of orgasm.

In addition, sexuality can be impaired by neuromuscular tension, particularly in the pelvic region. Although genital excitement may be strong, for many men it ends in premature ejaculation because a rigid pelvis cannot handle the sexual charge until that excitement can embrace the whole body. In women, anxiety about body image and sexual attractiveness, as well as feelings of inadequacy, guilt, and anger, can inhibit sexual responsiveness. When the male partner is not able to sustain sexual excitement or is insensitive to the stimulation requirements of the female partner, arousal does not reach the level required for a strong orgasm.

## Solving Sexual Problems

Because anxiety seems to be the basis of most sexual problems, and most sexual problems produce anxiety, therapy for sexual disorders includes anxiety reduction as part of the solution. Release of muscle tension is recommended for opening any blocks to the flow of life energy within the body, and exercises to accomplish this can focus on selected muscles. For releasing tension in the head and face, for example, repeatedly open the eyes wide and make frowns and grimaces with the face. Bioenergetic therapy also uses yelling, sucking, biting, and crying exercises to release tension in the jaw area.

Clinically, it is more difficult to release tension or armor in lower body areas, particularly in the pelvic region. Therapy to free up the sexual response, therefore, requires a multi-modal approach involving desensitization to physical arousal, changing attitudes toward sexuality, and helping people become more comfortable with feelings. These happen to be some of the components of effective anxiety treatment, discussed at various points elsewhere in this book, especially in Chapter 13.

A block in the natural flow of sexual energy creates a state of tension and numbness in the pelvic region. Once this pattern forms, sexual release becomes even more difficult and a vicious cycle develops in which tension and frustration intensify. To counteract this, some therapeutic exercises are suggested to relax the pelvis and improve sexual functioning.

In a normal state, the pelvis moves freely back and forth during sexual excitement, in harmony with breathing. During exhalation, the pelvis moves forward, and during inhalation the pelvis moves backwards. These rocking movements are subtle during normal breathing while sitting or standing. As breathing intensifies during sexual arousal, pelvic rocking also intensifies, and at the height of excitement and climax, they become rapid and powerful. However, anxiety immobilizes the pelvis, restraining its movement during sex. In this case, feeling during sex is cut off and full orgasmic release is prevented.

Bioenergetics is an approach to therapy that focuses on feelings and sexuality. Here is a bioenergetic exercise designed to assess mobility in the pelvic region:

### Exercise: *Assessing Your Pelvic Mobility*

- Stand in front of a mirror so you can see your back when you turn your head. Does your back look straight? Is your head held up? Is your pelvis back?

- Now make sure your feet are parallel and about six inches apart; then push your pelvis fully forward. Can you see or sense how your back rounds up or bends, causing you to lose height?

- Bring the pelvis backward slowly. Can you see the straightening of your back? What feeling is associated with each position? Which is your habitual pose?

- Now, as you stand, bend your knees slightly and try to let your pelvis hang loosely so it can move freely, like the hand at the wrist. Breathe deeply and slowly, trying to feel the respiratory wave go deep into the pelvis. Can you sense any movement in that structure? How does it feel? Can you sense any anxiety in that movement?

For people with significant overall tension, pelvic movement is likely to be restricted. However, for the person who is relatively free of tension, the orgasm reflex, or involuntary pelvic movement associated with orgasm, manifests while lying on a bed and breathing. You can check this for yourself with the following exercise:

### Exercise: *The Orgasm Reflex*

Lie on your back on a bed, with your knees raised so your feet make contact with the bed. Tilt your head back and place your arms at your sides. When your breathing is easy and deep, and no muscular tensions block the respiratory waves as they pass through the body, the pelvis moves spontaneously with each breath. It rises with the exhalation and falls on the inhalation. Your head moves in a reverse direction, upward with inhalation and backward with exhalation, with the exception that the throat moves forward with the exhalation. If you do not observe this pattern, your pelvic mobility is probably restricted by muscle tension.

Sexual activity is not the only mechanism for pelvic movement and associated pleasure. Dancing, which typically involves rhythmic movement of the pelvis, is also pleasurable for many people. It is no accident that the popularity of rock music—which rocks and rolls the pelvis— coincided with the so-called sexual revolution in the 1960s and 1970s. In fact, the early icons of rock and roll music, including Elvis Presley ("Elvis the Pelvis") and the Beatles, launched an era of music that is often associated with sexual expression and a defiance of "uptight" values and behavior. Rock music is not just for listening; it is felt in the body, especially the hips, which spontaneously move rhythmically as they do in sexual intercourse.

To help relax the pelvis and bring more feeling into sex, try the exercise on the next page.

As discussed in Chapter 8, yoga helps in developing and maintaining a flexible body, and there are a number of postures that specifically address the pelvic region. The plough (see page 135), bridge, fish, cobra, and bow postures all mobilize the hips and pelvic region. By lowering

### Exercise: *Relaxing Your Pelvis*

Stand with your feet parallel and about eight inches apart, your knees slightly bent and your weight forward. Let the pelvis drop backward, as described in the previous exercise. Try to push down the pelvic floor, while breathing deeply into the abdomen. At the same time, try to open the anal sphincter as if you would let some gas out. (Nothing will come out unless you are holding something in. I have conducted this exercise in my classes over many years, and no one has suffered any embarrassment.)

Then deliberately pull up the anus and pelvic floor by squeezing the buttocks. Can you feel tension develop? Now try to let the pelvic floor down. Does it feel more relaxed? Repeat this exercise several times to learn the difference between a tense pelvic floor and a relaxed one.

To become more aware of how you hold the pelvic floor during your normal activities, repeat this exercise a number of times during the day while walking, sitting at a desk, or engaged in any activity. You may need to pay a good deal of attention to the area before you can keep it fully relaxed, but the effort will yield a rich reward in increased sexual feeling.

body tension, yoga can help release muscular armor, mobilize feelings, and improve sexual functioning. Along with strength training and aerobic exercise, yoga can improve body image and self-confidence. In fact, any practice that improves health, self-esteem, and body image is likely to have a positive effect on a person's sexuality.

## Healing from Sexual Abuse

Sexual abuse was discussed in Chapter 5 as one potential cause of anxiety. Among the devastating effects of sexual abuse are conflicted feelings about sexual desire because of the emotional pain that can be evoked by a sexual experience or even arousal. To cope with such "pleasure anxiety," victims of sexual abuse may cut off sexual feelings altogether. Or they may develop strong needs for control in sexual relations. Trust can also become a significant issue.

In some cases, victims of sexual abuse reenact the trauma history with new partners, in an effort to work through the emotional pain and achieve a more comfortable outcome. The effect of sexual abuse can manifest in the body as muscular rigidity of the pelvis or other affected regions (muscles appear to have memory and can store the feelings involved in trauma). In addition, feelings of insecurity and inadequacy about body image are likely to develop in victims of sexual abuse. Furthermore, sexual abuse often triggers a post-traumatic stress reaction, causing anxiety symptoms that can interfere with a healthy sexual life.

### Rachel

*One of my patients, Rachel, had a history of sexual abuse that resulted in several emotional disorders, including depression, panic anxiety disorder, and PTSD. What brought Rachel for professional help was stress overload, resulting from a recent relocation; full-time work as a nurse while parenting two children; temporary housing in a new community while waiting for her old house to sell; and the loss of both parents, who passed away within the previous year.*

*Rachel had a successful therapy experience with significant reduction in anxiety and terminated therapy after approximately seven months. However, several months later, she contacted me in distress. Rachel was having dreams and memories about an older brother sexually abusing her. She recalled, one by one, the specifics of each incident, until she put the entire picture together. We worked together for several months to help her through this process, which included dealing with anger as well as sorting out the impact of the abuse history on various aspects of her personality, sexuality, and social functioning.*

*Not once during her initial treatment for anxiety did Rachel mention sexual abuse or reveal any signs of it, although many other issues were addressed. This turned out to mirror her family's emotional style, as reflected in statements Rachel made in therapy, such as, "My parents never told me they loved me," "We never talked about our feelings," and "I felt I couldn't tell my mother about the abuse."*

*What was notable about Rachel's case was her inability to face her sexual abuse history—or even remember it—until she acquired some emotional skills and achieved a degree of anxiety recovery. In other words, Rachel could only deal with the sexual abuse after she developed the skills that would permit her to handle the repressed emotional pain.*

## A Healthy Sex Life

In a healthy sex life, there is no anxiety about sexual excitement, intimate contact, and release of control during orgasm. Normal sex involves a complete convulsive discharge in the embrace of a love partner, with a momentary loss of consciousness. Control is joyfully surrendered as the trance of sexual excitement takes over. Although the genitals are sensitized by an infusion of blood, the whole body participates in healthy sex. The intensity of sexual feeling and build up of a powerful energy toward explosive release are pleasurable and without anxiety.

Likewise, no anxiety is associated with the sense of boundary loss and merging of two bodies into one. The ego loss in sex is called by the French *le petit mort,* meaning "the little death," and renewal following sexual release is like a rebirth. After an orgasm, there is a feeling of deep peacefulness, and a healing sleep may follow. In a sexually healthy person, all this takes place spontaneously and without conflict, ambivalence, or anxiety.

Clearly, a healthy and active sex life can make a difference in anxiety regulation. Orgasmic release maintains healthy biological equilibrium and counteracts the effects of stress. Sexual release also induces relaxation, which is essential for managing anxiety. In these ways, sex can be one of the most important and pleasurable aspects of stress control and creating a life beyond anxiety.

## Obstacles to a Healthy Sex Life

The full benefits of a healthy sex life are experienced by only a minority of Americans. Large surveys indicate that only 15 percent of women and 65 percent of men *always* have an orgasm during sex. The numbers improve if *often* is added to the statement. In this case, 61 percent of women and 93 percent of men always or often have orgasms during lovemaking. On the other hand, only 44 percent of women and 56 percent of men feel they are functioning at their biological maximum.

How often do Americans have sex? A definitive survey of 3,500 Americans, ranging in age from 18 to 59, suggests Americans fall into three groups. One-third have sex twice a week, one-third a few times a month, and one-third a few times a year. It appears that only one-third of Americans have sex at least once a week, as Reich advises. This is not the complete story, however, because having sex does not mean having orgasms. Even so, if Reich is right about the need for regular orgasmic release in order to maintain healthy biological equilibrium, approximately two-thirds of Americans do not meet the criteria.

Men and women differ biologically in their sexual response, and this must be understood and taken into consideration for a sexual relationship to be fulfilling. The male sexual response consists of a single cycle of excitation, during which tension and associated pleasure build up to a point of "ejaculatory inevitability," followed by orgasmic release. Recovery from orgasmic release in men is a relatively short period, during which interest in further stimulation drops sharply.

The female sexual response also consists of an excitation phase, but it is typically of longer duration, which means more time is usually required for women to reach the point of orgasm. In women, the point of orgasmic release can be a single moment or multiple moments, and the recovery phase is slower than in men, resulting in a more gradual loss of interest in sexual stimulation.

In heterosexual couples, men who assume their female partners have the same sexual response as their own are likely to climax too soon, resulting in loss of interest in their partners' sexual pleasure. Women who do not understand the differences between the male and female sexual response may think there is something wrong with them sexually, especially if they do not experience orgasm at the same time as their male partners. If we consider differences in couples' sexual histories, skills, and experiences, as well as differences in emotional and communication styles between men and women, the potential for conflict and anxiety about sexuality is high. These issues can occur in sexually healthy people, but complications and frustration are even more likely when other emotional problems are brought to bed.

For those who are not in an intimate relationship, masturbation serves as an option for pleasure and release of sexual tension. However,

I am frequently reminded in my therapy practice about how anxiety arousing this form of sexual release can be for those who are misinformed. Many people have been taught that masturbation is shameful and even sinful, and they experience guilt and anxiety about this totally natural act. The problem is complicated even more when sexually explicit stimuli are used to enhance arousal, as society seems to have a double standard about pornography.

For gay, lesbian, and bisexual couples, anxiety about sexuality can be reinforced by society's attitudes toward alternative lifestyles. Although people in some regions seem to be "gay and lesbian friendly," those in other regions are less tolerant if not outright hostile toward alternative lifestyles. To add to anxiety, it is actually illegal in some states to engage in sexual practices that are common among same-sex partners.

## Conclusion

Sexual issues can both cause and result from anxiety. As a source of anxiety, we discussed the impact of sexual abuse; lack of accurate sex education (leading to confusion, guilt, and anxiety about sexual functioning); and cultural attitudes toward nontraditional sexual orientation and certain practices such as masturbation. For many people, it is anxiety arousing to even discuss their sexuality.

Some theories view sexuality as an energy system in which anxiety is the result of accumulated sexual tension. When anxiety about sexual feelings or intense physical arousal is involved, discharge of sexual energy is blocked and orgasm can be difficult. This results in tension and anxiety.

"Pleasure anxiety" and tension are key factors in most sexual disorders (such as inhibited sexual desire, premature ejaculation, inorgasmia, and even pain). Some of these sexual problems can be addressed without professional help, using exercises designed to help people relax and develop a more natural sexual response. Professional counseling is advisable for some conditions, such as the effects of sexual abuse.

Sexuality can be a healing experience for those with anxiety. Sex is not only one of nature's mechanisms for releasing tension and stress, but is also a source of pleasure and well-being.

# CHAPTER 16

||||||||||||||||||||||||||||

# *Spirituality and Anxiety*

In this chapter I address anxiety as a faith issue, and I suggest that anxiety can be reduced by developing a spiritual attitude. This perspective raises questions about how to understand spirituality and how to cultivate spiritual qualities (such as faith, hope, peace, and trust) that can reduce our anxiety. In this chapter, we address such intriguing questions as:

- What are some key spiritual qualities and how can we cultivate them in ourselves?

- Can anxiety be reduced by faith or belief in a higher power?

- Does meaning and purpose in life reduce anxiety?

- How does fear of death correlate with worry, medical phobias, and other symptoms of anxiety?

- How can we view life and death in a way that reduces anxiety?

In addressing these questions, I express some opinions and share personal experiences, but my purpose is not to promote any particular religion. I distinguish between religion and spirituality, and I emphasize spiritual ideas and qualities that can be helpful in dealing with anxiety.

## Spiritual Qualities

To begin viewing anxiety from a spiritual perspective, let's consider the opposite of anxiety and fear. If we want to replace anxiety, with what would we replace it?

What comes to my mind when I think about the opposite of anxiety are inner qualities, such as peace, contentment, self-confidence, courage, optimism, hope, and the faith that things will work out. These are spiritual qualities and they coincide with the goals of anxiety recovery in most cases. Indeed, these qualities are desired by most people, although there is much confusion about how to achieve them. Anxiety inhibits these spiritual qualities, but the task of recovery is an opportunity to cultivate these qualities and enrich our lives.

Although anxiety is a form of emotional suffering, suffering is a powerful incentive for change and growth. Therefore, an anxiety disorder is an opportunity for self-improvement and spiritual growth. Our anxiety might be a signal that we are too stressed or that something is missing in our lives. Anxiety can alert us to reevaluate our priorities if our focus is on materialism at the expense of health or joy. If we view anxiety from a spiritual perspective—as an opportunity for reassessment of our values or lifestyle—it can become a gateway to greater satisfaction.

This perspective also applies to therapy for anxiety disorders. It is important to work with a therapist who understands the spiritual aspects of an anxiety disorder. Anxiety treatment needs to go beyond symptom reduction—though that is no simple accomplishment in itself. Therapy must encompass wholeness and spirituality, whereby anxiety is understood as a call to acquire skills for living more effectively and reaching a higher level of life satisfaction.

## My Spirituality

My spirituality developed without any religious training as a child. My father was an atheist who related to his Judaism as an ethnic rather than a religious identity. My mother referred to herself as an agnostic and celebrated Christian holidays, such as Christmas and Easter, as secular rather than religious events. Our family never went to synagogue or church, although we observed key Jewish and Christian holidays, such as Passover, Christmas, Chanukah, and Easter. Ours was an interfaith family, with no deep religious affiliations. However, there were clear moral and ethical values in my family, consistent with the fundamental tenets of most religions.

A challenging incident occurred when I was a senior at Yale. As the war in Vietnam intensified, the Selective Service System ended the student deferments, and I applied for a military service exemption as a conscientious objector. Such status normally required a recognized religious affiliation. I wrote my application honestly and based on the facts of my upbringing, and after a personal interview with my draft board, I was granted the conscientious objector classification. Apparently, the draft board considered the ethical principles by which I lived to be equivalent to a religion. As a conscientious objector, I served two years in alternative military service, working as a therapist with military dependents at a residential treatment center.

As an adult, I became a spiritual seeker, searching for answers to the existential questions of life by exploring many religious traditions and spiritual practices. My spiritual quest was part of my anxiety recovery process. As I began to answer the fundamental questions of life and death for myself, the ground became more solid and my insecurity, fears, and anxiety diminished. The fruits of my spiritual practices included a sense of purpose, more self-confidence, greater personal power, greater capacity for love, and trust that things would generally work out for me. As I cultivated these spiritual qualities, I began to worry less and enjoy life more.

## Buddhism and Anxiety Recovery

Although I studied a number of different spiritual traditions, I found Buddhism to be directly helpful in my anxiety recovery. What are the essential teachings of Buddhism and how do they help reduce anxiety?

After meditating for two years under the Bodhi tree, Gautama Buddha (the Enlightened One) declared the Four Noble Truths. The first noble truth is that "life is suffering," meaning that suffering is inherent in living. The second is that suffering is caused by "attachment," "craving," or "desire." This includes attachment to our own thoughts and separate identities, an issue of special relevance for anxiety. The third is that freedom can be attained through nonattachment, or learning how to go beyond craving, addiction, attachment, and separateness. Finally, the fourth noble truth is that the way to nonattachment is through meditation, moral conduct, and attaining wisdom.

Buddhism is a psychological approach that speaks to the heart of anxiety recovery. Its primary teachings include the ideas of nonjudgement, nonattachment, moral conduct, attaining wisdom, and practice of mindfulness. Mindfulness meditation, as discussed in Chapter 7, can help us recognize and step back from our obsessive thoughts, need to control, addictive attachments, and ways of avoiding anxious feelings. Meditation also leads to peace of mind, one of the opposites of anxiety. And the Buddhist emphasis on moral conduct and simplicity (these are universal spiritual principles) can serve to lower stress, guilt, and anxiety. Finally, cultivating wisdom is helpful in understanding the sources of anxiety and some of the solutions.

There are a number of parallels between Buddhist practice and psychotherapy for anxiety disorders. Both of these disciplines involve learning to observe, relax, let go, and attain equanimity (a nonjudgmental attitude toward anxiety). Both involve cognitive change, or changing the way we react to our thoughts. Both are processes for personal improvement that require patience and compassion toward oneself.

## The Purpose of Life

What is the purpose of life, and how does it relate to anxiety and fear?

As I see it, the purpose of life is to live a life with purpose. A life with purpose is one with a sense of meaning or direction. We know when we are serving a meaningful purpose because certain feelings, such as passion and enthusiasm, affirm we are on the right path. Our heart feels full when we have purpose, and empty when we are without purpose. The purpose of life is mysterious, in part because each person's purpose in life is unique. We must each discover our own personal life purpose.

I experience purpose as a beckoning or calling, as a magnetic pull in a particular direction, although I cannot always make out the details of the landscape ahead. I have moments of awareness about the degree to which I am on course, about the extent to which I am fulfilling my purpose. When I am aligned with my purpose, I have energy, passion for life, and a sense of direction. I feel a subtle gracefulness. On the other hand, when I deviate from my purpose, I become anxious, defensive, and tense.

## Being Anxious Does Not Always Mean
## We Are Going in the Wrong Direction

Sometimes anxiety arises as we face a new challenge or phobic situation, even while we are heading in the apparently right direction. In fact, sometimes anxiety means we are doing what is needed in order to grow and develop. In this sense, anxiety can play a significant role in helping us shape a life with purpose and meaning, and can keep us on track.

## What We Think We Want

I find it helpful to distinguish between what I *think* I want and what I *really* want. Material things, such as money, job or career, house, car, family, educational degree, and travel, may be desirable, but they are usually symbols of or methods to attain what I really want. What I really want are certain inner experiences, such as security, self-worth, contentment, freedom, self-respect, peace of mind, and love. These inner experiences are spiritual and deeply satisfying.

Material things tend to lose their luster, and our excitement about them wears off because they do not satisfy an inner longing for something more fulfilling, more spiritual. There is nothing wrong with having nice things—these are flowers on the path of life—but they do not necessarily lead to an enduring or deep satisfaction. In fact, I have found that possessing more things results in more stress and maintenance responsibilities, and less time for relaxing and enjoying the simple pleasures, such as taking walks, being with nature, meditating, and enjoying the company of my loved ones and friends.

Recognizing these distinctions helps us reduce stress and anxiety, feel more content, and focus more on cultivating spiritual qualities than on acquiring material possessions. We can also learn to appreciate what we already have and to become less dependent on external things.

## Spirituality and Control

One of the most pervasive aspects of the anxiety personality style is the need for control. Those who fit this profile tend to feel most comfortable when they are in control, and most vulnerable and threatened when they are not in control. Their strong control needs lead them to seek routine, structure, and predictability, and even make efforts to control other people in order to feel safe and secure. As a result, they spend considerable time and energy anticipating the future, scrutinizing other people, and anxiously monitoring the environment, as well as their own body changes, in order to feel prepared for what may happen.

A high need for control is at odds with life, which involves far too many variables beyond our influence to allow us to predict what will happen, let alone control it. As a more effective alternative, consider the idea that we are not in control, but can nevertheless feel safe and secure. What could provide such reassurance, other than a higher power before which we give up our futile attempts to control?

We can gain control by giving up control, by putting it in the hands of a higher power. This does not mean we become passive, but that we do our best while leaving room for life to unfold according to larger plans. Nor does this mean we should blindly trust or passively accept whatever happens. As a Sufi saying warns, "Trust in God, but tie your camel to a tree."

Research has demonstrated that belief in a higher power can improve health. For example, an analysis of more than 250 health studies found a positive relationship between "religious observance" (defined as praying, attending a house of worship, or simply belief in a higher power) and health (both physical and emotional). This overwhelmingly positive relationship between religious observance and health is found equally among men and women, different races, and people with different geographical, educational, and medical histories.

It appears that spirituality can help with fear and anxiety by giving us a place to put our worries. We can obtain control of anxiety by giving it up to a higher power.

Paradoxically, I find some people who were raised with religion have difficulty attaining spirituality and coming to terms with God or a higher power. Some religious background experiences, such as harsh discipline in religious school, boring church services, empty religious rituals, and moral teachings based on fear and threat, are traumatic for children. Such experiences can turn children off to spirituality or lead to a fear-based concept of God.

## *Paula*

*One of my patients exemplifies the way spirituality can be impaired by a negative religious background. Paula was a quiet and passive woman, who was raised in a strict Catholic environment. Unfortunately, she was disciplined abusively by a nun in Catholic school. In one instance, she was smacked with a ruler on her hands in front of her class. In another instance, she was given a spanking over the nun's knee, again in the presence of her peers. What was most astounding, however, was that Paula's parents condoned the school's discipline methods, and she felt they showed little concern for her feelings.*

*Paula also reported that, in her community, it was common practice for the Catholic priests to enter freely into the homes of parishioners, without knocking or prior notice. Combined with an abusive father and a passive mother, Paula's experience of religion was a mixture of fear, shame, and guilt. She was fearful of abandonment, as well as punishment by authority figures. God apparently existed, but He was violent, unkind, and unprotective. As a result of her background, Paula had much to overcome before she could see God as benevolent, as a source of strength and reassurance in her anxiety recovery.*

## Anxiety and Death

Death evokes tremendous fear and anxiety in many people. Why is death feared, and how does the fear of death contribute to anxiety?

Death represents the unknown, the ultimate loss of control, and separation from our physical identity. Considering the profile of the anxiety personality, particularly the need to be in control, discomfort with uncertainty, all-or-nothing thinking, and preference for structure and predictability, it is not a surprise that, for many people, death is cause for fear. As long as we fear death, we tend to experience anxiety about many aspects of life, such as illness or symptoms that might be life-threatening, as well as uncertainty, unpredictability, and the unknown in general.

Death is a mystery because no one knows for sure what happens after death. Who has the credibility to tell us what death, or beyond, is like? Some clues are provided by individuals who have survived near-death experiences. The consensus of such reports is that death, or at least the moments immediately after death, can be safe and uplifting. However, these anecdotal stories are limited to the experience of dying and do not answer the question of what happens beyond that. Let's explore some ways of thinking about death that can reduce anxiety.

Meher Baba, a revered Indian guru who lived from 1894 to 1969, said that death is "like throwing away clothes which have become useless through wear and tear." Commenting specifically on fear of death, he explained:

> Some people are particularly afraid of the exact moment of death because they anticipate unbearable pain at that instant. In reality, all physical suffering experienced during illness or just before death terminates at the moment of death. The process of the actual dropping of the body is quite painless, contrary to the superstition that a person experiences indescribable agonies in death.

Meher Baba adds, "If death has any value, it is to teach the individual the true art of life."

The issue of death is at the core of most, if not all, religious and wisdom teachings. The essence of Christian teachings about death, for example, is that the quality of our lives is judged after death, and our fate in the afterlife is based on how we conduct ourselves in this life. Heaven or hell is where we go in the next life, as determined by our choices and behavior in this life. There is one exception to final judgment, namely, forgiveness. Through repentance, we have an opportunity to counteract the consequences of wrongful conduct. Recognition of our errors and taking responsibility for changing our ways can lead to forgiveness and redemption. This is a hopeful idea that gives us some control over our own fate.

The teachings of Judaism are similar, but differ in an interesting way as far as the concepts of heaven and hell are concerned. Judaism is less preoccupied with the afterlife and more focused on the consequences of moral conduct in this life. Judaism takes life one year at a time, and each person is written annually into the "book of life," based on his or her conduct during the preceding year. In fact, there is a one-week window

**Exercise:** *Back from the Future*

Relax, breathe deeply, and close your eyes. Imagine, in whatever form it comes, that you are at a future point in time near the end of your life. Your physical incarnation is ending and it is time to say goodbye to what you have known. You are poised for going through the doorway into the next stage of existence.

What do you feel at this moment? How do you feel about the life you have lived so far? Was it the life you hoped for? Did you do what was important to you? If not, what was missing? Have you left anything unfinished? What would you have done differently? Is there anyone to whom you need to talk, and if so, what do you need to say? Reflect quietly on these questions for a while and take note of your answers.

Now, inexplicably, a miracle has occurred. You are being offered more time, another chance. You are not at the end. You can resume your life in the present.

Will you go on living as usual or will your visit to the threshold of death help you live differently? Will you worry as much or will you trust more? Will you avoid and hold back due to anxiety or will you follow your heart, even if that involves unknowns and risks?

between the high holidays of Rosh Hashanah and Yom Kippur when Jews have an opportunity to make amends for any wrongful behavior, in hopes of softening the consequences. In the Jewish religion, heaven and hell are not places after death, but states of mind while we are living. Life can be "heaven on earth" or a "living hell," depending on our own conduct.

Similarly, in Hinduism it is believed that we experience the consequences of our behavior in terms of *karma*. The belief is that our conduct while living determines the quality of our life in future incarnations. Put differently, our life circumstances, or karma, is determined by the choices we have made in the past. In this view, we can improve our condition by right action, although the rewards may not be immediate. This seems similar to Christianity, Judaism, and Islam in that all these religions speak of our power to make choices that come back to haunt or reward us in the future. Even Buddhism, which is not a theistic religion, emphasizes our power to relieve our own suffering through right action (moral conduct), mindfulness meditation, and compassion toward ourselves.

Anxiety recovery can be enhanced through a spiritual understanding of death. Most wisdom traditions seem to agree that we go on to subsequent stages of existence and that death is one step in this ongoing process. Death is not the end point and does not need to be feared. By our everyday choices, we can each create our future experience. This way of looking at life and death gives us more control and allows us to replace anxiety and helplessness with actions that can bring greater peace and less suffering.

In my clinical work with anxiety patients, I have created an exercise that uses awareness of death to help us live in the present with less anxiety. This exercise can be practiced safely at home.

### Seeing Your Own Divinity

It has been said that we are made in God's image. This means divinity is within each of us. How do we recognize the divine aspect in ourselves and in others?

As discussed in Chapter 4, the anxiety personality style is recognizable by its perfectionism, high standards, need to please others, fear of rejection, sensitivity to criticism, and other traits. Those with this personality style tend to focus on their shortcomings and imperfections, as well as judge themselves harshly. They may have difficulty being compassionate toward themselves when they make a mistake or "fail" to live up to unreasonably high standards.

We can accelerate our anxiety recovery through greater compassion, respect, and sensitivity toward ourselves. We can treat ourselves as God would or—to leave God out of it—we can treat ourselves the way we would treat a friend who is feeling self-critical about a "failure," "mistake," or "imperfection." What would we say to a friend under those conditions? We would be gentle, caring, and respectful, and we would offer a wider perspective by emphasizing our friend's good qualities and positive intentions. The next exercise is designed to help us treat ourselves as we would treat a friend.

### The Friend Principle

Imagine that a friend of yours is feeling down or disappointed about not doing well in a particular situation. Perhaps your friend feels shame, discouragement, or embarrassment about a mistake or poor choice. For some reason, your friend is exhibiting self-criticism and negative self-judgment.

What would you say to this friend? How would you treat him or her? Would you condemn your friend and reinforce his or her bad feelings or would you offer emotional support and a perspective on the situation to help him or her see a more balanced picture? Would you be patient or impatient? Would you try to help your friend learn from the experience or criticize him or her?

Think about or write down your responses before continuing this exercise.

In most cases, people find it natural to be kind, understanding, and emotionally supportive toward others in need. From now on, treat yourself the way you would treat your friend. Say only those things to your self that you would say to a friend. Be compassionate and respectful toward your self and view mistakes as learning opportunities.

## The Language of Spirituality

In what language does God or a higher power speak? How can we recognize divine presence in our lives? And how else can we call on a higher power to help reduce and manage anxiety?

God seems to speak in a variety of languages, including dreams; images; coincidences; and for some attuned listeners, actual words. These seem to be coded messages that require deciphering or interpretation.

It is said that God's voice can be heard most clearly in stillness and silence. This is what is meant by the biblical passage "Be still and know that I am God." In quiet moments, when we are relaxed and still, we are more open to receiving spiritual messages. Eileen Caddy, cofounder of Findhorn, a spiritual community in Scotland, shares a personal experience that illustrates this kind of communication:

I was aware of a great noise all around and then the noise died down and there was great stillness. In the stillness I could hear what seemed to be the faint ticking of a clock. As I listened very intently, the sound became louder and clearer.

Then I heard the words: "I am always here but unless you become consciously aware of Me and of My divine Presence, you cannot hear My voice. Therefore, still that which is without so that you can hear that which is within."

In my own life, a number of similar experiences stand out as illustrations of spiritual communication. These experiences usually occurred in quiet moments—during the night or early in the morning—while I was relaxed, open, and turned toward the higher power. In one instance I experienced a convincingly lucid conversation with God. The occurrence took place at a time of personal turmoil and high anxiety, when I had asked for guidance. The following dialogue is etched in my memory and continues to reassure me:

**Me:** Dear God, will you be there for me?

**God:** Yes, I am there every step and every minute.

**Me:** Will I be okay?

**God:** Yes, everything will be okay.

**Me:** What will happen?

**God:** Whatever happens, everything will be okay.

**Me:** Can you tell me what will happen?

**God:** There are many forces, currents, and crosswinds operating, which will affect the details. Look beyond and know that everything will be okay.

**Me:** I see the sun rising and I feel that things will be better for me. Can I trust that?

**God:** The rising sun represents hope and dreams coming true. Everything will be okay.

These words seemed to have both a universal and a personal quality. A higher power spoke to me with a broadly applicable truth that felt valid, profound in its simplicity, and reassuring. Since that experience, I worry less and trust that things will work out.

To help you to develop a personal relationship with God or a higher source of wisdom, I offer the following exercise:

### Exercise: *The Wise Friend*

Relax, breathe deeply, and close your eyes. Imagine the wisest and most benevolent Being possible. Perhaps this Being has a physical form or perhaps it is more of a "presence" without visible form. Feel or picture the qualities of wisdom, compassion, kindness, fairness, and love that radiate from this special Being. This Being is your Wise Friend.

Locate the coordinates of your Wise Friend. Is your Wise Friend within you, above you, behind you, over your shoulder, or all around you? Use all of your senses to experience the presence of your Wise Friend. Practice making contact with this Being through repeated visits and cultivate a relationship by spending time together.

From time to time, you may have a deep question and need for an answer. Bring it to your Wise Friend and quietly listen for an answer in the form of feelings, dreams, images, or even words that seem to come to you from this source.

### The Body as a Temple of Spirituality

Spirituality takes form in the human body, and we must understand this connection to fully understand anxiety. The idea that the physical body is a temple or dwelling place for spirit is found in the Bible. Here are several Biblical references to this idea:

> "Do you not know that you are the temple of God, and that the Spirit of God dwells in you?"

> "Do you not know that your body is the temple of the Holy Spirit who is in you, whom you have from God, and you are not your own?"

"If anyone defiles the temple of God, God will destroy him. For the temple of God is holy, which temple is you."

If the body is a dwelling place for spirit, what is the effect of anxiety on this relationship? In *The Spirituality of the Body,* Alexander Lowen says, "Fear has a paralyzing effect on the spirit. It freezes the body, contracting the muscles. When this state persists, the body becomes numb, and the individual no longer feels his fear. This is the state in which most people come to therapy."

In other words, fear diminishes spirituality by contracting the muscles, as though squeezing spirit out of its dwelling place. As discussed in Chapter 8, anxiety causes the body to develop a protective pattern of muscular tension, or body armor. This can be adaptive, but in extreme cases the door closes to feelings and spiritual energy.

Lowen proposed that it is possible to increase spirituality through muscle relaxation, as well as breath work, both of which open the body to an inflow of spiritual energy. Some specific techniques for accomplishing this are provided in Chapter 8. In addition, it is possible to reduce anxiety through infusion of spiritual energy. This may explain why certain spiritual practices, such as meditation (see Chapter 7) and yoga (see Chapter 8), help reduce anxiety. Anxiety can also be reduced by cultivating spiritual qualities and a personal relationship with a higher power. Guidelines and suggestions for accomplishing this are offered at the end of this chapter.

### Faith

From a spiritual point of view, lack of faith is the root of anxiety and fear. What is faith and how can it counteract anxiety?

Faith is based on the assumption that there is a higher power or a natural order in the universe, and that there is a reason why things happen the way they do. Faith helps us to accept what is beyond our control and to be positive about the future. Faith allows us to take negative outcomes in stride because it is based on the idea of a higher plan. Having faith gives us security and reassurance that things will work out. With faith, we can trust that whatever happens was meant to be.

Some people have difficulty with faith because it implies that our lives are predetermined by a higher power, and that we have little control over what happens to us. However, it is reasonable to think that our life experience is determined by a collaboration or combination of personal responsibility and divine intervention. Even so, for those who are uncomfortable with the idea of a higher power, I suggest thinking of having faith in ourselves. We can have faith in ourselves based on confidence in our skills and resources for handling whatever may happen.

Faith and anxiety are incompatible. Having faith, as outlined above, makes it unnecessary to worry or feel anxious about what may happen in the future. Faith allows us to trust that things will work out either as intended by a higher power, or by own influence, or by a combination of both.

### Cultivating Spiritual Vitality

How can we increase our spirituality, and thereby reduce our anxiety? Are there any specific practices for cultivating the spiritual qualities discussed in this chapter?

Many practices and activities contribute to spiritual awareness and help develop the qualities of faith, hope, acceptance, security, and a sense of purpose—qualities that counteract anxiety. The following are some suggestions based on my personal experience as well as research on spirituality:

*Meditate:* Meditation is the most essential spiritual practice and should be practiced daily. In the quiet stillness of meditation, it is easy to attune to higher vibrations and the inner voice of God. Instructions for meditation practice are found in Chapter 7.

*Spend time with nature:* Spending time with nature brings you in contact with higher energies and the world "as it is." Contact with nature increases awareness of forces larger than yourself. This was known to naturalists, such as Henry Thoreau, John Muir, Ansel Adams, and others, and is the basis for the preservation of nature in our national parks system. In addition, fresh air invigorates the spirit by increasing intake of prana, or spiritual energy.

*Read and study works that cultivate spirituality:* The possibilities for spiritually inspiring reading are endless. They include biographies of great spiritual figures—such as Mahatma Gandhi, the Dalai Lama, Dr. Martin Luther King, Jr., Sri Aurobindo, the Buddha, Black Elk, the Prophet Muhammed, the Baal Shem Tov, Moses, and Jesus Christ—and other books about spirituality as well as spiritual texts themselves. A page or two a day can feed your growing spirituality.

*Practice relaxation:* You are more open to spirituality when your body is relaxed and free of tension. The flow of life forces is greatest in a loose and receptive state. Stretch your muscles and exercise regularly. Check your breathing frequently to ensure it is deep and full. See Chapters 7 and 8 for guidance on relaxation, exercise, and breathing practices.

*Develop physical strength and health:* Good health, energy, and strength are necessary for overcoming anxiety, as well as for joyful living. Developing these qualities increases personal power and enables you to do the work of anxiety recovery. Proper nutrition, adequate rest, and exercise are ways of building and maintaining these capacities. Hatha yoga, strength training, and the martial arts are also effective approaches. See Chapters 7, 8, and 10 for more information.

*Seek out social and spiritual support groups:* Spiritual energy often works through and between people. This is expressed in the biblical passage, "Wherever two or more are gathered in My name, there shall I be." It is helpful to participate in a support group, preferably one with spiritual inclinations. Book discussion groups, therapy groups, self-help groups, and church or temple activity groups are all supportive.

*Volunteer service:* Some professions, such as psychology, call for a percentage of "gratis work," service that is offered free of charge to those in need. When you volunteer your time and energy without material gain, or even perform a simple act to help another, you profit spiritually. Some examples include coaching an athletic team, chaperoning a school event, participating in a "green-up day," and providing meals-on-wheels.

*Donate to causes that reflect your values:* Giving to a spiritual cause is another way to increase your spirituality. This can include charitable donations of money or goods to organizations that represent your spiritual values, including a church or temple, as well as secular organizations, such as groups working to preserve the environment, public radio and television, and community service organizations. Whereas paying taxes is a legal obligation, spiritual giving comes from the heart, and therefore enlarges your spiritual dimension.

*Travel:* An excellent way to gain spiritual perspective is to travel, so you can see how people in other cultures live and deal with life. Travel expands your awareness, and usually your appreciation for what you have. If you can afford to travel, you are likely to notice that the majority of people in other parts of the world are less fortunate in a material sense. This can open your heart. However, you do not have to go to exotic places to expand your awareness. Visiting any major American inner city can be a startling reality check. On the other hand, seeing the awesome beauty of the world can also draw you closer to God.

*Open up emotionally:* Getting out of your head and into your feelings and intuition can help develop your spirituality. Learn how to identify, experience, and express your feelings as a path to spiritual openness. Some techniques are offered in Chapter 13.

*Practice love:* Love is the primary vehicle through which spirituality is expressed. Practicing a loving attitude toward others, as well as toward yourself, is a powerful way to cultivate your spirituality. Remember that you usually get back what you give.

*Interact with God or a higher power:* It can be helpful to actively communicate with God by asking questions and listening for answers. I have a running dialogue with God in which I ask for guidance with virtually every act and decision. You can consciously dedicate every act to enhancing your spirituality. It can also be helpful to place symbols of your relationship with a higher power in locations you encounter daily, such as doorways, refrigerator, desk, computer, car, bathroom mirror, and so on. The symbol can be a flower, cross, Star of David, holy name, or something else of your own choosing. Each time you notice the symbol, take a second to remember God or affirm your spirituality.

## Conclusion

Overcoming anxiety means more than learning how to manage stress, face our phobic situations, and think positively. It also means developing spiritual qualities, such as serenity, wisdom, nonattachment, trust, faith, hope, and a sense of purpose. Spiritual practice is the wellspring from which these essential qualities are drawn.

As a therapist, I try to create a proper environment and provide a map for recovery, but there is something more to the process. There is a third force in the therapy office. Together, patient, therapist, and a higher power are the alchemy for anxiety recovery.

# CHAPTER 17

# Should You Take Medication
# for Anxiety — or Not?

People tend to have strong feelings—negative or positive—about medication. The use of medication for anxiety is controversial even among health-care professionals, who differ in their view of what role medication should play in anxiety treatment. Physicians and psychiatrists, for example, tend to value medication as a primary tool for helping people with anxiety, while psychotherapists lean toward non-drug treatments for anxiety. In this chapter, I try to present a balanced picture of the benefits and pitfalls of medications for anxiety.

### Biological Approaches and Medication for Anxiety

Treatment with medications is based on a biological view of anxiety. It has been hypothesized that anxiety sufferers have a unique brain chemistry—perhaps a highly sensitive amygdala, or the "smoke alarm" in the limbic (emotional) area of the brain—that predisposes them to react strongly to many types of stimuli.

When it appropriated funds for brain research, the United States Congress declared the 1990s the "decade of the brain." During those years, exciting advances in brain-imaging technology and in understanding brain chemistry fueled optimism about using drugs to treat depression, anxiety, and other emotional disorders. For example, brain research showed that anxiety and depression are associated with lower levels of the neurotransmitter, serotonin. In sufficient quantity, serotonin seems to contribute to positive mood and feelings of well-being. Although these drugs can be helpful in controlling some anxiety symptoms, they have some significant pitfalls, which are discussed later in this chapter.

In my view, changes in brain chemistry could reasonably be considered a result of anxiety, rather than a cause of anxiety. Although anxiety symptoms can be reduced by medications, that does not mean anxiety is caused by inadequate supplies of arousal-inhibiting chemicals in the body. In fact, anxiety symptoms may reflect good biological response capabilities—quick fight/flight reactions—that have been activated by trauma, stress, or misperceptions of danger.

It is appealing to think of eliminating anxiety by using drugs to alter brain chemistry or short-circuit the biological sensitivity component of anxiety. How convenient it would be if we could resolve anxiety by controlling the body's reactions. Indeed, one type of drug used in treating panic disorder (the beta-blocker) does inhibit some physical symptoms associated with anxiety. Due to their effect on heart rate and blood pressure, beta-blockers are widely prescribed for controlling hypertension. Propranolol (Inderal) and atenolol (Tenormin) are two common beta-blockers. See the table on page 253 for more information about dosage and target symptoms.

## The Popularity of Anxiety Medications

In addition to advances in brain research, there are some cultural explanations for the popularity of drug treatments for anxiety, as well as for other emotional and medical problems.

One reason is a loosening of regulations on drug advertising. Drug manufacturers have in recent years advertised directly to the public using television and print media. Such ads typically target anxiety disorders; they identify the symptoms of anxiety and imply the disorder will be relieved by a particular drug. One compelling example is a television ad that shows a number of distressed adults wearing name tags such as "Worried," "Shy," "Panicky," "Obsessive," and "Phobic." These images are followed by a party scene in which all the people appear to be interacting happily after taking the drug (Paxil).

Most drug ads end with the suggestion, "Ask your doctor if *(name of medication)* is right for you," or "Ask your doctor about *(name of medication)*." This type of direct advertising is designed to create a market for drugs, and some critics consider this practice unethical because the public is not trained to diagnose emotional disorders or to understand the complications and dangers associated with medicines.

Another trend is managed care, an attempt by the health-insurance industry to control the cost of health care. As a psychologist who deals regularly with health insurance, I am familiar with the policies and procedures used by managed-care companies. One strategy has been an emphasis on medication as a lower-cost approach to mental-health treatment. For example, one insurance company sends me computer-generated letters reminding me to consider medication for my patients.

Finally, it is important to understand the way drug manufacturers promote their products. One way is to fund conferences and seminars at elegant facilities with fine food, where doctors can receive information about new drugs. There has also been a pattern of offering financial incentives and gifts to doctors, such as coupons for free medical supplies and equipment, in exchange for attending sessions with speakers paid by drug companies. These marketing practices apply to all drugs, not just those used to treat anxiety. Nevertheless, these marketing strategies are intended to promote a drug-based approach to treating anxiety, even though it is known that a cognitive-behavioral skills approach can be equally effective.

## When to Consider Medication for Anxiety

Early in my career as a psychologist, my idealism and enthusiasm for the benefits of psychotherapy caused me to hesitate when it came to drug treatment. However, I have learned there are a number of situations in which medication for anxiety can make a significant difference in therapy outcome. I now consider referring anxiety patients for a medication evaluation under the following conditions:

- Acute or chronic sleep problems (insomnia or night waking)
- Impaired concentration and energy for psychotherapy
- Depression with suicidal feelings

These conditions make it difficult for patients to focus on the education, insights, and new skills involved in psychological counseling.

Before I recommend medication, however, I usually try other interventions and strategies. For example, steps a person can take to counteract a sleep problem include establishing a regular sleep cycle, relaxing or meditating before sleep, lowering light levels before bedtime, and avoiding stimulating media exposure before bed. Refer to Chapter 6 for a list of recommendations for improving sleep.

Other health habits and lifestyle changes can go a long way toward reducing troublesome anxiety symptoms. For example, regular exercise (see Chapter 9), dietary changes (see Chapter 10), and relaxation practices (see Chapter 7) can reduce anxiety symptoms. These health practices should be addressed before medication is recommended, or at least they should be considered as part of the overall treatment plan.

Because I am licensed as a psychologist, I do not personally prescribe medication. Instead, when appropriate, I refer patients to psychiatrists for medication evaluations or I confer with my patients' physicians regarding the treatment plan and medication.

As discussed in Chapter 3, depression can develop as a secondary symptom of anxiety. Depression can interfere with sleep, learning ability, concentration, and energy for therapy. Typically, secondary depression subsides when the anxiety condition is addressed, but it may be necessary in some cases to treat the depression directly with appropriate medication as an adjunct to anxiety therapy.

### Special Medication Issues with Children

Are medications for anxiety and depression safe for children? Safety became an issue when it was learned that suicidal thinking increased in some children involved in the clinical trials of paroxetine (Paxil), an antidepressant approved for anxiety in adults. Although no suicides occurred, the finding was alarming enough to limit FDA approval of most anxiety medications for children. Because of safety concerns, only two medications—fluvoxamine (Luvox) and sertraline (Zoloft)—are currently approved for those under the age of eighteen, and the approval is limited to obsessive-compulsive disorder.

Beta-blockers and benzodiazepines are generally not considered safe for children because their cardiovascular systems are considered vulnerable to the effects of these drugs. For a more detailed discussion of safety concerns regarding medications with children, readers are referred to my book, *The Worried Child* (Hunter House, 2004). A chapter in that book ("Biochemistry, Medications, and Nature's Remedies") is devoted to this topic.

Physicians and other health-care professionals who prescribe drugs face liability concerns when prescribing drugs for young patients with or without anxiety symptoms. In fact, there is some evidence that the number of prescriptions written for children is decreasing. Some physicians are addressing these concerns by requiring young patients to participate in psychotherapy while taking a medication. I think this is a positive trend that helps coordinate care as well as increase the likelihood of successful treatment.

Because a high percentage of children with anxiety disorders (about 80 percent) can be successfully treated without medication, my opinion is that drugs should be used with this age group as a last resort and with special attention to side effects and risks.

## Types of Medication for Anxiety

We turn now to the specific medications that are used to treat anxiety. There are several types of medications, and I list them below followed by a brief discussion of each.

Medications used to treat anxiety fall into three broad types:

- Beta-blockers
- Benzodiazepines
- Antidepressants (monoamine oxidase inhibitors, selective serotonin reuptake inhibitors, and tricyclics)

### Beta-Blockers

For an infrequently occurring anxiety problem, such as a fear of flying, there may be little opportunity for exposure and desensitization practice. In such cases, a quick-acting beta-blocker can counteract the arousal symptoms of anxiety and help a person to face the phobic situation, and perhaps replace the need for a more complete course of therapy.

Beta-blockers are a class of drug commonly used to control hypertension. They act by suppressing the autonomic nervous system, which controls functions such as heart rate, blood pressure, muscle tension, and sweating. They are nonaddictive and do not have any sedating effects. The usefulness of beta-blockers in anxiety treatment lies in their ability to control the body's reactivity, which in turn can reduce the subjective experience of anxious feelings. On the other hand, their effects may not be sufficient to counteract the anticipatory anxiety associated with a phobic situation.

### Maria

*Beta-blockers were used by Maria, whom I introduced in Chapter 3 as someone with a flying phobia. Maria was a competent woman who worked as a supervisor at a large insurance company. She had no history of anxiety problems. However, a turbulent flight from New York to Miami triggered a panic reaction that evolved into a flying phobia. Maria did have all the prerequisites for an anxiety disorder: biological sensitivity, anxiety personality traits, and stress.*

*Maria came to see me after five years of avoiding air travel. She was motivated to overcome the flying phobia because she wanted to be able to join friends and family on vacations.*

*Flying phobia can be difficult to treat using the usual desensitization approaches because practice opportunities are limited. However, a combination of therapy and a sedative or arousal-blocker can be used in such cases. My work with Maria included cognitive and behavior therapy to understand the problem and provide skills for managing anxiety. This was followed by use of a benzodiazepine during Maria's test flight. The drug helped to reduce the intensity of her anxiety symptoms and she completed an enjoyable vacation with friends that involved a round-trip flight from Boston to Bermuda. She used the medication on the departing flight, but not on the return flight. Maria had faced her biggest fear and formed a new attitude toward flying.*

A variation of the above approach to flying phobia would have been for Maria to carry the medication but not take it immediately when she became anxious. The plan would be for her to delay taking the medication by fifteen to thirty minutes. Within that timeframe, the anxiety might subside, especially if she could engage in conversation or another activity to take attention away from the anxiety. If the anxious feelings were too persistent, she could either take the medication or delay taking it for another period of time. The objective would be to develop some anxiety tolerance before taking the medication, and the goal would be to develop confidence in using skills and inner resources to control anxiety when it occurs. When a person has that confidence, the likelihood of anxiety is significantly reduced.

### Benzodiazepines

Another type of drug used in the treatment of anxiety is the benzodiazepine, also called an *antianxiety* drug. These drugs have a tranquilizing effect, and because the primary physical mechanism in anxiety is arousal, they can bring relief. Some examples of this drug type are alprazolam (Xanax), lorazepam (Ativan), chlordiazepoxide (Librium), clonazepam (Klonopin), prazepam (Centrax), oxazepam (Serax), chlorazepate (Tranxene), and diazepam (Valium). Sertraline (Xanax) has also been found to be particularly effective for panic disorder.

Benzodiazepines have the advantage of acting quickly, even within minutes in some cases. In addition, the benzodiazepines are generally well-tolerated and have fewer side effects, compared with other drugs used in anxiety treatment. On the other hand, benzodiazepines can be habit-forming. They can also cause drowsiness or a groggy feeling (which can impair concentration and motivation and interfere with the effectiveness of psychotherapy or self-help).

### Antidepressants

Although it may seem counterintuitive, antidepressant drugs are effective for some anxiety disorders. Three subtypes are discussed: monoamine oxidase inhibitors, selective serotonin reuptake inhibitors, and tricyclics.

### Monoamine Oxidase Inhibitors

The monoamine oxidase inhibitors (MAOIs) are thought to increase concentration of certain hormones, such as epinephrine, norepinephrine, and serotonin, in storage sites throughout the nervous system. This, in theory, is the basis for their antidepressant action. They have been used effectively for panic disorder and social phobia.

A significant disadvantage to these drugs is that they are dangerous if combined with certain foods, such as cheese, red wines, and foods containing MSG, as well as certain over-the-counter medicines. Also, these drugs have a high number of unpleasant side effects, which makes many physicians hesitant to prescribe them. The MAOIs tend to be reserved for people who do not respond favorably to other antidepressant medications.

### Selective Serotonin Reuptake Inhibitors

Selective serotonin reuptake inhibitors (SSRIs) have become popular in the treatment of anxiety disorders. These include fluoxetine (Prozac), sertraline (Zoloft), and paroxetine (Paxil), escitalopram (Lexapro), venlafaxine (Effexor), and citalopram (Celexa). These drugs generally produce fewer side effects than the other antidepressants and they do not cause physical dependency as do benzodiazepines. As discussed earlier, the SSRIs are designed to block the reabsorption of serotonin and maintain a higher level of this mood-enhancing brain hormone.

One significant problem with SSRIs is their propensity to cause an initial hyperarousal reaction in which the user can become even more anxious and agitated than before taking the drug. This can be counteracted to some extent by starting with very low doses of the drug and increasingly slowly. Another problem is the extended time period usually required before the medication reaches a therapeutic level. This can take several months, far longer than the two to four weeks generally believed to be the adjustment period. Many users do not have the patience to get through this adjustment period. Troublesome side effects, such as headaches, increased anxiety, and sleep problems, can also occur during the adjustment period, although these usually diminish with time.

*Tricyclics*

Like SSRIs, tricyclic drugs (TCAs) maintain higher levels of certain neurotransmitters, such as serotonin and norepinephrine. This is the basis
for their antidepressant effect. However, this type of antidepressant is
older than the SSRIs and they have significant disadvantages. They have
dangerous interaction effects when used with alcohol, aspirin, antihista-
mines, tobacco, and other drugs.

Some examples of tricyclic drugs are amitriptyline (Elavil), clomip-
ramine (Anafranil), and desipramine (Norpramin). Their use for anxiety
is diminishing due to less troublesome alternatives, notably SSRIs.

*Nonprescription Drugs*

It should be acknowledged that some people with anxiety attempt to control their symptoms with nonprescription drugs, such as alcohol or marijuana. It is estimated that up to one-third of those with alcohol dependence are anxiety sufferers who turned to this drug as a form of self-
medication. Anxiety sufferers use nonprescription drugs for the same
reason as they use prescription medications: symptom relief. Unfortunately, this coping strategy is ineffective in the long run because it does
not promote the learning of any new skills for preventing or controlling
anxiety and because the potential for addiction is high.

## Problems with Medication

Although medications can certainly play a helpful role in anxiety treatment, there are some issues that interfere with their effectiveness, in
addition to the troublesome side effects discussed in previous sections.

Many anxious people have negative feelings about drugs. Relying on
a drug to cope runs against the grain of their anxiety-prone personality.
For example, most anxiety sufferers have a strong need to feel in control.
Taking drugs can be objectionable because it conflicts with such control
needs or because of resistance to outside forces, including chemicals.

Another issue is high biological sensitivity in many anxiety sufferers, which raises the probability of strong reactions to drug effects.
The side effects of imipramine (Tofranil), for example, can include dry
mouth, constipation, blurred vision, weight gain, lower blood pressure,

decreased sexual responsiveness, and difficulty urinating, all of which can intensify anxiety in people who react strongly to changes within the body. Even the intended effects of drugs can increase anxiety because of their biochemical impact.

Another issue is the cumbersome trial-and-error process that is often involved in finding a workable drug choice and dosage. Even after an acceptable drug and dosage is in place, the effect of some drugs decreases with time, requiring further adjustments. Many anxiety sufferers simply do not get through this process, especially if unpleasant side effects or an initial arousal reaction are involved. These are not only inconveniences, but can serve as another source of anxiety.

In addition, the *rebound effect* (sudden increase in anxiety symptoms) is another potential problem when people do not withdraw gradually from some drugs. Rebound or withdrawal symptoms are likely to increase the *second fear* reaction (fear of having the anxiety), which can set the anxiety cycle in motion again. This is a significant problem with the benzodiazepines, for which close medical supervision is advised during the tapering-off period. The addictive quality of some drugs, such as diazepam (Valium), is also frightening to those with a high need for control. Many patients who are taking drugs when they initially come to my anxiety treatment center express concerns about discontinuing the medication. Will they have a relapse? Will they be able to function without the drugs?

### Christine

*Christine, who we met in Chapter 9, was a college professor who came to see me with a fear of discontinuing drugs. She had been relying on drugs to cope with stress for many years and was taking two drugs, one for insomnia and one for generalized anxiety. Despite her obvious competencies as a person—intelligence, social skills, drive, and resourcefulness—Christine believed she would be unable to function without drugs. However, she desperately wanted to discontinue her reliance on them.*

*Christine's history revealed that her mother had used tranquilizing drugs, which set a precedent for her reliance on them. Moreover, Christine had a traumatic experience several years before I met her, when she attempted to stop taking her drugs. Two weeks after she stopped the medication, she became overwhelmed with panic anxiety. Nevertheless, Christine felt drugs were limiting her ability to feel emotionally "alive."*

*This was, in fact, Christine's basic problem. Having been raised in a family in which feelings were suppressed and denied, she became uncomfortable with feelings. As an adolescent, she began using alcohol, followed in adulthood by prescription drugs, to subdue her feelings. With this history, she felt she would not be able to cope with feelings if she discontinued the drugs.*

*In our work together, we focused on Christine's dual fears of discontinuing drugs and experiencing emotional stress. As part of her treatment plan, I emphasized exposure to feelings by having Christine slow down and focus on her inner experiences, instead of distracting herself. This step proved helpful and was followed by Christine learning some new skills to replace medication as a means of coping with stress and feelings. She was finally able to discontinue the drugs, after relying on them for about 20 years. What is more, she did not resume using alcohol as a coping mechanism.*

*On a post-therapy evaluation, Christine wrote, "I feel more in control of my thoughts and feelings than before. I feel I have a more positive attitude in general and spend less time worrying about things, particularly those I can't change. I feel I like myself better and am not so hard on myself, and when I do have negative thoughts about myself, I am able to dismiss them more easily. I find I brood less. I feel more physically comfortable, less tense, and less nervous." The last word I received from Christine was that she had made a successful professional trip to Europe to present at a conference, without medication.*

## The Medications Used to Treat Anxiety

To help readers understand the variety of medications used to treat anxiety, I have prepared the table on pages 253–54, which displays their generic and trade names, the anxiety disorders they target, and their drug classifications.

## THE MEDICATIONS USED TO TREAT ANXIETY

||||||||||||||||||||||||||||||||||||||||||||||||||||||||||||||||||||||||||||||||

| GENERIC NAME | BRAND NAME | PRESCRIBED FOR (see key) | USUAL DOSE* | DRUG CLASS |
|---|---|---|---|---|
| alprazolam | Xanax | PD, GAD, D | 0.5–5 | Benzodiazepine |
| amitriptyline | Elavil | PTSD | 150–200 | Tricyclic antidepressant |
| atenolol | Tenormin | HBP, SP, PA | 50–100 | Beta-blocker |
| buspirone | Buspar | GAD | 30–60 | Antianxiety (tranquilizer) |
| chlorazepate | Tranxene | GAD | 15–60 | Benzodiazepine |
| chlordiazepoxide | Librium | GAD | 60–100 | Benzodiazepine ** |
| citalopram | Celexa | OCD, PD | 20–60 | SSRI |
| clomipramine | Anafranil | D, OCD, PD, GAD | 100–300 | Tricyclic antidepressant |
| clonazepam | Klonopin | PD, GAD | 1–6 | Benzodiazepine |
| desipramine | Norpramine | D, PD | 100–300 | Tricyclic antidepressant |
| diazepam | Valium | GAD, PD | 2–20 | Benzodiazepine |
| escitalopram | Lexapro | GAD, PD | 5–20 | SSRI |
| fluoxetine | Prozac | D, OCD, PD | 20–80 | SSRI |
| fluvoxamine | Luvox | OCD | 50–300 | SSRI |
| imipramine | Tofranil | D, PD, GAD | 100–300 | Tricyclic antidepressant |
| labetalol | Normodyne | HBP, PA | 200–800 | Beta-alpha blocker |
| lorazepam | Ativan | PD | 1–10 | Benzodiazepine |
| mirtazapine | Remeron | D, S | 30–45 | Antidepressant |
| nortriptyline | Pamelor | D, PD | 25–150 | Tricyclic antidepressant |
| oxazepam | Serax | GAD | 30–120 | Benzodiazepine |
| paroxetine | Paxil | D, GAD, OCD, PD, PTSD, SP, PH | 20–50 | SSRI |

*(cont'd.)*

## THE MEDICATIONS USED TO TREAT ANXIETY (cont'd.)

| GENERIC NAME | BRAND NAME | PRESCRIBED FOR (see key) | USUAL DOSE* | DRUG CLASS |
|---|---|---|---|---|
| phenelzine | Nardil | D, PD, SP | 45–90*** | MAOI |
| prazepam | Centrax | GAD | 20–60 | Benzodiazepine |
| propranolol | Inderal | HBP, PA | 40–240 | Beta-blocker |
| sertraline | Zoloft | D, OCD, PTSD | 50–200 | SSRI |
| tranylcypromine | Parnate | D | 20–50 | MAOI |
| trazodone | Desyrel | D | 150–400 | Antidepressant |
| venlafaxine | Effexor | GAD, SP, D | 75–150 | SSRI |

KEY:

PD = panic disorder
GAD = generalized anxiety disorder
OCD = obsessive-compulsive disorder
SP = social phobia
PH = specific phobia
D = depression
PA = performance anxiety
S = sleep disturbance

HBP = high blood pressure
MAOI = monoamine oxidase inhibitor
SSRI = selective serotonin reuptake inhibitor
* Dosages are shown in milligrams per day
** Includes a sedative
*** 1 milligram per 2.2 pounds of body weight

## When Is It Time to Discontinue Medication?

Most people would rather not rely on medication to manage anxiety or depression, so there is usually an interest in discontinuing it as soon as possible. My suggestion is to think in terms of acquiring anxiety-control skills—and the confidence to use them effectively—in order to minimize the possibility of a relapse when you stop using medication. In other words, if you are going to stop using medication, you want to have alternative ways to stay in control. And the best time to learn and practice new skills is while still taking medication, when your symptoms are under control.

In most cases, the cue for discontinuing medication comes from my patients. There seems to be an intuitive awareness or sense of readiness to stop using drugs, even though a person may be anxious about a recurrence of anxiety symptoms. If I feel the person has acquired some anxiety control skills, I usually recommend a "taper test" so that we can monitor anxiety levels during the tapering-off process. If my patient feels unready, he or she can resume medication, continue to practice key skills, and try tapering off medication again later.

It is important to withdraw gradually from any medication, except for drugs that have been used only occasionally. Medical supervision is recommended to monitor for withdrawal symptoms and adjust the taper schedule, as needed. The general guideline is to reduce the dosage of your medication by one-half for two weeks, then by half again for another two weeks, for a total tapering period of one month.

## Alternative Medicine Approaches

There are some time-tested alternative medicine approaches that are applicable to anxiety disorders. Herbal preparations, for example, are widely used in Europe, where medical doctors have a long history of prescribing them. Herbs are regulated as medicines in Switzerland, Germany, France, and other European countries, where they are manufactured under strict quality controls. In these countries, medical training includes these forms of treatment.

In contrast, American medical practice has been slow to recognize the value of alternative, or "natural," treatments, and many physicians are skeptical about their usefulness. However, this is changing. Approximately two-thirds of the 125 medical schools in the United States have introduced some form of alternative or complementary medicine in their curricula.

In addition, there is a growing public interest in complimentary or alternative medicine (CAM). CAM is broadly defined as use of nontraditional forms of health care, such as chiropractic, acupuncture, herbal therapy, and homeopathy. It is estimated that more than one-third of American adults use some form of CAM.

*Herbal Medicine*

Herbs have been valued as remedies for anxiety symptoms such as nervousness and insomnia since ancient times. Modern medical science, however, has only recently acknowledged their medicinal properties. Nevertheless, contemporary interest in herbs as part of a natural approach to health care is increasing, especially in response to dissatisfaction with the side effects of prescription drugs. In addition, health care in the United States is shifting to incorporate self-education and self-care. Herbal medicine seems to fit naturally into this new paradigm. A brief review of herbs for anxiety is included here to orient readers to this option for anxiety.

One problem with herbal preparations is that, at present, the FDA does not regulate them or consider them to be medicines. As a result, no official quality standards exist for herbs in the United States, and they must be sold as supplements. Furthermore, current law prevents the labeling of herbs as capable of treating or preventing diseases or symptoms, although manufacturers can claim their products enhance well-being or help improve body functions, as long as such claims are supported by scientific evidence.

Readers considering the use of herbs are advised to consult with a knowledgeable health-care professional, such as a naturopathic doctor (N.D.). Also, further self-education about herbs for anxiety is recommended. As a general rule, herbal remedies should not be combined with prescription drugs because of potentially adverse interactions.

### Some Herbs That Can Help Anxiety

*St. John's wort:* a perennial plant (wort means "plant") with a 2,400-year history of use for anxiety, sleep disturbances, and worry. Hippocrates recommended St. John's wort for "nervous unrest." The herb apparently enhances three key neurotransmitters—serotonin, norepinephrine, and dopamine—and has also been shown to be effective for depression. It has an exceptional safety record, confirmed by many studies.

*Kava:* approved by English, German, Swiss, and other European health boards for treating anxiety and insomnia, kava is a member of the pepper tree family. It is native to Fiji, Samoa, and other South Pacific islands, where it is made into a beverage and exported as a natural tranquilizer. Researchers are not sure how kava reduces anxiety symptoms, but one theory is that it has a soothing effect on the amygdala (the brain's alarm center). Studies have shown kava to be effective for anxiety disorders such as GAD, social phobia, specific phobias, and agoraphobia.

*Valerian:* the most widely used herbal sedative in Europe, where more than one hundred valerian preparations are sold in pharmacies. Its popularity is growing worldwide as a treatment for anxiety and insomnia. Valerian was popular in the United States as a sedative until it was replaced by synthetic drugs after World War II. Like St. John's wort, valerian has a long history of safety.

*California poppy:* from the same family as opiates, but with no narcotic properties. This herb has been used for its ability to induce sleep, relieve nervous tension, and reduce mild anxiety.

*Hops:* approved in Europe for anxiety, restlessness, and sleep disturbances. When combined with valerian, it can promote and improve sleep quality.

*Passionflower:* a native North American flower popular for reducing nervous tension. In Europe, passionflower is combined with valerian root as a remedy for insomnia, anxiety, and irritability.

## Homeopathy

Like herbal therapy, homeopathy is an alternative healing science that uses natural ingredients. One difference, however, is that homeopathy involves carefully prepared and administered substances that can have adverse effects in large quantities, but that stimulate self-healing and balance in very minute dosages. Another difference is that homeopathic medicines are defined and regulated as drugs by the FDA.

Homeopathic remedies are prepared through a process called *potentization*—a series of systematic dilutions and "succussions" (forceful shaking actions). This procedure reportedly removes the risk of chemical toxicity, while activating the remedy substance, enabling it to affect the body therapeutically. The first step in producing a homeopathic remedy is to make a pure extract from the therapeutic substance. The extract is then put through a measured series of dilutions, alternating with succussions, until the desired potency is reached.

Paradoxically, potency increases the more the substance is diluted. Higher potencies of homeopathic remedies have been diluted past the point at which molecules of the original substance are measurable in the solution. This fact is a major stumbling block for skeptics when it comes to understanding homeopathy. Homeopathic remedies often do work and the effects can be measured, but it is unclear why or how.

Homeopathic remedies are usually selected based on a close match with the target symptoms, and unless otherwise specified by the physician, can be taken according to instructions printed on the label. Some examples of homeopathic remedies for anxiety are as follows:

### Some Homeopathic Remedies for Anxiety

*Aconitum napellus:* Acute anxiety, bad dreams, and sleep problems can be helped with this remedy.

*Pulsatilla:* Anxiety expressed as insecurity and clinginess, with a need for constant support and comforting, can benefit from this remedy. Anxiety around the time of hormonal changes (puberty, menstrual periods) is often helped with pulsatilla.

*Gelsemium:* Feelings of weakness, trembling, or feeling "paralyzed by fear" can be helped with this remedy. It is considered helpful for test anxiety, anxiety associated with dental or medical visits, and stage fright before a public performance or interview, or other stressful event.

*Natrum muriaticum:* Emotional sensitivity, self-protective shyness, and social phobia are indications for this remedy, which also helps reduce claustrophobia, anxiety at night, migraines, and insomnia.

*Phosphorus:* This remedy is prescribed for people who are open-hearted, imaginative, excitable, easily startled, and experiencing intense and vivid fears. It is also appropriate for some anxiety personality traits, such as a tendency to overextend oneself, suggestibility, habitual worry, and negative thinking.

Homeopathic drug products must be chosen on a case-by-case basis, and the decision to use them should be made in consultation with a trained homeopathic physician. Homeopathic doctors can be located in local telephone directories (yellow pages) under "naturopathic physicians." See also the national organizations for alternative health care listed in the Resources section at the end of this book.

## Conclusion

Medication is not a good long-term solution for anxiety disorders because it does not in itself teach people the skills needed to manage stress and anxiety. But medication can play a vitally important role in supporting people as they learn new skills in therapy or on their own.

Three different types of prescription medications are used to treat anxiety: beta-blockers, benzodiazepines, and antidepressants. Each type has advantages and disadvantages. Regardless of type, most drugs have side effects that can be troublesome for the biologically sensitive person. With certain drugs, notably the benzodiazepines, addiction is a potential problem if they are used regularly.

The idea of using medication does not sit well with some people. They may have strong feelings about being controlled by drugs, or concerns about becoming drug dependent. It is important to make sure the decision to take medication is based on accurate information, rather than misconceptions.

On the other hand, some safe alternative medicines are available. Herbs and homeopathic medicines have a long history of use and documented effectiveness for anxiety. Because herbs are not regulated for quality control, it is advisable to consult with a knowledgeable professional such as a naturopathic physician. Medical schools in the United States are slowly introducing alternative medicines into their curricula and it is anticipated that physicians will become more knowledgeable about these options.

## CHAPTER 18

||||||||||||||||||||||||||

# *Toward a Life Beyond Panic and Anxiety*

How can we describe what life is like without abnormal anxiety? Is there a language for what is beyond symptom reduction? Is there a lifestyle that counteracts anxiety? How will we know if we are making progress toward it? These are the key questions to be addressed in this final chapter.

The National Institute of Mental Health reports an encouraging 80 percent recovery rate for anxiety disorders when people receive appropriate help. They define successful anxiety recovery as "a significant reduction in symptoms." Recovery from panic disorder, for example, consists of a significant reduction in the frequency, intensity, and duration of anxiety episodes. When an agoraphobia component is involved, a successful outcome also includes a reduction in avoidant behavior. Similarly, recovery from OCD is measured by a significant decrease in obsessive or compulsive behavior. In other words, for each anxiety disorder, we think of recovery in terms of symptom relief. This is good, but is it good enough? What will we gain and what will replace the anxiety symptoms?

The field of mental health was built on the foundation of the medical approach, or the "disease model." In this approach, health is defined as the absence of disease. There is no vocabulary for a positive description of health in the medical model. Instead, health is the undefined vacuum that is left when there are no more symptoms. Naturally, a person suffering from a disease is happy to have the symptoms reduced or eliminated, and to resume daily routines. The medical terminology for this is *premorbid condition*. But in many cases, it is that this very lifestyle that creates the disease.

Let's consider, for example, an overweight person who does not exercise or eat properly. There is a high probability such a person will develop poor health, such as high blood pressure or heart disease. If the high blood pressure is treated and controlled with medication, is that a good enough outcome? Is the reduction of symptoms a guarantee of health?

We face the same question with anxiety disorders. Most patients and therapists are competent at identifying the symptoms of an anxiety disorder. We have a system for diagnosing anxiety disorders based on symptom patterns, as discussed in Chapter 3. But we are not good at describing life beyond the anxiety disorder. We focus on symptom reduction because we do not have a language for describing the goals of anxiety recovery in any other way.

As we discussed in Chapter 4, anxiety disorders develop from the interaction of three ingredients: biological sensitivity, personality style, and stress overload. Therefore, simply reducing anxiety symptoms does not guarantee a long-term solution because the potential for an anxiety relapse always exists for the biologically sensitive person with those personality traits. We need to change our lifestyle so the three ingredients do not reach a critical threshold and trigger a relapse. We need to create a lifestyle that prevents anxiety by managing our biological disposition, our personality traits, and our stress. What does this lifestyle look like?

We can begin to describe life beyond anxiety by generating a vocabulary that describes the alternatives to anxiety. Here is an exercise designed to generate this vocabulary list.

### Exercise: *Alternatives to Anxiety*

- Close your eyes, relax, and begin to think of words or expressions that represent the opposite of anxiety.
- Write down the words as they come to mind.
- Compare what you have written to the following vocabulary list I have gathered from participants at many of my anxiety workshops.

The following list of alternatives was collected from many mental-health professionals with whom I have worked in my anxiety workshops, as well as patients in my clinical practice. See which of these characteristics or states speak to you. Which would you like to have more of in your life?

### List of Alternatives to Anxiety

- Peace of mind
- Trust
- Serenity
- Ability to live in the present
- Assertiveness
- Emotional self-regulation
- Creativity
- Contentment
- Empowerment
- Experience of "flow"
- High self-esteem

- Relaxation
- Calm
- Self-confidence
- Flexibility
- Positive attitude
- Optimism
- Tranquility
- Centeredness
- Ability to take risks
- Nonjudgment
- Acceptance

The concepts and skills discussed in this book are intended to help reduce anxiety, but are ultimately directed toward increasing these positive characteristics. And having a vocabulary for such qualities increases the chances for achieving them. Let's put them together into a composite picture of a life beyond anxiety.

Having overcome your anxiety disorder, you are more relaxed, more optimistic about the future, and more comfortable socially. With improved confidence, you are able to communicate more effectively. As a result of better stress-management skills and health practices, you have more energy and a more positive body image. You are able to take more risks and view mistakes as learning experiences. You are nonjudgmental and, in turn, less concerned about how others view you. In addition, you are able to pursue activities that bring you joy, pleasure, and satisfaction. You live life passionately and your emotional life is rich. You are free to follow your dreams, become your true self, and find meaning and purpose in life.

It can be helpful and inspiring to learn about other people who have been successful in creating a life beyond anxiety. One way to do this is to read some first-person success stories. Here are some books that can provide such inspiration (full publication information is located in the Bibliography): *Free from Fears* (Seagrave and Covington), *Triumph Over Fear* (Ross), *Living Fully with Shyness and Social Anxiety* (Hilliard), *Conquering Panic and Anxiety Disorders* (Glatzer).

Another helpful way to receive reassurance and inspiration is to hear it from others who have been successful in anxiety recovery. In my practice, I sometimes offer to put new patients in contact with former patients who want to share their success with others. These personal stories about anxiety recovery are among the most credible sources of inspiration, hope, and reassurance to the new anxiety patient. Group therapy is another opportunity for new patients to learn first-hand about progress made by others with similar disorders.

### When to Consider Professional Help

Individual anxiety cases vary widely in frequency, intensity, and duration of symptoms, as well as motivation, stress level, and learning style. Some people are self-motivated learners who can take the information and suggestions from this book (and other resources) and implement a personal program for anxiety recovery. Many people, however, benefit from professional guidance and support for making the changes that can lead to a life beyond anxiety. How do you decide if professional help is appropriate for you?

Professional help is appropriate when an anxiety disorder persists or when self-help efforts have not been productive. The test is whether anxiety symptoms are interfering with daily functioning on a frequent or chronic basis. Here are some indicators for determining whether anxiety is serious enough to seek professional help:

- Social withdrawal or isolation

- Inability to concentrate or perform at work

- Difficulty sleeping on a regular or prolonged basis

Indicators
of Serious
Anxiety

- Avoidance of situations despite a desire to experience them

- Difficulty relaxing or chronic hyperarousal

- Significant signs of depression (loss of motivation, low energy)

- Low self-esteem

- Frequent illness

- Loss of appetite or under-eating

- Overeating or weight gain

- Significant relationship problems

### How to Choose a Therapist for Anxiety

A variety of mental-health professionals are able to provide therapy and related services for anxiety disorders. Differing primarily in training and focus, they include psychologists, clinical mental-health counselors, marriage and family therapists, clinical social workers, and psychiatrists. The choices and options can be confusing to the average person seeking professional help. The number of specialties in psychology alone is staggering. For example, there are more than 150,000 members of the American Psychological Association, a professional organization with fifty-five different divisions, representing a vast array of fields and specialties. Most psychologists who provide therapy services for the public are members of the divisions of clinical psychology, or psychologists in independent practice.

I recommend asking around in your community, consulting with your physician, and researching professional listings, such as the Anxiety Disorders Association of America, as well as state associations for psychologists, mental-health counselors, clinical social workers, and psychiatrists (see Resources).

Feel free to interview a prospective therapist—by phone or in person—before deciding whether to go forward with that particular professional. Here are some questions to ask when you call or meet with a mental-health professional:

- How long have you been in practice?

- With what age range do you work?

- What percentage of your patients have an anxiety disorder?

- Do you have any data on your success rate with anxiety disorders?

- Do you have any specific training or credentials in anxiety treatment?

- What is your approach to helping with anxiety problems?

- On average, how long does it take you to help a person control anxiety?

- How often do you refer your anxiety patients for medication?

- Under what conditions do you refer anxiety clients for medication?

Questions
to Ask a
Prospective
Therapist

Therapy involves a personal and confidential relationship and you should feel comfortable with your therapist. If after meeting with a new therapist, you do not feel comfortable, either discuss your feelings with that professional or move on to another. Therapists want their patients to feel comfortable and they generally support you in switching to another professional. You also have a legal right to see your clinical record and to request (in writing) that a copy be sent to another therapist.

### Components of Effective Therapy

Therapists differ in their approach to anxiety disorders, but there are some generally accepted standards and practices. In one form or another, effective therapy for anxiety disorders should include the following components:

- Assessment and diagnosis

- Prognosis (the projected outcome of treatment)

- Insights about your particular anxiety disorder

- Individualized stress management skills, including relaxation

- Behavioral health recommendations (e.g., sleep, diet, exercise)

- Focus on personality traits that contribute to anxiety

- Cognitive change, as needed

- Development of emotional skills, as needed

- Desensitization or exposure for phobic avoidance, if appropriate

During my initial diagnostic interview, I make sure my patients have been medically evaluated and cleared of an organic or physical basis for their anxiety condition. This is an important step in helping to dispel unrealistic fears about having a life-threatening disease or illness. After the anxiety condition is diagnosed, my next intervention is to reassure people that treatment for anxiety disorders has a high success rate. I use my own case as an example, if appropriate, or describe other examples of successful recovery. The initial interview is also important for establishing trust and rapport because a good working relationship is essential when dealing with anxiety.

I find that it helps immeasurably to offer appropriate reassurance early in therapy. But I also emphasize that successful anxiety recovery is a collaborative effort in which the patient must play a key role. I dispel the myth that therapy works by magic, and I point out that the patient must do the work that leads to recovery.

As therapy is a collaborative effort, the patient and therapist both have responsibilities for the success of anxiety treatment. The therapist's responsibility begins with conducting a proper assessment, making an accurate diagnosis, and developing an appropriate treatment plan. If the primary problem is an anxiety disorder and the therapist is not skilled in this area, he or she is responsible for referring the patient to an anxiety treatment specialist. Unfortunately, this does not happen as often as it should, which contributes to the high percentage of anxiety sufferers who receive inappropriate or ineffective care. A number of organizations have formed to correct this, including the National Institute of Mental Health's Panic Disorder Education Program, the Anxiety Disorders Association of America, The Obsessive-Compulsive Foundation, Freedom From Fear, the National Anxiety Council, and others. The mission of these organizations includes public and professional education about anxiety disorders and effective treatment, with the hope of increasing the number of people who receive appropriate care. Some of these organizations maintain lists of anxiety treatment specialists, although they do not set any practice standards.

The anxiety specialist's next responsibility is to provide a therapy process that includes the tools and skills known to be effective for overcoming anxiety. The components of effective therapy are listed in an earlier section of this chapter.

In many cases, it is important to combine a structured self-help program with therapy. The CHAANGE (Center for Help for Anxiety/Agoraphobia through New Growth Experiences) anxiety treatment program, for example, is a comprehensive, 16-week homework program that contains most of the components for effective therapy. A nice feature is that a patient's progress is monitored by self-evaluations at the beginning, middle, and end of the process. The CHAANGE program also offers the advantage of providing learning materials to be used by patients at home—between therapy sessions—to ensure daily effort and increase the likelihood of success. In addition, the information is delivered in a personal style by other patients who were successful in their own recoveries. This format provides hope, inspiration, and an opportunity for new patients to identify with others' success.

Other self-help options include anxiety workbooks that provide structure and appropriate homework activities. Some examples are *The Anxiety and Phobia Workbook* (Bourne), and *Mind Over Mood: A Cognitive Therapy Treatment Manual for Clients* (Greenberger and Padesky). These workbooks are listed in the Bibliography.

The therapy patient's role is to make a commitment to the recovery process and stay with it even when progress seems slow or inconsistent.

The patient is also responsible for daily practice of prescribed skills and exercises. Some of my patients demonstrate responsibility by recording questions and comments from their homework and personal experiences and bringing them to therapy sessions for discussion. Some keep a diary of their progress and some make cue cards with inspiring affirmations, as well as instructions to themselves, which many of them carry in a pocket or purse as daily reminders. As a therapy patient, you must recognize that progress takes place as a result of efforts that only you can make. No one can do it for you.

## Realistic Expectations

What can you realistically expect to achieve in anxiety recovery? Anxiety recovery can be defined as having the confidence to know you can handle anxiety if and when it occurs. This confidence comes from practicing the skills necessary for dancing with fear and by successfully facing fears and phobias with those skills. Anxiety recovery also means a new understanding of the mind-body relationship, and making behavioral changes to manage stress and support a healthy lifestyle.

It is possible to manage fear, but it is not possible to live without periodic anxiety. To a certain extent, anxiety is inherent in life and cannot be eliminated completely. We are all subject to imperfection, disappointment, illness, loss, decay, and death, and we are not in total control of our destinies. Therefore, we live with constant vulnerability. On the other hand, despite our lack of control, an optimistic attitude is possible. For those who understand this and who acquire the skills for accepting and dancing with fear, there can be joy and inner peace in daily living.

The ever-present potential for anxiety is high in people who have the personality traits discussed in Chapter 4. To review the anxiety personality briefly, the profile includes biological and emotional sensitivity; an active and creative mind; fear of rejection; sensitivity to criticism; a high need to please other people; a need to feel in control; perfectionism; suggestibility; and a strong preference for certainty, structure, and predictability. When these traits control us, we are at risk for stress and anxiety. Our personality cannot be remade entirely, but we can modify these traits so we are more in control of them and, therefore, of our stress and anxiety.

Stress is an inevitable part of life, adding to our potential for experiencing anxiety. The natural, biological reaction to stress involves the same body arousal and symptoms as anxiety. However, anxiety recovery means no longer fearing the body's reactions to stress. This is accomplished by learning to trust that the body's reaction to stress is not life-threatening, as well as by learning to recognize the early warning signs of stress and intervening with skills that reduce stress and minimize its impact. As the world around us becomes more stressful, these skills are increasingly necessary for dancing without fear.

### The Factors Affecting Success in Anxiety Recovery

Whether you are using a self-help book or receiving professional help, success in the relearning process is influenced by three factors:

1. Motivation

2. Concurrent stress

3. Chronicity (not severity)

The first factor is *motivation,* which translates into commitment, effort, and taking responsibility for having an anxiety disorder and for recovery. The higher the motivation, the more likely it is that a person will do the work and stay with it. Motivation is the most important ingredient in overcoming anxiety.

The probability of successful recovery from anxiety is also influenced by the amount of *stress* in a person's life during the recovery program. Medical conditions, relationship problems, financial hardship, illness in the family, or recent death or loss of a loved one all take up energy required to absorb new information and learn new skills. Under such conditions, anxiety treatment may need to focus first on the other issues. This may affect the length of treatment and the time needed to practice and apply new skills. However, as long as you are motivated to succeed, you have every reason to be optimistic about attaining recovery.

Success in recovery is also affected by *chronicity,* or the length of time you have had an anxiety disorder. A long-standing anxiety disorder usually means a person has developed habitual coping patterns and defense mechanisms that can be difficult to modify. Therefore, a longer period of relearning may be required. On the other hand, I have often had the satisfaction of working with people who recovered within months, despite years of living with fear and anxiety. In fact, most adults with an anxiety disorder have a long history of symptoms they may not have recognized earlier. Regardless of how long you have had an anxiety disorder, recovery is a realistic goal if motivation is high.

## Pitfalls and Obstacles to Recovery

A number of obstacles and pitfalls can interfere with anxiety recovery. One pitfall is the temptation to stop practicing new skills when we feel better or when our anxiety symptoms subside. This can happen at any time after some progress has been made and we begin to feel less anxious. It is natural to become less consistent about self-help efforts when things are going well. Motivation for managing stress, exercising, eating properly, thinking positively, and daily practice of relaxation or meditation can drop when anxiety is reduced. However, this pitfall should be recognized and avoided because basic sensitivity and other personality traits will not change, and because the potential for anxiety remains high under new stress.

Another pitfall is feeling discouraged by anxiety setbacks. Anxiety setbacks are inevitable during recovery and can be viewed as practice opportunities. A resurgence of anxiety provides an opportunity to apply newly acquired skills, such as using the relaxation response, changing inner dialogue, thinking positively, floating through, trusting ourselves, and keeping faith in the universe. We must experience anxiety in order to overcome it and to develop the skills and confidence to know we can handle it. Creating a life beyond anxiety is a life-long process that may not always go as smoothly as we wish.

We must also identify unrealistic expectations. For example, it is unrealistic to expect to never experience anxiety again. As discussed in Chapter 17, anxiety is sometimes a signal that we are on the right track and facing a change or challenge that is good for us even though it may take us out of our comfort zone. It is also important to remember that some anxiety is normal for everyone under certain circumstances, such as making a presentation to a large group of people or going to an important interview. In such situations, we can change our view of the anxiety and see it as energy that can help us prepare and have a positive experience.

One final caution to keep in mind is that stress is inevitable and we are likely to periodically react with arousal symptoms. On the other hand, stress will not confuse us or make us more anxious if we understand it and have the skills to manage it. As discussed in Chapter 6, stress is not just about external stressors, but also about how we react to them.

## Conclusion

A life beyond anxiety cannot be described using the medical or disease model in which health is the vacuum left after symptoms are reduced. To imagine a life beyond anxiety, we need a positive language that describes the alternative states of being. We need words to represent what will replace anxiety symptoms.

Some terms have been generated by therapists in my workshops and patients in my clinical practice. These include peace of mind, emotional self-regulation, serenity, optimism, acceptance, self-confidence, trust, and faith.

With just a few qualifications, as discussed in this chapter, it is absolutely possible to create a life beyond anxiety using the concepts and skills discussed in this book. You will recognize progress toward this goal when you feel more relaxed, less stressed, and more in control of your body's reactions. You will notice that your thinking is more optimistic and less focused on worries about what may happen in the future. You will become less judgmental and more accepting, and this will help you be less concerned about how others may judge you. In turn, you will feel more comfortable around other people. As you practice new skills, your self-confidence is likely to improve. And as this all comes together, you will experience more joy, pleasure, and satisfaction; you will find that rather than being anxious, you are dancing with fear.

# Bibliography

Allione, T. *Women of Wisdom*. New York: Snow Lion, 2000.

Aron, E. *The Highly Sensitive Child*. New York: Broadway Books (Random House), 2004.

Aron, E. *The Highly Sensitive Person*. New York: Broadway Books (Random House), 1996.

Axt, P., and M. Axt-Gadermann. *The Joy of Laziness*. Alameda, CA: Hunter House, 2003.

Barefoot, J. C., W. G. Dahlstrom, and R. B. Williams, Jr. "Hostility, CHD Incidence, and Total Mortality: A 25-Year Follow-Up Study of 255 Physicians." *Psychosomatic Medicine* 45 (1983): 59–63.

Bass, C. "Chest Pain and Breathlessness: Relationship to Psychiatric Illness." *The American Journal of Medicine* 92 (1992): 12–19.

Beck, A. *Cognitive Therapy and the Emotional Disorders*. New York: Meridian, 1979.

Beck, J. *Cognitive Therapy: Basics and Beyond*. New York: Guilford Press, 1995.

Benson, H. *Beyond the Relaxation Response*. New York: Times Books, 1984.

Benson, H. *The Relaxation Response*. New York: William Morrow, 1975.

Bloomfield, H. *Healing Anxiety with Herbs*. New York: HarperCollins, 1998.

Borysenko, J. *Minding the Body, Mending the Mind*. Reading, PA: Addison-Wesley, 1987.

Bradley, D. *Self-Help for Hyperventilation Syndrome*. Alameda, CA: Hunter House, 2001.

Brandon, N. *The Psychology of Self-Esteem*. New York: Nash, 1969.

Burns, D. *Feeling Good*. New York: Signet, 1981.

Caddy, E. *The Living Word*. Forres, Scotland: Findhorn Foundation, 1977.

Canfield, J. *Self-Esteem and Peak Performance* (Audio CD). CareerTrack (www.careertrack.com), 1990.

Cloninger, R. *Feeling Good: The Science of Well-Being.* New York: Oxford University Press, 2004.

Cousins, N. *Anatomy of an Illness.* New York: Norton, 1979.

Cousins, N. *The Healing Heart.* New York: Norton, 1983.

Covey, S. *The Seven Habits of Highly Effective People.* New York: Simon and Schuster, 1989.

Covey, S., A. Merrill, and R. Merrill. *First Things First.* New York: Simon and Schuster, 1996.

Csikszentmihalyi, M. *Flow: The Psychology of Optimal Experience.* New York: Harper and Row, 1990.

Dass, R. *Be Here Now.* New York: Crown Publishing, 1971.

*Diagnostic and Statistical Manual of Mental Disorders*, 4th ed. Washington, DC: American Psychiatric Association, 1994.

Dossey, L. *Healing Words: The Power of Prayer.* New York: HarperCollins, 1993.

Eadie, B. *Embraced by the Light.* New York: Bantam Books, 1993.

Elkind, D. *The Hurried Child: Growing Up Too Fast Too Soon.* Reading, PA: Addison-Wesley, 1981.

Epstein, M. *Thoughts without a Thinker.* New York: Basic Books, 1995.

Erikson, E. H. *Childhood and Society.* New York: Norton, 1950.

Fekete, Michael. *Strength Training for Seniors.* Alameda, CA: Hunter House Publishers, 2006.

Foxman, P. "Tolerance for Ambiguity: Implications for Mental Health." In *Encyclopedia of Clinical Assessment*, ed. R. Woody, 455–462. San Francisco, CA: Jossey-Bass, 1980.

Foxman, P. "Tolerance for Ambiguity and Self-Actualization." *Journal of Personality Assessment* 40, no. 1 (1976): 67–72.

Freud, S. "Formulations Regarding the Two Principles of Mental Functioning." *Standard Edition of Complete Works,* 7th ed. London: Hogarth Press, 1911.

Freud, S. *A General Introduction to Psychoanalysis*. New York: Liveright, 1935.

Gardner, R. W., P. S. Holzman, G. S. Klein, H. Linton, and D. P. Spence. "Cognitive Control: A Study of Individual Consistencies in Cognitive Behavior." *Psychological Issues* 1, no. 4, mono. 4 (1959).

Gawain, S. *Creative Visualization*. New York: Bantam Books, 1978.

Gendlin, E. *Focusing*. New York: Bantam Books, 1978.

Glatzer, J., ed. *Conquering Panic and Anxiety Disorders*. Alameda, CA: Hunter House, 2002.

Goleman, D. *Emotional Intelligence*. New York: Bantam Books, 1995.

Greenberger, D., and C. Padesky. *Mind over Mood: A Cognitive Therapy Treatment Manual for Clients*. New York: Guilford, 1995.

Hamer, D. *The God Gene: How Faith Is Hardwired Into Our Genes*. New York: Doubleday, 2004.

Hanh, T. N. *Being Peace*. Berkeley, CA: Parallax, 1987.

Hauri, P., and S. Linde. *No More Sleepless Nights*. New York: John Wiley & Sons, 1996.

Hay, L. *You Can Heal Your Life*. Santa Monica, CA: Hay House, 1987.

Hilliard, E. *Living Fully with Shyness and Social Anxiety*. New York: Marlowe and Company, 2005.

Holmes, T., and M. Masuda. "Psychosomatic Syndrome." *Psychology Today* (April 1972).

Holmes, T., and M. Masuda. "The Social Readjustment Rating Scale." *Journal of Psychosomatic Research* 2 (1967): 213–218.

Isaacs, A. "Studies: Religion, Health Go Hand in Hand." *Maturity News Service*. Washington, DC., October 10, 1994.

Janus, S., and C. Janus. *The Janus Report on Sexual Behavior*. New York: John Wiley & Sons, 1993.

Kabat-Zinn, J. *Full Catastrophe Living: Using the Wisdom of your Body and Mind to Face Stress, Pain, and Illness*. New York: Delacorte, 1994.

Kabat-Zinn, J. *Wherever You Go, There You Are: Mindfulness Meditation in Everyday Life*. New York: Hyperion, 1994.

Kaplan, H. *The New Sex Therapy*. New York: Bruner/Mazel, 1974.

Keesling, B. *Sexual Healing*, 3rd ed. Alameda, CA: Hunter House Publishers, 2006.

Kornfield, J. *A Path with Heart: A Guide Through the Perils and Promises of Spiritual Life*. New York: Bantam Books, 1993.

Laney, M. *The Introvert Advantage: How to Thrive in an Extrovert World*. New York: Workman, 2002.

Lappe, F. M. *Diet for a Small Planet*. New York: Ballantine Books, 1971.

Lee, J. *Expressing Anger Appropriately* (Recorded workshop). Boulder, CO: Sounds True Recordings, 1990.

Lerner, H. *The Dance of Intimacy*. New York: Harper and Row, 1989.

Levin, J. "Religion and Health: Is There an Association, Is It Valid, and Is It Causal?" *Social and Scientific Medicine*, 38, no. 11 (1994): 1475–1482.

Levitt, J., L. Smith, and C. Warren. *Kripalu Kitchen: A Natural Foods Cookbook and Nutritional Guide*. Lenox, MA: Kripalu Publications, 1980.

Lidell, L. *The Sivananda Companion to Yoga*. New York: Simon and Schuster, 1983.

Lowen, A. *Bioenergetics*. New York: Penguin Books, 1975.

Lowen, A. *The Spirituality of the Body*. New York: Macmillan, 1990.

Maddi, S., and S. Kobasa. *The Hardy Executive: Health under Stress*. Homewood, IL: Dow Jones-Irwin, 1984.

Marshall, F., and P. Cheevers. *Positive Options for Seasonal Affective Disorder (SAD)*. Alameda, CA: Hunter House, 2003.

Mason, J. W. "A Historical View of the Stress Field." *Journal of Human Stress*, 1 (1975): 6–36.

Masters, W., and V. Johnson. *Human Sexual Inadequacy*. Boston: Little, Brown and Company, 1970.

Masters, W., and V. Johnson. *Human Sexual Response*. Boston: Little, Brown and Company, 1966.

Michael, R., J. Gagnon, E. Laumann, and G. Kolata. *Sex in America: A Definitive Survey*. Boston: Little, Brown and Company, 1995.

Moyers, B. *Healing and the Mind*. New York: Doubleday, 1993.

Muggeridge, M. *Something Beautiful for God.* New York: Image/Harper and Row, 1977.

Muktananda, S. *Does Death Really Exist?* South Fallsburg, NY: Siddha Yoga Publications, 1995.

Muktananda, S. *God is With You.* South Fallsburg, NY: Siddha Yoga Publications, 1993.

Muller, W. *Legacy of the Heart: The Spiritual Advantage of a Painful Childhood.* New York: Simon and Schuster, 1992.

Neil, A. S. *Summerhill: A Radical Approach to Child Rearing.* New York: Hart Publishing Company, 1960.

Ornstein, R., and D. Sobel. *Healthy Pleasures.* Reading, PA: Addison-Wesley, 1989.

Peale, N. V. *The Power of Positive Thinking.* New York: Prentice-Hall, 1952.

Pearce, J. C. *The Bond of Power.* New York: Dutton, 1981.

Pearce, J. C. *Magical Child: Rediscovering Nature's Plan for Our Children.* New York: Dutton, 1977.

Pearl, B., and G. Moran. *Getting Stronger.* Bolinas, CA: Shelter Publications, 1986.

Peck, M. S. *The Road Less Traveled.* New York: Touchstone/Simon and Schuster, 1978.

Pelletier, K. *Mind as Healer, Mind as Slayer: A Holistic Approach to Preventing Stress Disorders.* New York: Delta, 1977.

Piaget, J. *The Origins of Intelligence in Children.* New York: Norton, 1952.

Piaget, J. *Play, Dreams, and Imitation in Childhood.* New York: Norton, 1962.

Ponichtera, B. *Quick and Healthy Recipes and Ideas.* Dalles, OR: Scale-Down, 1991.

Preston, J., and J. Johnson. *Clinical Psychopharmacology Made Ridiculously Simple,* 5th Edition. Sacramento, CA: Alliant International University, 2005.

Reich, W. *Character Analysis,* 3rd ed. New York: Farrar, Straus and Giroux, 1972.

Reich, W. *The Function of the Orgasm.* New York: Farrar, Straus and Giroux, 1961.

Reiter, S., S. Kutcher, and D. Gardner. "Anxiety Disorders in Children and Adolescents: Clinical and Related Issues in Pharmacological Treatment." *Canadian Journal of Psychiatry* 37 (1992): 431–438.

Rinpoche, S. *The Tibetan Book of Living and Dying.* New York: Harper-Collins, 1992.

Robertson, L., C. Flinders, and B. Godfrey. *Laurel's Kitchen: A Handbook for Vegetarian Cookery and Nutrition.* Berkeley, CA: Nilgiri Press, 1976.

Rodale, J. *The Complete Book of Food and Nutrition.* Emmaus, PA: Rodale Books, 1971.

Rodegast, P., and J. Stanton. *Emmanuel's Book: A Manual for Living Comfortably in the Cosmos.* New York: Bantam Books, 1985.

Roger, J., and P. McWilliams. *Life 101: Everything We Wish We Had Learned About Life in School—But Didn't.* Los Angeles, CA: Prelude Press, 1991.

Ross, J. *Triumph over Fear.* New York: Bantam, 1994.

Rubin, T. *The Angry Book.* New York: Collier Books, 1969.

Satir, V. *Making Contact.* Berkeley, CA: Celestial Arts, 1976.

Schwartz, J. *Brainlock: Free Yourself from Obsessive-Compulsive Behavior.* New York: Regan Books, 1996.

Seagrave, A., and F. Covington. *Free from Fears.* New York: Pocket Books, 1987.

Seligman, M. *Learned Optimism: How to Change Your Mind and Your Life.* New York: Pocket Books, 1998.

Selye, H. *The Stress of Life.* New York: McGraw-Hill, 1956.

Shekelle, R. B., M. Gale, A. M. Ostfield, and O. Paul. "Hostility, Risk of CHD, and Mortality." *Psychosomatic Medicine* 45 (1983): 109–114.

Shurtleff, W., and A. Aoyagi. *The Book of Tofu: Food for Mankind.* Brookline: Autumn Press, 1975.

Siegel, B. *Love, Medicine and Miracles.* New York: Harper and Row, 1986.

St. James, E. *Simplify Your Life: 100 Ways to Slow Down and Enjoy the Things that Really Matter.* New York: Hyperion, 1994.

Steiner, R. *The Education of the Child in the Light of Anthroposophy.* London: Rudolf Steiner Press, 1975.

Steiner, R. *Knowledge of the Higher Worlds and its Attainment,* 3rd ed. New York: Anthroposophic Press, 1947.

Steinsaltz, A. *The Strife of the Spirit.* Northvale, NJ: Jason Aronson, 1988.

Stern, C. *Gates of Repentance.* New York: Central Conference of American Rabbis, 1978.

Stevens, D. E., ed. *Listen, Humanity—Meher Baba.* New York: Harper and Row, 1957.

Tavris, C. *Anger: The Misunderstood Emotion.* New York: Simon and Schuster, 1982.

Valenstein, E. *Blaming the Brain: The Truth about Drugs and Mental Health.* New York: Free Press, 1998.

Vissell, B., and J. Vissell. *The Shared Heart: Relationship Initiations and Celebrations.* Aptos, CA: Ramira Publishing, 1984.

Wallerstein, J., and S. Blakeslee. *Second Chances: Men, Women and Children a Decade after Divorce.* New York: Ticknor and Fields, 1989.

Wallerstein, J., and S. Blakeslee. *What About the Kids?: Raising Your Children Before, During, and After Divorce.* New York: Hyperion, 2003.

Watts, A. "Letting Go: The Art of Playful Living." *East West Journal* (April 1983).

Watts, A. *The Way of Liberation.* New York: Weatherhill, 1983.

Weekes, C. "Simple, Effective Treatment of Agoraphobia." *American Journal of Psychotherapy* 23, no. 3 (1978): 357–369.

Wegscheider, S. *Another Chance—Hope and Health for the Alcoholic Family.* Palo Alto, CA: Science and Behavior Books, 1981.

Williams, R. B., T. L. Haney, K. I. Lee, Y. Kong, J. A. Blumenthal, and R. E. Walen. "Type A Behavior, Hostility, and Coronary Atherosclerosis." *Psychosomatic Medicine* 42 (1980): 539–549.

Wurtman, J. *Managing Your Mind and Mood through Food.* New York: Perennial Library, 1988.

# *Resources*

## National Organizations for Anxiety Education and Treatment

**American Psychological Association (APA)**
750 First St. NE, Washington DC 20002-4242
(800) 374-2721 ■ Website: www.apa.org

The APA is a professional organization whose Office of Public Affairs disseminates information to the public about various psychological disorders, including anxiety. The website is useful with many articles on anxiety disorders, depression, and related issues.

**Anxiety Disorders Association of America (ADAA)**
8730 Georgia Ave., Suite 600, Silver Spring MD 20910
(240) 485-1001 ■ (240) 485-1035, fax ■ Website: www.adaa.org

The ADAA is a nonprofit organization whose mission is to promote the prevention and cure of anxiety disorders, and to improve the lives of all people who suffer from them. The organization disseminates information and facilitates access to treatment by providing a National Professional Membership Directory, including a state-by-state listing of mental-health professionals who specialize in the treatment of anxiety disorders. Website is useful with many articles on topics related to anxiety disorders. The ADAA sponsors an annual conference open to both the public and professionals. Publishes free electronic newsletter, *Triumph*.

**Anxiety Disorders Education Program Library**
National Institute of Mental Health
6001 Executive Blvd., Rm. 8184, MSC 9663, Bethesda MD 20892-9663
(866) 615-6464 ■ (301) 443-4279, fax
E-mail: nimhinfo@nih.gov ■ Website: www.nimh.nih.gov

NIMH is a government agency whose mission is to improve mental health through biomedical research on mind, brain, and behavior. The NIMH website provides useful and up-to-date information on anxiety and related disorders.

**CHAANGE**
1360 Rosecrans St., Suite I, San Diego CA 92106
(619) 224-2216 ■ (619) 224-2215, fax ■ Website: www.chaange.com

CHAANGE (Center for Help for Anxiety/Agoraphobia through New Growth Experiences) is a national organization dedicated to effective treatment for anxiety disorders. CHAANGE provides a state-by-state listing of professionals who specialize in anxiety treatment using the CHAANGE program. An online brochure is available on their website. A children's anxiety recovery program, LifeSkills, is also available from CHAANGE. The organization also offers a catalogue of books and tapes related to anxiety recovery.

**Freedom From Fear**
308 Seaview Ave., Staten Island NY 10305
(718) 351-1717 ■ (718) 980-5022, fax
Website: www.freedomfromfear.org

Freedom From Fear is "a nonprofit organization dedicated to helping those who suffer from fears, phobias, anxiety, and depression." Cosponsor of annual Anxiety and Depression Awareness Days offering public information and a free diagnostic screening. The website is informative with many articles about anxiety and depression.

**National Anxiety Foundation**
3135 Custer Dr., Lexington KY 40517-4001
(606) 272-7166 ■ Website: www.lexington-on-line.com/naf.html

This organization is a "nonprofit public health education and research institution" that provides information on panic disorder and other anxiety conditions, as well as a list of anxiety treatment specialists in the United States.

**Obsessive-Compulsive Foundation, Inc.**
676 State St., New Haven CT 06511
(203) 401-2070 ■ (203) 401-2076, fax
E-mail: info@ocfoundation.org ■ Website: www.ocfoundation.org

This nonprofit organization is devoted to research, treatment, and public information about the nature of obsessive-compulsive disorder (OCD), and it publishes the *OCD Newsletter*.

**Social Phobics Anonymous**
Website: www.healsocialanxiety.com

This web-based organization offers information and telephone support groups for those dealing with social phobia

## National Associations of Mental-Health Professionals

The organizations listed below will provide names of practitioners in the caller's area, or will refer callers to local offices for referral information.

**American Psychiatric Association**
1000 Wilson Blvd., Suite 1825, Arlington VA 22209-3901
(703) 907-7300 ■ Website: www.psych.org

**American Psychological Association (APA)**
750 First St. NE, Washington DC 20002-4242
(800) 374-2721 ■ Website: www.apa.org

**Anxiety Disorders Association of America (ADAA)**
8730 Georgia Ave., Suite 600, Silver Spring MD 20910
(240) 485-1001 ■ (240) 485-1035, fax ■ Website: www.adaa.org

**Association for Behavioral and Cognitive Therapies (ABCT)**
305 Seventh Ave., 16th Fl., New York NY 10001
(212) 647-1890 ■ Website: www.aabt.org

**CHAANGE\* National Office**
1360 Rosecrans St., Suite I, San Diego CA 92106-2639
(800) 276-7800 ■ (619) 224-2216 ■ (619) 224-2215, fax
Website: www.chaange.com

\* Center for Help for Anxiety and Agoraphobia through New Growth Experiences

**The Lazarus Institute**
98 Tamarack Circle, Skillman NJ 08858
(609) 683-9122 ■ Website: www.thelazarusinstitute.com

**National Association of Cognitive-Behavior Therapists**
P.O. Box 2195, Weirton WV 26062
(800) 853-1135 ■ (304) 723-3982, fax
Website: www.nacbt.org

**National Association of Social Workers (NASW)**
750 First St. NE, Suite 700, Washington DC 20002-4241
(202) 408-8600 ■ Website: www.naswdc.org

## National Organizations for Alternative Health Care

The organizations listed below represent alternative health-care
approaches:

**Alliance for Alternative Medicine**
160 N.W. Widmer Pl., Albany OR 97321
(503) 926-4678

**American Association of Naturopathic Physicians**
4435 Wisconsin Ave. NW, Suite 403, Washington DC 20016
(866) 538-2267 ■ Website: www.naturopathic.org

**American Foundation for Alternative Health Care**
25 Landfield Ave., Monticello NY 12701
(914) 794-8181

**American Holistic Medical Association**
4101 Lake Boone Trail, Suite 201, Raleigh NC 27607
(919) 787-5146

**American Holistic Health Association**
P.O. Box 17400, Anaheim CA 92817-7400
(714) 779-6152 ■ Website: www.ahha.org

**Aromatherapy Institute of Research**
P.O. Box 2354, Fair Oaks CA 95628
(916) 965-7546

**Bach Centre**
P.O. Box 320, Woodmere NY 11598
(516) 825-2229

**Bach International Education Program**
Nelson Bach USA, Ltd.
100 Research Dr., Wilmington MA 01887
(800) 334-0843 ■ (978) 988-0233, fax
Website: www.bachfloweressences.co.uk

**Homeopathic Association of Naturopathic Physicians**
14653 S. Graves Rd., Mulino OR 97041
(503) 829-7326

**International Association of Holistic Health Practitioners**
5020 Spring Mountain Rd., Las Vegas NV 89121
(702) 873-4542

**National Center for Homeopathy**
801 North Fairfax St., Suite 306, Alexandria VA 22314
(703) 548-7790

**National College of Natural Medicine**
049 SW Porter St., Portland OR 97201
(503) 552-1555 ■ Website: www.ncnm.edu

## Other Resources

**Center for Anxiety Disorders**
Paul Foxman, Ph.D., Director
86 Lake St., Burlington VT 05401
(802) 865-3450 ■ Website: www.centerforanxiety.com

This center, directed by the author, is a private practice specializing in the treatment of anxiety disorders, stress-related conditions, and relationship problems.

# Index

## A

abuse, physical: and children, 68, 71; contributing factors, 73; and post-traumatic stress disorder, 37–39; as risk factor for anxiety disorder, 10, 72–73

abuse, sexual: and anxiety about sex, 215; healing from, 219–221; and post-traumatic stress disorder, 37–39; as risk factor for anxiety disorder, 73–74

*Aconitum napellus,* 258

acupuncture, 255

acute stress disorder, 39

Adams, Ansel, 238

adoption, 81

adrenaline, 18, 20

adult children of alcoholism, 71

advertising, drug, 243–244

aerobic exercise, 131–133

affairs, extramarital, 81

affirmations, 160, 165, 167

agoraphobia: described, 26–29; and sensitization, 17, 171

alcohol, 15, 41, 70–71, 81, 144, 250

all-or-nothing thinking, 23, 71, 167–168

alprazolam (Xanax), 248, 253

alternative medicine, *xiv,* 255–259

Amazon.com, *xiv*

ambiguity, tolerance for, 168

American Academy of Sports Medicine, 140

American Psychiatric Association, 25, 33, 281

American Psychological Association, 264–265, 279, 281

amitriptyline (Elavil), 250, 253

amphetamines, 41

amygdala, 18, 19, 242

anabolism, 87–88

anger: and depression, 198; expressing, 198–200; passive-aggressiveness, 197–198; and reactions similar to anxiety, 21, 51; sources of, 197; as symptom of post-traumatic stress disorder, 37

angina, 106

animals, fear of, 31

anorexia, 37, 142, 146

antidepressants, 4–5, 248–250, 259

anxiety: alternatives to, 261–263; about death, 230–233; defined, 15–18; and eating disorders, 146–148; and emotions, 21; fear of, 172, 174–175; in parents, 77–79; physical symptoms of, 1; prevention of, 91–99; statistics on, 4; and thought patterns, 21–23

*Anxiety and Phobia Workbook* (Bourne), 267

anxiety disorder: acute stress disorder, 39; and anxiety personality style, 46–57; associated with medical conditions, 40–41; biological sensitivity to, 44–46; and breathing, 115–118; components of, *xv,* 2, 8, 44–62, 261; developmental factors contributing to, 66–81; diagnosis of, 3; in family members, 208–210; generalized anxiety disorder (GAD), 29–30, 42; life after recovery, 14, 84, 261; medications for, 242–259; panic disorder, 5, 26–29, 42, 56; recovery rates, 5, 8, 260; self-medicating, 15; separation

## THE WORRIED CHILD: Recognizing Anxiety in Children and Helping Them Heal *by Paul Foxman, Ph.D.*

Anxiety in children affects their health and intellectual, emotional, and social development. Today's triggers include family

breakdown, and a failing school system. The result? A shell-shocked generation of children, many of whom suffer from significant anxiety.

Dr. Foxman shows that this anxiety is preventable — or can at least be minimized. He uses exercises, sample dialogues, and case studies to outline steps that can be taken by parents, schools, health professionals, and children themselves. For example, parents will learn positive ways to

— communicate effectively and discipline without creating anxiety

— manage the impact of TV and movies, the Internet, and video games

— discuss drugs, alcohol, and sexuality with children

**304 pages ... 2 illus. ... Paperback $17.95**

## CONQUERING PANIC AND ANXIETY DISORDERS: Success Stories, Strategies and Other Good News *by Jenna Glatzer, Editor, with commentaries by Paul Foxman, Ph.D.*

Anxiety disorders affect 1 out of 9 people in America. This unique book presents the success stories of women and men who have overcome a wide range of anxiety disorders, from panic attacks, agoraphobia, and obsessive-compulsive disorder to social anxiety disorder and PTSD. Their stories offer hope and valuable tips, and each features a commentary by Dr. Paul Foxman, who explains how the techniques used work and how they can be adapted by others.

**256 pages ... Paperback $17.95**

## MANTRACARDS©

MantraCards — a tool for living without anxiety — are a set of reminders and suggestions from Dr. Foxman's book *Dancing with Fear*. Each deck contains 52 cards — one for each week of the year — with 44 thoughts from the book and 8 formatted blank cards that allow you to create your own personal inspirations.

You can use your cards in several ways:

— Flip through the deck of MantraCards often to keep yourself focused on living without worry or anxiety.

— Display selected MantraCards in a conspicuous location (such as on a desk or night table).

— Select a card at random from your set of MantraCards whenever you feel anxious.

— Write your own mantras on the formatted blank MantraCards as you identify what you need to practice or remember.

After you pick a card, read it, close your eyes, breathe deeply, and reflect on how you can implement the mantra in your everyday life. Repeat often.

**52 cards ... $10.00**

## ~ How to Order ~

**THE WORRIED CHILD and CONQUERING PANIC AND ANXIETY DISORDERS may be ordered directly from Hunter House. Please call 1-800-266-5592 or visit our website at www.hunterhouse.com**

**To order *MANTRACARDS* or to request free information on the CHAANGE anxiety recovery program, contact**

**Paul Foxman, Ph.D.**
**86 Lake Street, Burlington, VT 05401**
**Tel.: (802) 865-3450 ... Fax: (802) 860-5011**
**(Please note that the PO address on the cards is no longer current). There is a $4.00 shipping charge.**

**You can also order and pay for MantraCards at Dr. Foxman's website, www.drfoxman.com**

**Please order MantraCards from Dr. Foxman; they are not available from Hunter House.**